FREE Test Taking Tips DVD Offer

To help us better serve you, we have developed a Test Taking Tips DVD that we would like to give you for FREE. **This DVD covers world-class test taking tips that you can use to be even more successful when you are taking your test.**

All that we ask is that you email us your feedback about your study guide. Please let us know what you thought about it – whether that is good, bad or indifferent.

To get your **FREE Test Taking Tips DVD**, email freedvd@studyguideteam.com with "FREE DVD" in the subject line and the following information in the body of the email:

    a. The title of your study guide.

    b. Your product rating on a scale of 1-5, with 5 being the highest rating.

    c. Your feedback about the study guide. What did you think of it?

    d. Your full name and shipping address to send your free DVD.

If you have any questions or concerns, please don't hesitate to contact us at freedvd@studyguideteam.com.

Thanks again!

GED Preparation 2018 & 2019 All Subjects Study Questions

Three Full-Length Practice Tests for GED Test Prep 2018 & 2019

Test Prep Books Study Guide 2018 All Subjects Prep Team

Table of Contents

Quick Overview

As you draw closer to taking your exam, effective preparation becomes more and more important. Thankfully, you have this study guide to help you get ready. Use this guide to help keep your studying on track and refer to it often.

This study guide contains several key sections that will help you be successful on your exam. The guide contains tips for what you should do the night before and the day of the test. Also included are test-taking tips. Knowing the right information is not always enough. Many well-prepared test takers struggle with exams. These tips will help equip you to accurately read, assess, and answer test questions.

A large part of the guide is devoted to showing you what content to expect on the exam and to helping you better understand that content. Near the end of this guide is a practice test so that you can see how well you have grasped the content. Then, answer explanations are provided so that you can understand why you missed certain questions.

Don't try to cram the night before you take your exam. This is not a wise strategy for a few reasons. First, your retention of the information will be low. Your time would be better used by reviewing information you already know rather than trying to learn a lot of new information. Second, you will likely become stressed as you try to gain a large amount of knowledge in a short amount of time. Third, you will be depriving yourself of sleep. So be sure to go to bed at a reasonable time the night before. Being well-rested helps you focus and remain calm.

Be sure to eat a substantial breakfast the morning of the exam. If you are taking the exam in the afternoon, be sure to have a good lunch as well. Being hungry is distracting and can make it difficult to focus. You have hopefully spent lots of time preparing for the exam. Don't let an empty stomach get in the way of success!

When travelling to the testing center, leave earlier than needed. That way, you have a buffer in case you experience any delays. This will help you remain calm and will keep you from missing your appointment time at the testing center.

Be sure to pace yourself during the exam. Don't try to rush through the exam. There is no need to risk performing poorly on the exam just so you can leave the testing center early. Allow yourself to use all of the allotted time if needed.

Remain positive while taking the exam even if you feel like you are performing poorly. Thinking about the content you should have mastered will not help you perform better on the exam.

Once the exam is complete, take some time to relax. Even if you feel that you need to take the exam again, you will be well served by some down time before you begin studying again. It's often easier to convince yourself to study if you know that it will come with a reward!

Test-Taking Strategies

1. Predicting the Answer

When you feel confident in your preparation for a multiple-choice test, try predicting the answer before reading the answer choices. This is especially useful on questions that test objective factual knowledge or that ask you to fill in a blank. By predicting the answer before reading the available choices, you eliminate the possibility that you will be distracted or led astray by an incorrect answer choice. You will feel more confident in your selection if you read the question, predict the answer, and then find your prediction among the answer choices. After using this strategy, be sure to still read all of the answer choices carefully and completely. If you feel unprepared, you should not attempt to predict the answers. This would be a waste of time and an opportunity for your mind to wander in the wrong direction.

2. Reading the Whole Question

Too often, test takers scan a multiple-choice question, recognize a few familiar words, and immediately jump to the answer choices. Test authors are aware of this common impatience, and they will sometimes prey upon it. For instance, a test author might subtly turn the question into a negative, or he or she might redirect the focus of the question right at the end. The only way to avoid falling into these traps is to read the entirety of the question carefully before reading the answer choices.

3. Looking for Wrong Answers

Long and complicated multiple-choice questions can be intimidating. One way to simplify a difficult multiple-choice question is to eliminate all of the answer choices that are clearly wrong. In most sets of answers, there will be at least one selection that can be dismissed right away. If the test is administered on paper, the test taker could draw a line through it to indicate that it may be ignored; otherwise, the test taker will have to perform this operation mentally or on scratch paper. In either case, once the obviously incorrect answers have been eliminated, the remaining choices may be considered. Sometimes identifying the clearly wrong answers will give the test taker some information about the correct answer. For instance, if one of the remaining answer choices is a direct opposite of one of the eliminated answer choices, it may well be the correct answer. The opposite of obviously wrong is obviously right! Of course, this is not always the case. Some answers are obviously incorrect simply because they are irrelevant to the question being asked. Still, identifying and eliminating some incorrect answer choices is a good way to simplify a multiple-choice question.

4. Don't Overanalyze

Anxious test takers often overanalyze questions. When you are nervous, your brain will often run wild, causing you to make associations and discover clues that don't actually exist. If you feel that this may be a problem for you, do whatever you can to slow down during the test. Try taking a deep breath or counting to ten. As you read and consider the question, restrict yourself to the particular words used by the author. Avoid thought tangents about what the author *really* meant, or what he or she was *trying* to say. The only things that matter on a multiple-choice test are the words that are actually in the question. You must avoid reading too much into a multiple-choice question, or supposing that the writer meant something other than what he or she wrote.

5. No Need for Panic

It is wise to learn as many strategies as possible before taking a multiple-choice test, but it is likely that you will come across a few questions for which you simply don't know the answer. In this situation, avoid panicking. Because most multiple-choice tests include dozens of questions, the relative value of a single wrong answer is small. Moreover, your failure on one question has no effect on your success elsewhere on the test. As much as possible, you should compartmentalize each question on a multiple-choice test. In other words, you should not allow your feelings about one question to affect your success on the others. When you find a question that you either don't understand or don't know how to answer, just take a deep breath and do your best. Read the entire question slowly and carefully. Try rephrasing the question a couple of different ways. Then, read all of the answer choices carefully. After eliminating obviously wrong answers, make a selection and move on to the next question.

6. Confusing Answer Choices

When working on a difficult multiple-choice question, there may be a tendency to focus on the answer choices that are the easiest to understand. Many people, whether consciously or not, gravitate to the answer choices that require the least concentration, knowledge, and memory. This is a mistake. When you come across an answer choice that is confusing, you should give it extra attention. A question might be confusing because you do not know the subject matter to which it refers. If this is the case, don't eliminate the answer before you have affirmatively settled on another. When you come across an answer choice of this type, set it aside as you look at the remaining choices. If you can confidently assert that one of the other choices is correct, you can leave the confusing answer aside. Otherwise, you will need to take a moment to try to better understand the confusing answer choice. Rephrasing is one way to tease out the sense of a confusing answer choice.

7. Your First Instinct

Many people struggle with multiple-choice tests because they overthink the questions. If you have studied sufficiently for the test, you should be prepared to trust your first instinct once you have carefully and completely read the question and all of the answer choices. There is a great deal of research suggesting that the mind can come to the correct conclusion very quickly once it has obtained all of the relevant information. At times, it may seem to you as if your intuition is working faster even than your reasoning mind. This may in fact be true. The knowledge you obtain while studying may be retrieved from your subconscious before you have a chance to work out the associations that support it. Verify your instinct by working out the reasons that it should be trusted.

8. Key Words

Many test takers struggle with multiple-choice questions because they have poor reading comprehension skills. Quickly reading and understanding a multiple-choice question requires a mixture of skill and experience. To help with this, try jotting down a few key words and phrases on a piece of scrap paper. Doing this concentrates the process of reading and forces the mind to weigh the relative importance of the question's parts. In selecting words and phrases to write down, the test taker thinks about the question more deeply and carefully. This is especially true for multiple-choice questions that are preceded by a long prompt.

9. Subtle Negatives

One of the oldest tricks in the multiple-choice test writer's book is to subtly reverse the meaning of a question with a word like *not* or *except*. If you are not paying attention to each word in the question, you can easily be led astray by this trick. For instance, a common question format is, "Which of the following is...?" Obviously, if the question instead is, "Which of the following is not...?," then the answer will be quite different. Even worse, the test makers are aware of the potential for this mistake and will include one answer choice that would be correct if the question were not negated or reversed. A test taker who misses the reversal will find what he or she believes to be a correct answer and will be so confident that he or she will fail to reread the question and discover the original error. The only way to avoid this is to practice a wide variety of multiple-choice questions and to pay close attention to each and every word.

10. Reading Every Answer Choice

It may seem obvious, but you should always read every one of the answer choices! Too many test takers fall into the habit of scanning the question and assuming that they understand the question because they recognize a few key words. From there, they pick the first answer choice that answers the question they believe they have read. Test takers who read all of the answer choices might discover that one of the latter answer choices is actually *more* correct. Moreover, reading all of the answer choices can remind you of facts related to the question that can help you arrive at the correct answer. Sometimes, a misstatement or incorrect detail in one of the latter answer choices will trigger your memory of the subject and will enable you to find the right answer. Failing to read all of the answer choices is like not reading all of the items on a restaurant menu: you might miss out on the perfect choice.

11. Spot the Hedges

One of the keys to success on multiple-choice tests is paying close attention to every word. This is never truer than with words like almost, most, some, and sometimes. These words are called "hedges" because they indicate that a statement is not totally true or not true in every place and time. An absolute statement will contain no hedges, but in many subjects, like literature and history, the answers are not always straightforward or absolute. There are always exceptions to the rules in these subjects. For this reason, you should favor those multiple-choice questions that contain hedging language. The presence of qualifying words indicates that the author is taking special care with his or her words, which is certainly important when composing the right answer. After all, there are many ways to be wrong, but there is only one way to be right! For this reason, it is wise to avoid answers that are absolute when taking a multiple-choice test. An absolute answer is one that says things are either all one way or all another. They often include words like *every*, *always*, *best*, and *never*. If you are taking a multiple-choice test in a subject that doesn't lend itself to absolute answers, be on your guard if you see any of these words.

12. Long Answers

In many subject areas, the answers are not simple. As already mentioned, the right answer often requires hedges. Another common feature of the answers to a complex or subjective question are qualifying clauses, which are groups of words that subtly modify the meaning of the sentence. If the question or answer choice describes a rule to which there are exceptions or the subject matter is complicated, ambiguous, or confusing, the correct answer will require many words in order to be expressed clearly and accurately. In essence, you should not be deterred by answer choices that seem excessively long. Oftentimes, the author of the text will not be able to write the correct answer without offering some qualifications and modifications. Your job is to read the answer choices thoroughly and completely and to select the one that most accurately and precisely answers the question.

13. Restating to Understand

Sometimes, a question on a multiple-choice test is difficult not because of what it asks but because of how it is written. If this is the case, restate the question or answer choice in different words. This process serves a couple of important purposes. First, it forces you to concentrate on the core of the question. In order to rephrase the question accurately, you have to understand it well. Rephrasing the question will concentrate your mind on the key words and ideas. Second, it will present the information to your mind in a fresh way. This process may trigger your memory and render some useful scrap of information picked up while studying.

14. True Statements

Sometimes an answer choice will be true in itself, but it does not answer the question. This is one of the main reasons why it is essential to read the question carefully and completely before proceeding to the answer choices. Too often, test takers skip ahead to the answer choices and look for true statements. Having found one of these, they are content to select it without reference to the question above. Obviously, this provides an easy way for test makers to play tricks. The savvy test taker will always read the entire question before turning to the answer choices. Then, having settled on a correct answer choice, he or she will refer to the original question and ensure that the selected answer is relevant. The mistake of choosing a correct-but-irrelevant answer choice is especially common on questions related to specific pieces of objective knowledge, like historical or scientific facts. A prepared test taker will have a wealth of factual knowledge at his or her disposal, and should not be careless in its application.

15. No Patterns

One of the more dangerous ideas that circulates about multiple-choice tests is that the correct answers tend to fall into patterns. These erroneous ideas range from a belief that B and C are the most common right answers, to the idea that an unprepared test-taker should answer "A-B-A-C-A-D-A-B-A." It cannot be emphasized enough that pattern-seeking of this type is exactly the WRONG way to approach a multiple-choice test. To begin with, it is highly unlikely that the test maker will plot the correct answers according to some predetermined pattern. The questions are scrambled and delivered in a random order. Furthermore, even if the test maker was following a pattern in the assignation of correct answers, there is no reason why the test taker would know which pattern he or she was using. Any attempt to discern a pattern in the answer choices is a waste of time and a distraction from the real work of taking the test. A test taker would be much better served by extra preparation before the test than by reliance on a pattern in the answers.

FREE DVD OFFER

Don't forget that doing well on your exam includes both understanding the test content and understanding how to use what you know to do well on the test. We offer a completely FREE Test Taking Tips DVD that covers world class test taking tips that you can use to be even more successful when you are taking your test.

All that we ask is that you email us your feedback about your study guide. To get your **FREE Test Taking Tips DVD**, email freedvd@studyguideteam.com with "FREE DVD" in the subject line and the following information in the body of the email:

- The title of your study guide.
- Your product rating on a scale of 1-5, with 5 being the highest rating.
- Your feedback about the study guide. What did you think of it?
- Your full name and shipping address to send your free DVD.

Introduction to the GED

Function of the Test

The General Education Development (GED) test is an exam developed and administered by the GED Testing Service, a joint venture of the American Council on Education and Pearson VUE. The GED offers those without a high school diploma the chance to earn a high school equivalency credential by evaluating their knowledge of core high school subjects. In 2014, the test was updated to become computer-based only and to align with current high school graduation standards.

The GED is the only nationally recognized high school equivalency credential, and GED test takers represent a wide age group with diverse goals. Generally, the GED is appropriate for people who did not graduate from high school but who wish to pursue advancement in their career and/or education. According to MyGED, approximately 98% of U.S. colleges and universities accept a GED as the equivalent of a high school diploma (other schools may require additional preparation courses in addition to a passing GED score in order to be considered for admission). Over 20 million adults have earned GED credentials, and the latest reported pass rates for the 2014 GED are around 60%.

Test Administration

GED tests are widely offered throughout the United States and Canada, although jurisdictions (state, province, etc.) may vary in terms of things like pricing, scheduling, and test rules. For international students and US military, international testing options are also available. Official GED Testing Centers are often operated by community colleges, adult education centers, and local school boards; GED Testing Service offers a comprehensive search of nearby test centers.

Keeping in mind that rules may vary between jurisdictions, all tests are administered in-person and taken on a computer. Tests are scheduled throughout the year; refer to local testing centers for available test times. Generally, test takers are able to take any test module three times without any restrictions on retesting. However, after three failed attempts, testers must wait a minimum of 60 days to retake the test. GED testing centers can also offer accommodations for students with disabilities, such as additional test time or Braille format tests. The GED may also be offered in Spanish or in French (verify availability with local testing centers). (http://www.gedtestingservice.com/testers/mygedfaqs)

Test Format

The GED consists of four sections, or modules: Mathematical Reasoning, Science, Social Studies, and Reasoning Through Language Arts. Although the complete test is offered together, it is not necessary to take all four modules at once. Test subjects vary in length:

Subject	Time	Topics
Math	115 minutes	Quantitative and algebraic problem solving; data analysis of charts, graphs, and tables; geometry
Science	90 minutes	Life science, physical science, earth and space science
Social Studies	70 minutes	Civics and government, U.S. history, economics, world geography
Reasoning Through Language Arts	150 minutes	Ability to closely read, comprehend, and edit written text; ability to write clearly

A ten-minute break is given between each module.

On the testing day, test takers are not permitted to eat, drink, smoke, or use their cell phones during the test. Test takers are permitted to bring a handheld calculator (TI-30XS Multiview Scientific Calculator) to the test; testing centers will not provide handheld calculators, although an on-screen calculator will be available on the computer. Students will also be provided with three erasable note boards to use during the test.

Scoring

Because the GED is now a computer-based test, scores will be available on MyGED within 24 hours of completing the test. The four modules of the GED are scored on a scale of 100–200. In order to earn high school equivalency, it is necessary to achieve a passing score on all of the four modules, and scores cannot be made up between modules—that is, a high score on one subject cannot be used to compensate for a low score on another subject. Scores are divided into four ranges:

> 1. A score lower than 145 points earns a score of "Not Passing." It is necessary to retake the test to earn high school equivalency.

> 2. A score at or higher than 145 points earns "GED Passing Score/High School Equivalency."

> 3. A score of 165-175 is deemed "GED College Ready." This designation advises colleges and universities that the test taker is ready to begin a degree program without further placement testing or preparation courses (policies vary among schools).

> 4. A score over 175 earns the test taker "GED College Ready + Credit." For some institutions, a score at this level allows the GED graduate to earn college credit for certain courses (policies vary among schools).

GED Practice Test #1

Reading Comprehension

Questions 1–6 are based upon the following passage:

What is Gulliver up to?

My gentleness and good behaviour had gained so far on the emperor and his court, and indeed upon the army and people in general, that I began to conceive hopes of getting my liberty in a short time. I took all possible methods to cultivate this favourable disposition. The natives came, by degrees, to be less apprehensive of any danger from me. I would sometimes lie down, and let five or six of them dance on my hand; and at last the boys and girls would venture to come and play at hide-and-seek in my hair. I had now made a good progress in understanding and speaking the language. The emperor had a mind one day to entertain me with several of the country shows, wherein they exceed all nations I have known, both for dexterity and magnificence. I was diverted with none so much as that of the rope-dancers, performed upon a slender white thread, extended about two feet, and twelve inches from the ground. Upon which I shall desire liberty, with the reader's patience, to enlarge a little.

This diversion is only practised by those persons who are candidates for great employments, and high favour at court. They are trained in this art from their youth, and are not always of noble birth, or liberal education. When a great office is vacant, either by death or disgrace (which often happens,) five or six of those candidates petition the emperor to entertain his majesty and the court with a dance on the rope; and whoever jumps the highest, without falling, succeeds in the office. Very often the chief ministers themselves are commanded to show their skill, and to convince the emperor that they have not lost their faculty. Flimnap, the treasurer, is allowed to cut a caper on the straight rope, at least an inch higher than any other lord in the whole empire. I have seen him do the summerset several times together, upon a trencher fixed on a rope which is no thicker than a common packthread in England. My friend Reldresal, principal secretary for private affairs, is, in my opinion, if I am not partial, the second after the treasurer; the rest of the great officers are much upon a par.

from Jonathan Swift's Gulliver's Travels into Several Remote Nations of the World

1. Which of the following statements best summarize the central purpose of this text?
    a. Gulliver details his fondness for the archaic yet interesting practices of his captors.
    b. Gulliver conjectures about the intentions of the aristocratic sector of society.
    c. Gulliver becomes acquainted with the people and practices of his new surroundings.
    d. Gulliver's differences cause him to become penitent around new acquaintances.

2. What is the word *principal* referring to in the following text?

> My friend Reldresal, principal secretary for private affairs, is, in my opinion, if I am not partial, the second after the treasurer; the rest of the great officers are much upon a par.

   a. Primary or chief
   b. An acolyte
   c. An individual who provides nurturing
   d. One in a subordinate position

3. What can the reader infer from this passage?

> I would sometimes lie down, and let five or six of them dance on my hand; and at last the boys and girls would venture to come and play at hide-and-seek in my hair.

   a. The children tortured Gulliver.
   b. Gulliver traveled because he wanted to meet new people.
   c. Gulliver is considerably larger than the children who are playing around him.
   d. Gulliver has a genuine love and enthusiasm for people of all sizes.

4. What is the significance of the word *mind* in the following passage?

> The emperor had a mind one day to entertain me with several of the country shows, wherein they exceed all nations I have known, both for dexterity and magnificence.

   a. The ability to think
   b. A collective vote
   c. A definitive decision
   d. A mythological question

5. Which of the following assertions does not support the fact that games are a commonplace event in this culture?
   a. My gentlest and good behavior . . . short time.
   b. They are trained in this art from their youth . . . liberal education.
   c. Very often the chief ministers themselves are commanded to show their skill . . . not lost their faculty.
   d. Flimnap, the treasurer, is allowed to cut a caper on the straight rope . . . higher than any other lord in the whole empire.

6. How do the roles of Flimnap and Reldresal serve as evidence of the community's emphasis in regards to the correlation between physical strength and leadership abilities?
   a. Only children used Gulliver's hands as a playground.
   b. The two men who exhibited superior abilities held prominent positions in the community.
   c. Only common townspeople, not leaders, walk the straight rope.
   d. No one could jump higher than Gulliver.

Questions 7–12 are based upon the following passage:

Who will save the birds?

Three years ago, I think there were not many bird-lovers in the United States, who believed it possible to prevent the total extinction of both egrets from our fauna. All the known rookeries accessible to plume-hunters had been totally destroyed. Two years ago, the secret discovery of several small, hidden colonies prompted William Dutcher, President of the National Association of Audubon Societies, and Mr. T. Gilbert Pearson, Secretary, to attempt the protection of those colonies. With a fund contributed for the purpose, wardens were hired and duly commissioned. As previously stated, one of those wardens was shot dead in cold blood by a plume hunter. The task of guarding swamp rookeries from the attacks of money-hungry desperadoes to whom the accursed plumes were worth their weight in gold, is a very chancy proceeding. There is now one warden in Florida who says that "before they get my rookery they will first have to get me."

Thus far the protective work of the Audubon Association has been successful. Now there are twenty colonies, which contain all told, about 5,000 egrets and about 120,000 herons and ibises which are guarded by the Audubon wardens. One of the most important is on Bird Island, a mile out in Orange Lake, central Florida, and it is ably defended by Oscar E. Baynard. To-day, the plume hunters who do not dare to raid the guarded rookeries are trying to study out the lines of flight of the birds, to and from their feeding-grounds, and shoot them in transit. Their motto is—"Anything to beat the law, and get the plumes." It is there that the state of Florida should take part in the war.

The success of this campaign is attested by the fact that last year a number of egrets were seen in eastern Massachusetts—for the first time in many years. And so to-day the question is, can the wardens continue to hold the plume-hunters at bay?

from Our Vanishing Wildlife, by William T. Hornaday

7. The author's use of first person pronoun in the following text does NOT have which of the following effects?

Three years ago, I think there were not many bird-lovers in the United States, who believed it possible to prevent the total extinction of both egrets from our fauna.

a. The phrase *I think* acts as a sort of hedging, where the author's tone is less direct and/or absolute.
b. It allows the reader to more easily connect with the author.
c. It encourages the reader to empathize with the egrets.
d. It distances the reader from the text by overemphasizing the story.

8. What purpose does the quote serve at the end of the first paragraph?
a. The quote shows proof of a hunter threatening one of the wardens.
b. The quote lightens the mood by illustrating the colloquial language of the region.
c. The quote provides an example of a warden protecting one of the colonies.
d. The quote provides much needed comic relief in the form of a joke.

9. What is the meaning of the word *rookeries* in the following text?

To-day, the plume hunters who do not dare to raid the guarded rookeries are trying to study out the lines of flight of the birds, to and from their feeding-grounds, and shoot them in transit.

a. Houses in a slum area
b. A place where hunters gather to trade tools
c. A place where wardens go to trade stories
d. A colony of breeding birds

10. What is on Bird Island?
    a. Hunters selling plumes
    b. An important bird colony
    c. Bird Island Battle between the hunters and the wardens
    d. An important egret with unique plumes

11. What is the main purpose of the passage?
    a. To persuade the audience to act in preservation of the bird colonies
    b. To show the effect hunting egrets has had on the environment
    c. To argue that the preservation of bird colonies has had a negative impact on the environment.
    d. To demonstrate the success of the protective work of the Audubon Association

12. Why are hunters trying to study the lines of flight of the birds?
    a. To study ornithology, one must know the lines of flight that birds take.
    b. To help wardens preserve the lives of the birds
    c. To have a better opportunity to hunt the birds
    d. To builds their homes under the lines of flight because they believe it brings good luck

Questions 13–18 are based upon the following passage:

What's the life cycle of insects?

Insects as a whole are preeminently creatures of the land and the air. This is shown not only by the possession of wings by a vast majority of the class, but by the mode of breathing to which reference has already been made, a system of branching air-tubes carrying atmospheric air with its combustion-supporting oxygen to all the insect's tissues. The air gains access to these tubes through a number of paired air-holes or spiracles, arranged segmentally in series.

It is of great interest to find that, nevertheless, a number of insects spend much of their time under water. This is true of not a few in the perfect winged state, as for example aquatic beetles and water-bugs ('boatmen' and 'scorpions') which have some way of protecting their spiracles when submerged, and, possessing usually the power of flight, can pass on occasion from pond or stream to upper air. But it is advisable in connection with our present subject to dwell especially on some insects that remain continually under water till they are ready to undergo their final moult and attain the winged state, which they pass entirely in the air. The preparatory instars of such insects are aquatic; the adult instar is aerial. All may-flies, dragon-flies, and caddis-flies, many beetles and two-winged flies, and a few moths thus divide their life-story between the water and the air. For the present we confine attention to the Stone-flies, the May-flies, and the Dragon-flies, three well-known orders of insects respectively called by systematists the Plecoptera, the Ephemeroptera and the Odonata.

In the case of many insects that have aquatic larvae, the latter are provided with some arrangement for enabling them to reach atmospheric air through the surface-film of the water. But the larva of a stone-fly, a dragon-fly, or a may-fly is adapted more completely than these for aquatic life; it can, by means of gills of some kind, breathe the air dissolved in water.

from *The Life-Story of Insects*, by Geo H. Carpenter

13. Which statement best details the central idea in this passage?
    a. It introduces certain insects that transition from water to air.
    b. It delves into entomology, especially where gills are concerned.
    c. It defines what constitutes as insects' breathing.
    d. It invites readers to have a hand in the preservation of insects.

14. Which definition most closely relates to the usage of the word *moult* in the passage?
    a. An adventure of sorts, especially underwater
    b. Mating act between two insects
    c. The act of shedding part or all of the outer shell
    d. Death of an organism that ends in a revival of life

15. What is the purpose of the first paragraph in relation to the second paragraph?
    a. The first paragraph serves as a cause and the second paragraph serves as an effect.
    b. The first paragraph serves as a contrast to the second.
    c. The first paragraph is a description for the argument in the second paragraph.
    d. The first and second paragraphs are merely presented in a sequence.

16. What does the following sentence most nearly mean?
    The preparatory instars of such insects are aquatic; the adult instar is aerial.

    a. The volume of water is necessary to prep the insect for transition rather than the volume of the air.
    b. The abdomen of the insect is designed like a star in the water as well as the air.
    c. The stage of preparation in between molting is acted out in the water, while the last stage is in the air.
    d. These insects breathe first in the water through gills yet continue to use the same organs to breathe in the air.

17. Which of the statements reflect information that one could reasonably infer based on the author's tone?
    a. The author's tone is persuasive and attempts to call the audience to action.
    b. The author's tone is passionate due to excitement over the subject and personal narrative.
    c. The author's tone is informative and exhibits interest in the subject of the study.
    d. The author's tone is somber, depicting some anger at the state of insect larvae.

18. Which statement best describes stoneflies, mayflies, and dragonflies?
    a. They are creatures of the land and the air.
    b. They have a way of protecting their spiracles when submerged.
    c. Their larvae can breathe the air dissolved in water through gills of some kind.
    d. The preparatory instars of these insects are aerial.

Questions 19–25 are based on the following passage.

What is the "Business of the Holes"?

In the quest to understand existence, modern philosophers must question if humans can fully comprehend the world. Classical western approaches to philosophy tend to hold that one can understand something, be it an event or object, by standing outside of the phenomena and observing it. It is then by unbiased observation that one can grasp the details of the world. This seems to hold true for many things. Scientists conduct experiments and record their findings, and thus many natural phenomena become comprehendible. However, several of these observations were possible because humans used tools in order to make these discoveries.

This may seem like an extraneous matter. After all, people invented things like microscopes and telescopes in order to enhance their capacity to view cells or the movement of stars. While humans are still capable of seeing things, the question remains if human beings have the capacity to fully observe and see the world in order to understand it. It would not be an impossible stretch to argue that what humans see through a microscope is not the exact thing itself, but a human interpretation of it.

This would seem to be the case in the "Business of the Holes" experiment conducted by Richard Feynman. To study the way electrons behave, Feynman set up a barrier with two holes and a plate. The plate was there to indicate how many times the electrons would pass through the hole(s). Rather than casually observe the electrons acting under normal circumstances, Feynman discovered that electrons behave in two totally different ways depending on whether or not they are observed. The electrons that were observed had passed through either one of the holes or were caught on the plate as particles. However, electrons that weren't observed acted as waves instead of particles and passed through both holes. This indicated that electrons have a dual nature. Electrons seen by the human eye act like particles, while unseen electrons act like waves of energy.

This dual nature of the electrons presents a conundrum. While humans now have a better understanding of electrons, the fact remains that people cannot entirely perceive how electrons behave without the use of instruments. We can only observe one of the mentioned behaviors, which only provides a partial understanding of the entire function of electrons. Therefore, we're forced to ask ourselves whether the world we observe is objective or if it is subjectively perceived by humans. Or, an alternative question: can man understand the world only through machines that will allow them to observe natural phenomena?

Both questions humble man's capacity to grasp the world. However, those ideas don't take into account that many phenomena have been proven by human beings without the use of machines, such as the discovery of gravity. Like all philosophical questions, whether man's reason and observation alone can understand the universe can be approached from many angles.

19. What is the author's motivation for writing the passage?
    a. Bring to light an alternative view on human perception by examining the role of technology in human understanding.
    b. Educate the reader on the latest astroparticle physics discovery and offer terms that may be unfamiliar to the reader.
    c. Argue that humans are totally blind to the realities of the world by presenting an experiment that proves that electrons are not what they seem on the surface.
    d. Reflect on opposing views of human understanding.

20. Which of the following most closely resembles the way in which paragraph four is structured?
    a. It offers one solution, questions the solution, and then ends with an alternative solution.
    b. It presents an inquiry, explains the detail of that inquiry, and then offers a solution.
    c. It presents a problem, explains the details of that problem, and then ends with more inquiry.
    d. It gives a definition, offers an explanation, and then ends with an inquiry.

21. For the classical approach to understanding to hold true, which of the following must be required?
    a. A telescope.
    b. The person observing must prove their theory beyond a doubt.
    c. Multiple witnesses present.
    d. The person observing must be unbiased.

22. Which best describes how the electrons in the experiment behaved like waves?
    a. The electrons moved up and down like actual waves.
    b. The electrons passed through both holes and then onto the plate.
    c. The electrons converted to photons upon touching the plate.
    d. Electrons were seen passing through one hole or the other.

23. The author mentions "gravity" in the last paragraph in order to do what?
    a. In order to show that different natural phenomena test man's ability to grasp the world.
    b. To prove that since man has not measured it with the use of tools or machines, humans cannot know the true nature of gravity.
    c. To demonstrate an example of natural phenomena humans discovered and understand without the use of tools or machines.
    d. To show an alternative solution to the nature of electrons that humans have not thought of yet.

24. Which situation best parallels the revelation of the dual nature of electrons discovered in Feynman's experiment?
    a. A man is born color-blind and grows up observing everything in lighter or darker shades. With the invention of special goggles he puts on, he discovers that there are other colors in addition to different shades.
    b. The coelacanth was thought to be extinct, but a live specimen was just recently discovered. There are now two living species of coelacanth known to man, and both are believed to be endangered.
    c. In the Middle Ages, blacksmiths added carbon to iron, thus inventing steel. The consequences of this important discovery would have its biggest effects during the industrial revolution.
    d. In order to better examine and treat broken bones, the x-ray machine was invented and put to use in hospitals and medical centers.

25. Which statement about technology would the author likely disagree with?
    a. Technology can help expand the field of human vision.
    b. Technology renders human observation irrelevant.
    c. Developing tools used in observation and research indicates growing understanding of our world in itself.
    d. Studying certain phenomena necessitates the use of tools and machines.

Questions 26–31 are based upon the following passage:

What to the Slave is the Fourth of July?

Fellow citizens—Pardon me, and allow me to ask, why am I called upon to speak here today? What have I, or those I represent, to do with your national independence? Are the great principles of political freedom and of natural justice embodied in that Declaration of Independence, Independence extended to us? And am I therefore called upon to bring our humble offering to the national altar, and to confess the benefits, and express devout gratitude for the blessings, resulting from your independence to us?

Would to God, both for your sakes and ours, ours that an affirmative answer could be truthfully returned to these questions! Then would my task be light, and my burden easy and delightful. For who is there so cold that a nation's sympathy could not warm him? Who so obdurate and dead to the claims of gratitude that would not thankfully acknowledge such priceless benefits? Who so stolid and selfish, that would not give his voice to swell the hallelujahs of a nation's jubilee, when the chains of servitude had been torn from his limbs? I am not that man. In a case like that, the dumb may eloquently speak, and the lame man leap as an hart.

But, such is not the state of the case. I say it with a sad sense of the disparity between us. I am not included within the pale of this glorious anniversary. Oh pity! Your high independence only reveals the immeasurable distance between us. The blessings in which you this day rejoice, I do not enjoy in common. The rich inheritance of justice, liberty, prosperity, and independence, bequeathed by your fathers, is shared by *you*, not by *me*. This Fourth of July is *yours*, not *mine*. You may rejoice, *I* must mourn. To drag a man in fetters into the grand illuminated temple of liberty, and call upon him to join you in joyous anthems, were inhuman mockery and sacrilegious irony. Do you mean, citizens, to mock me, by asking me to speak today? If so there is a parallel to your conduct. And let me warn you that it is dangerous to copy the example of a nation whose crimes, towering up to heaven, were thrown down by the breath of the Almighty, burying that nation and irrecoverable ruin! I can today take up the plaintive lament of a peeled and woe-smitten people.

By the rivers of Babylon, there we sat down. Yea! We wept when we remembered Zion. We hanged our harps upon the willows in the midst thereof. For there, they that carried us away captive, required of us a song; and they who wasted us required of us mirth, saying, "Sing us one of the songs of Zion." How can we sing the Lord's song in a strange land? If I forget thee, O Jerusalem, let my right hand forget her cunning. If I do not remember thee, let my tongue cleave to the roof of my mouth.

From "What to the Slave is the Fourth of July?" by Frederick Douglass, Rochester, New York July 5, 1852

26. What is the tone of the first paragraph of this passage?
    a. Exasperated
    b. Inclusive
    c. Contemplative
    d. Nonchalant

27. Which word CANNOT be used synonymously with the term *obdurate* as it is conveyed in the text below?

> Who so obdurate and dead to the claims of gratitude, that would not thankfully acknowledge such priceless benefits?

    a. Steadfast
    b. Stubborn
    c. Contented
    d. Unwavering

28. What is the central purpose of this text?
    a. To demonstrate the author's extensive knowledge of the Bible
    b. To address the feelings of exclusion expressed by African Americans after the establishment of the Fourth of July holiday
    c. To convince wealthy landowners to adopt new holiday rituals
    d. To explain why minorities often relished the notion of segregation in government institutions

29. Which statement serves as evidence of the question above?
    a. By the rivers of Babylon . . . down.
    b. Fellow citizens . . . today.
    c. I can . . . woe-smitten people.
    d. The rich inheritance of justice . . . *not by me.*

30. The statement below features an example of which of the following literary devices?

> Oh pity! Your high independence only reveals the immeasurable distance between us.

    a. Assonance
    b. Parallelism
    c. Amplification
    d. Hyperbole

31. The speaker's use of biblical references, such as "rivers of Babylon" and the "songs of Zion," helps the reader to do all of the following EXCEPT:
    a. Identify with the speaker through the use of common text.
    b. Convince the audience that injustices have been committed by referencing another group of people who have been previously affected by slavery.
    c. Display the equivocation of the speaker and those that he represents.
    d. Appeal to the listener's sense of humanity.

The next question is based on the following passage.

Which statement can we infer?

A famous children's author recently published a historical fiction novel under a pseudonym; however, it did not sell as many copies as her children's books. In her earlier years, she had majored in history and earned a graduate degree in Antebellum American History, which is the time frame of her new novel. Critics praised this newest work far more than the children's series that made her famous. In fact, her new novel was nominated for the prestigious Albert J.

Beveridge Award, but still isn't selling like her children's books, which fly off the shelves because of her name alone.

32. Which one of the following statements might be accurately inferred based on the above passage?
    a. The famous children's author produced an inferior book under her pseudonym.
    b. The famous children's author is the foremost expert on Antebellum America.
    c. The famous children's author did not receive the bump in publicity for her historical novel that it would have received if it were written under her given name.
    d. People generally prefer to read children's series than historical fiction.

Questions 33–38 are based on the following passage:

What is the current state of poetry?

Dana Gioia argues in his article that poetry is dying, now little more than a limited art form confined to academic and college settings. Of course, poetry remains healthy in the academic setting, but the idea of poetry being limited to this academic subculture is a stretch. New technology and social networking alone have contributed to poets and other writers' work being shared across the world. YouTube has emerged to be a major asset to poets, allowing live performances to be streamed to billions of users. Even now, poetry continues to grow and voice topics that are relevant to the culture of our time. Poetry is not in the spotlight as it may have been in earlier times, but it's still a relevant art form that continues to expand in scope and appeal.

Furthermore, Gioia's argument does not account for live performances of poetry. Not everyone has taken a poetry class or enrolled in university—but most everyone is online. The Internet is a perfect launching point to get all creative work out there. An example of this was the performance of Buddy Wakefield's *Hurling Crowbirds at Mockingbars*. Wakefield is a well-known poet who has published several collections of contemporary poetry. One of my favorite works by Wakefield is *Crowbirds*, specifically his performance at New York University in 2009. Although his reading was a campus event, views of his performance online number in the thousands. His poetry attracted people outside of the university setting.

Naturally, the poem's popularity can be attributed both to Wakefield's performance and the quality of his writing. *Crowbirds* touches on themes of core human concepts such as faith, personal loss, and growth. These are not ideas that only poets or students of literature understand, but all human beings: "You acted like I was hurling crowbirds at mockingbars / and abandoned me for not making sense. / Evidently, I don't experience things as rationally as you do" (Wakefield 15-17). Wakefield weaves together a complex description of the perplexed and hurt emotions of the speaker undergoing a separation from a romantic interest. The line "You acted like I was hurling crowbirds at mockingbars" conjures up an image of someone confused, seemingly out of their mind . . . or in the case of the speaker, passionately trying to grasp at a relationship that is fading. The speaker is looking back and finding the words that described how he wasn't making sense. This poem is particularly human and gripping in its message, but the entire effect of the poem is enhanced through the physical performance.

At its core, poetry is about addressing issues/ideas in the world. Part of this is also addressing the perspectives that are exiguously considered. Although the platform may look different, poetry continues to have a steady audience due to the emotional connection the poet shares with the audience.

33. Which one of the following best explains how the passage is organized?
    a. The author begins with a long definition of the main topic, and then proceeds to prove how that definition has changed over the course of modernity.
    b. The author presents a puzzling phenomenon and uses the rest of the passage to showcase personal experiences in order to explain it.
    c. The author contrasts two different viewpoints, then builds a case showing preference for one over the other.
    d. The passage is an analysis of another theory in which the author has no stake in.

34. The author of the passage would likely agree most with which of the following?
    a. Buddy Wakefield is a genius and is considered at the forefront of modern poetry.
    b. Poetry is not irrelevant; it is an art form that adapts to the changing time while containing its core elements.
    c. Spoken word is the zenith of poetic forms and the premier style of poetry in this decade.
    d. Poetry is on the verge of vanishing from our cultural consciousness.

35. Which one of the following words, if substituted for the word *exiguously* in the last paragraph, would LEAST change the meaning of the sentence?
    a. Indolently
    b. Inaudibly
    c. Interminably
    d. Infrequently

36. Which of the following is most closely analogous to the author's opinion of Buddy Wakefield's performance in relation to modern poetry?
    a. Someone's refusal to accept that the Higgs Boson will validate the Standard Model.
    b. An individual's belief that soccer will lose popularity within the next fifty years.
    c. A professor's opinion that poetry contains the language of the heart, while fiction contains the language of the mind.
    d. A student's insistence that psychoanalysis is a subset of modern psychology.

37. What is the primary purpose of the passage?
    a. To educate readers on the development of poetry and describe the historical implications of poetry in media.
    b. To disprove Dana Gioia's stance that poetry is becoming irrelevant and is only appreciated in academia.
    c. To inform readers of the brilliance of Buddy Wakefield and to introduce them to other poets that have influence in contemporary poetry.
    d. To prove that Gioia's article does have some truth to it and to shed light on its relevance to modern poetry.

38. What is the author's main reason for including the quote in the passage?
    a. The quote opens up opportunity to disprove Gioia's views.
    b. To demonstrate that people are still writing poetry even if the medium has changed in current times.
    c. To prove that poets still have an audience to write for even if the audience looks different than it did centuries ago.
    d. The quote illustrates the complex themes poets continue to address, which still draws listeners and appreciation.

Questions 39–43 are based on the following passage:

What is Boethianism?

The Middle Ages were a time of great superstition and theological debate. Many beliefs were developed and practiced, while some died out or were listed as heresy. Boethianism is a Medieval theological philosophy that attributes sin to gratification and righteousness with virtue and God's providence. Boethianism holds that sin, greed, and corruption are means to attain temporary pleasure, but that they inherently harm the person's soul as well as other human beings.

In *The Canterbury Tales,* we observe more instances of bad actions punished than goodness being rewarded. This would appear to be some reflection of Boethianism. In the "Pardoner's Tale," all three thieves wind up dead, which is a result of their desire for wealth. Each wrong doer pays with their life, and they are unable to enjoy the wealth they worked to steal. Within his tales, Chaucer gives reprieve to people undergoing struggle, but also interweaves stories of contemptible individuals being cosmically punished for their wickedness. The thieves idolize physical wealth, which leads to their downfall. This same theme and ideological principle of Boethianism is repeated in the "Friar's Tale," whose summoner character attempts to gain further wealth by partnering with a demon. The summoner's refusal to repent for his avarice and corruption leads to the demon dragging his soul to Hell. Again, we see the theme of the individual who puts faith and morality aside in favor for a physical prize. The result, of course, is that the summoner loses everything.

The examples of the righteous being rewarded tend to appear in a spiritual context within the *Canterbury Tales*. However, there are a few instances where we see goodness resulting in physical reward. In the Prioress' Tale, we see corporal punishment for barbarism *and* a reward for goodness. The Jews are punished for their murder of the child, giving a sense of law and order (though racist) to the plot. While the boy does die, he is granted a lasting reward by being able to sing even after his death, a miracle that marks that the murdered youth led a pure life. Here, the miracle represents eternal favor with God.

Again, we see the theological philosophy of Boethianism in Chaucer's *The Canterbury Tales* through acts of sin and righteousness and the consequences that follow. When pleasures of the world are sought instead of God's favor, we see characters being punished in tragic ways. However, the absence of worldly lust has its own set of consequences for the characters seeking to obtain God's favor.

39. What would be a potential reward for living a good life, as described in Boethianism?
  a. A long life sustained by the good deeds one has done over a lifetime
  b. Wealth and fertility for oneself and the extension of one's family line
  c. Vengeance for those who have been persecuted by others who have a capacity for committing wrongdoing
  d. God's divine favor for one's righteousness

40. What might be the main reason why the author chose to discuss Boethianism through examining The Canterbury Tales?
  a. *The Canterbury Tales* is a well-known text.
  b. *The Canterbury Tales* is the only known fictional text that contains use of Boethianism.
  c. *The Canterbury Tales* presents a manuscript written in the medieval period that can help illustrate Boethianism through stories and show how people of the time might have responded to the idea.
  d. Within each individual tale in *The Canterbury Tales*, the reader can read about different levels of Boethianism and how each level leads to greater enlightenment.

41. What "ideological principle" is the author referring to in the middle of the second paragraph when talking about the "Friar's Tale"?
  a. The principle that the act of ravaging another's possessions is the same as ravaging one's soul.
  b. The principle that thieves who idolize physical wealth will be punished in an earthly sense as well as eternally.
  c. The principle that fraternization with a demon will result in one losing everything, including his or her life.
  d. The principle that a desire for material goods leads to moral malfeasance punishable by a higher being.

42. Which of the following words, if substituted for the word *avarice* in paragraph two, would LEAST change the meaning of the sentence?
  a. Perniciousness
  b. Pithiness
  c. Parsimoniousness
  d. Precariousness

43. Based on the passage, what view does Boethianism take on desire?
  a. Desire does not exist in the context of Boethianism
  b. Desire is a virtue and should be welcomed
  c. Having desire is evidence of demonic possession
  d. Desire for pleasure can lead toward sin

44. The following exchange occurred after the Baseball Coach's team suffered a heartbreaking loss in the final inning.

Reporter: The team clearly did not rise to the challenge. I'm sure that getting zero hits in twenty at-bats with runners in scoring position hurt the team's chances at winning the game. What are your thoughts on this devastating loss?

Baseball Coach: Hitting with runners in scoring position was not the reason we lost this game. We made numerous errors in the field, and our pitchers gave out too many free passes. Also, we did not even need a hit with runners in scoring position. Many of those at-bats could have driven in the run by simply making contact. Our team did not deserve to win the game.

Which of the following best describes the main point of dispute between the reporter and baseball coach?
- a. Whether the loss was heartbreaking.
- b. Whether getting zero hits in twenty at-bats with runners in scoring position caused the loss.
- c. Numerous errors in the field and pitchers giving too many free passes caused the loss.
- d. Whether the team deserved to win the game.

45. Conservative Politician: Social welfare programs are destroying our country. These programs are not only adding to the annual deficit, which increases the national debt, but they also discourage hard work. Our country must continue producing leaders who bootstrap their way to the top. None of our country's citizens truly *need* assistance from the government; rather, the assistance just makes things easier.

Liberal Politician: Our great country is founded on the principle of hope. The country is built on the backs of immigrants who came here with nothing, except for the hope of a better life. Our country is too wealthy not to provide basic necessities for the less fortunate. Recent immigrants, single mothers, historically disenfranchised, disabled persons, and the elderly all require an ample safety net.

What is the main point of dispute between the politicians?
- a. Spending on social welfare programs increases the national debt.
- b. Certain classes of people rely on social welfare programs to meet their basic needs.
- c. Certain classes of people would be irreparably harmed if the country failed to provide a social welfare program.
- d. All of the country's leaders have bootstrapped their way to the top.

Extended Response

There are two passages below. Read both of the passages carefully all the way through. Then, choose which passage you think is better supported by evidence. In your response, be sure to use your own evidence from the passages. You will have forty-five minutes to plan, write, and edit your response. Your essay should be around 500 words.

Passage I

Lethal force, or deadly force, is defined as the physical means to cause death or serious harm to another individual. The law holds that lethal force is only accepted when you or another person are in immediate and unavoidable danger of death or severe bodily harm. For example, a person could be beating a weaker person in such a way that they are suffering severe enough trauma that could result in death or serious harm. This would be an instance where lethal force would be acceptable and possibly the only way to save that person from irrevocable damage.

Another example of when to use lethal force would be when someone enters your home with a deadly weapon. The intruder's presence and possession of the weapon indicate mal-intent and the ability to inflict death or severe injury to you and your loved ones. Again, lethal force can be used in this situation. Lethal force can also be applied to prevent the harm of another individual. If a woman is being brutally assaulted and is unable to fend off an attacker, lethal force can be used to defend her as a last-ditch effort. If she is in immediate jeopardy of rape, harm, and/or death, lethal force could be the only response that could effectively deter the assailant.

The key to understanding the concept of lethal force is the term *last resort*. Deadly force cannot be taken back; it should be used only to prevent severe harm or death. The law does distinguish whether the means of one's self-defense is fully warranted, or if the individual goes out of control in the process. If you continually attack the assailant after they are rendered incapacitated, this would be causing unnecessary harm, and the law can bring charges against you. Likewise, if you kill an attacker unnecessarily after defending yourself, you can be charged with murder. This would move lethal force beyond necessary defense, making it no longer a last resort but rather a use of excessive force.

Passage II

Assault is the unlawful attempt of one person to apply apprehension on another individual by an imminent threat or by initiating offensive contact. Assaults can vary, encompassing physical strikes, threatening body language, and even provocative language. In the case of the latter, even if a hand has not been laid, it is still considered an assault because of its threatening nature.

Let's look at an example: A homeowner is angered because his neighbor blows fallen leaves into his freshly mowed lawn. Irate, the homeowner gestures a fist to his fellow neighbor and threatens to bash his head in for littering on his lawn. The homeowner's physical motions and verbal threat heralds a physical threat against the other neighbor. These factors classify the homeowner's reaction as an assault. If the angry neighbor hits the threatening homeowner in retaliation, that would constitute an assault as well because he physically hit the homeowner.

Assault also centers on the involvement of weapons in a conflict. If someone fires a gun at another person, it could be interpreted as an assault unless the shooter acted in self-defense. If an individual drew a gun or a knife on someone with the intent to harm them, it would be considered assault. However, it's also considered an assault if someone simply aimed a weapon, loaded or not, at another person in a threatening manner.

Science

Passage 1

Questions 1–5 pertain to the following information:

Worldwide, fungal infections of the lung account for significant mortality in individuals with compromised immune function. Three of the most common infecting agents are *Aspergillus*, *Histoplasma*, and *Candida*. Successful treatment of infections caused by these agents depends on an early and accurate diagnosis. Three tests used to identify specific markers for these mold species include ELISA (enzyme-linked immunosorbent assay), GM Assay (Galactomannan Assay), and PCR (polymerase chain reaction).

Two important characteristics of these tests include sensitivity and specificity. Sensitivity relates to the probability that the test will identify the presence of the infecting agent, resulting in a true positive result. Higher sensitivity equals fewer false-positive results. Specificity relates to the probability that if the test doesn't detect the infecting agent, the test is truly negative for that agent. Higher specificity equals fewer false-negatives.

Figure 1 shows the timeline for the process of infection from exposure to the pathogen to recovery or death.

Figure 1:
Natural History of the Process of Infection

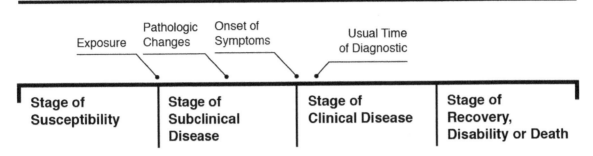

Figure 2 (below) shows the sensitivity and specificity for ELISA, GM assay and PCR related to the diagnosis of infection by *Aspergillus*, *Histoplasma* and *Candida*.

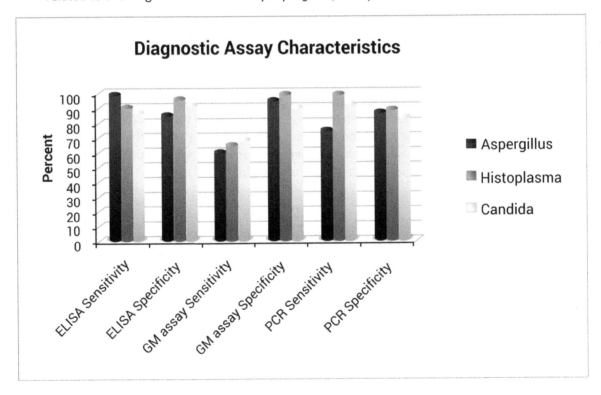

The table below identifies the process of infection in days from exposure for each of the species.

Process of Infection – Days Since Pathogen Exposure			
	Aspergillus	Histoplasma	Candida
Sub-clinical Disease	Day 90	Day 28	Day 7
Detection Possible	Day 118	Day 90	Day 45
Symptoms Appear	Day 145	Day100	Day 120

Figure 3 (below) identifies the point at which each test can detect the organism. Time is measured in days from the time an individual is exposed to the pathogen.

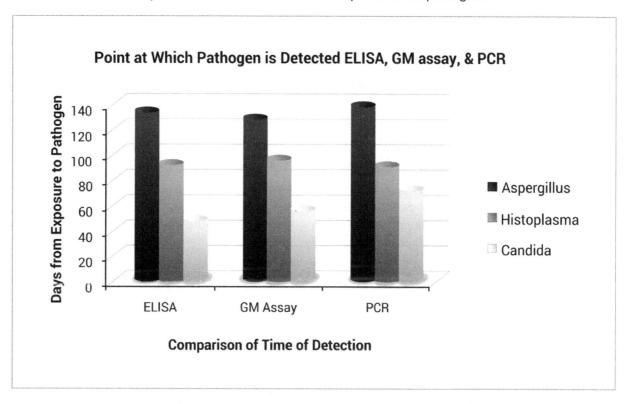

1. Which of the following statements is supported by Figure 2?
   a. For *Candida*, the GM assay will provide the most reliable results.
   b. ELISA testing for *Aspergillus* is the most specific of the three tests.
   c. PCR is the most sensitive method for testing *Histoplasma*.
   d. True positive rates were greater than 75% for all three testing methods.

2. In reference to the table and Figure 3, which pathogen can be detected earlier in the disease process, and by which method?
   a. *Candida* by PCR testing
   b. *Aspergillus* by ELISA testing
   c. *Candida* by GM assay
   d. *Histoplasma* by PCR testing

3. In reference to Figure 2, which statement is correct?

   a. There is a 20% probability that ELISA testing will NOT correctly identify the presence of *Histoplasma*.

   b. When GM assay testing for *Candida* is conducted, there is a 31% probability that it will NOT be identified if the organism is present.

   c. The probability that GM assay testing for *Aspergillus* will correctly identify the presence of the organism is 99%.

   d. The false-negative probabilities for each of the three testing methods identified in Figure 2 indicate that the organism will be detected when present less than 70% of the time.

4. Physicians caring for individuals with suspected *Histoplasma* infections order diagnostic testing prior to instituting treatment. PCR testing results will not be available for 10 days. GM assay results can be obtained more quickly. The physicians opt to wait for the PCR testing. Choose the best possible rationale for that decision.

   a. The treatment will be the same regardless of the test results.

   b. The individual was not exhibiting any disease symptoms.

   c. The probability of PCR testing identifying the presence of the organism is greater than the GM assay.

   d. The subclinical disease phase for *Histoplasma* is more than 100 days.

5. Referencing the data in Figures 2 and 3, if ELISA testing costs twice as much as PCR testing, why might it still be the best choice to test for *Candida*?

   a. ELISA testing detects the presence of *Candida* sooner than PCR testing.

   b. ELISA testing has fewer false-positives than PCR testing.

   c. There is only a 69% probability that PCR testing will correctly identify the presence of *Candida*.

   d. PCR testing is less sensitive than ELISA testing for *Candida*.

Passage 2

Questions 6–12 pertain to the following information:

> Scientists disagree about the cause of Bovine Spongiform Encephalopathy (BSE), also known as "mad cow disease." Two scientists discuss different explanations about the cause of the disease.

Scientist 1

> Mad cow disease is a condition that results in the deterioration of brain and spinal cord tissue. This deterioration manifests as sponge-like defects or holes that result in irreversible damage to the brain. The cause of this damage is widely accepted to be the result of an infectious type of protein, called a prion. Normal prions are located in the cell wall of the central nervous system and function to preserve the myelin sheath around the nerves. Prions are capable of turning normal proteins into other prions by a process that is still unclear, thereby causing the proteins to be "refolded" in abnormal and harmful configurations. Unlike viruses and bacteria, the harmful prions possibly don't contain DNA or RNA, based on the observation of infected tissues in the laboratory that remain infected after immersion in formaldehyde or exposure to ultraviolet light. The transformation from normal to abnormal protein structure and function in a given individual is thought to occur as the result of proteins that are genetically weak or abnormally prone to mutation, or through transmission from

another host through food, drugs or organ transplants from infected animals. The abnormal prions also don't trigger an immune response. After prions accumulate in large enough numbers, they form damaging conglomerations that result in the sponge-like holes in tissues, which eventually cause the loss of proper brain function and death.

Figure 1 depicts formation of abnormal prions that results from the abnormal (right) folding of amino acids.

Figure 1:
Configurations of Normal and Abnormal Prions

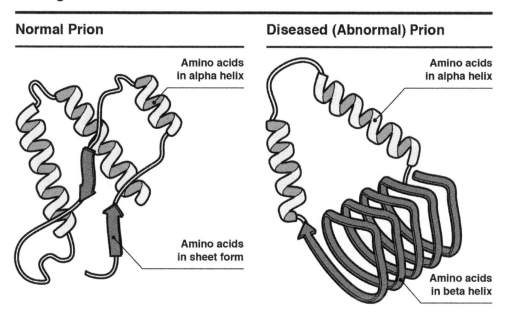

Normal Prion | Diseased (Abnormal) Prion

Amino acids in alpha helix

Amino acids in sheet form

Amino acids in alpha helix

Amino acids in beta helix

Scientist 2

The degeneration of brain tissue in animals afflicted with mad cow disease is widely considered to be the result of prion proteins. This theory fails to consider other possible causes, such as viruses. Recent studies have shown that infected tissues often contain small particles that match the size and density of viruses. In order to demonstrate that these viral particles are the cause of mad cow disease, researchers used chemicals to inactivate the viruses. When the damaged, inactivated viruses were introduced into healthy tissue, no mad cow disease symptoms were observed. This result indicates that viruses are likely the cause of mad cow disease. In addition, when the infected particles from an infected animal are used to infect a different species, the resulting particles are identical to the original particles. If the infecting agent was a protein, the particles would not be identical because proteins are species-specific. Instead, the infective agent is viewed as some form of a virus that has its own DNA or RNA configuration and can reproduce identical infective particles.

6. Which statement below best characterizes the main difference in the scientists' opinions?
    a. The existence of species-specific proteins
    b. Transmission rates of mad cow disease
    c. The conversion process of normal proteins into prions
    d. The underlying cause of mad cow disease

7. Which of the following statements is INCORRECT?
    a. Scientist 2 proposes that viruses aren't the cause of mad cow disease because chemicals inactivated the viruses.
    b. Scientist 1 suggests that infectious proteins called prions are the cause of mad cow disease.
    c. Scientist 1 indicates that the damaging conglomerations formed by prions eventually result in death.
    d. Scientist 2 reports that infected tissues often contain particles that match the size profile of viruses.

8. which of the following is true according to Scientist 1?
    a. Normal proteins accumulate in large numbers to produce damaging conglomerations.
    b. Prions can change normal proteins into prions.
    c. Species-specific DNA sequences of infected tissues indicate that proteins cause mad cow disease.
    d. Prions are present only in the peripheral nervous system of mammals.

9. Which of the following statements would be consistent with the views of BOTH scientists?
    a. Resulting tissue damage is reversible.
    b. The infecting agent is composed of sheets of amino acids in an alpha helix configuration.
    c. Species-specific DNA can be isolated from infected tissue.
    d. Cross-species transmission of the illness is possible.

10. How does the *conglomeration* described in the passage affect function?
    a. Synapses are delayed
    b. Sponge-like tissue formations occur
    c. Space-occupying lesions compress the nerves
    d. The blood supply to surrounding tissues is decreased

11. What evidence best supports the views of Scientist 2?
    a. Species-specific DNA is present in the infected particles.
    b. Prions are present in the cell membrane.
    c. Prions can trigger an immune response.
    d. The infected particles were inactivated and didn't cause disease.

12. Which of the following statements is supported by this passage?
    a. Scientist 1 favors the claim that viruses are the cause of mad cow disease.
    b. Prions are a type of infectious virus.
    c. The process that results in the formation of the abnormal prion is unclear.
    d. Mad cow disease is caused by normal proteins.

Passage 3

Questions 13–17 pertain to the following information:

Scientists have long been interested in the effect of sleep deprivation on overeating and obesity in humans. Recently, scientists discovered that increased levels of the endocannabinoid 2-Arachidonoylglycerol (2-AG) in the human body is related to overeating. The endocannabinoids play an important role in memory, mood, the reward system, and metabolic processes including glucose metabolism and generation of energy. The endocannabinoid receptors CB1-R and CB2-R are protein receptors located on the cell membrane in the brain, the spinal cord and, to a lesser extent, in the peripheral neurons and the organs of the immune system. The two principal endogenous endocannabinoids are AEA (Anandamide) and 2-Arachidonoylglycerol (2-AG). The endocannabinoids can affect the body's response to chronic stress, mediate the pain response, decrease GI motility, and lessen the inflammatory response in some cancers.

Figure 1 (below) identifies the chemical structure of the endogenous cannabinoids including 2-AG.

Figure 1:
Chemical Structure of Common Endogenous Cannabinoids

The Five-Best known Endocannabinoids Showing the Common 19 - C Backbone Structure and specific R-group Constituents

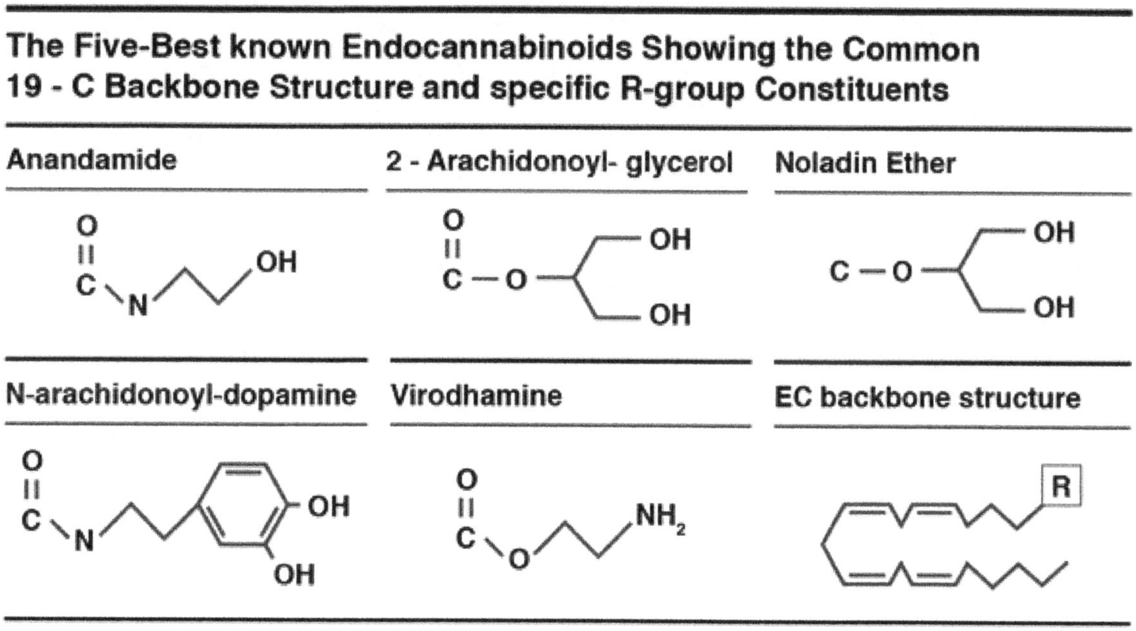

Recent research has also examined the relationship between sleep deprivation and the levels of 2-AG present in blood, as these conditions relate to obesity. The circadian fluctuations of 2-AG are well-known. Levels normally increase in late afternoon and evening. This physiological increase is thought to contribute to late-day snacking behaviors even after adequate calories have been consumed. The relationship between sleep deprivation and 2-AG appears to relate to the effect of 2-AG on the stress response, represented by sleep deprivation in this study. In order to examine this relationship, university scientists conducted an experiment to identify the influence of injections of 2-AG and sleep deprivation on overeating in a population of non-obese male and female participants that ranged in age from 20–40 years old. To accomplish this, human research subjects (participants) were allowed to eat their favorite junk foods in addition to consuming sufficient calories each day. All of the participants were injected daily with a solution of either sterile normal saline or 2-AG. Daily weight gain was recorded for the three treatment groups that included: participants A–E who received sterile normal saline injections, participants F–J who received 2-AG injections, and participants K–O who received 2-AG injections and were limited to 4.5 hours of sleep each night for 7 nights. The results of the three trials are shown below.

Figure 2 identifies the daily weight gain (in grams) of participants receiving sterile normal saline injections.

Daily Weight Gain for Patients Receiving Sterile Normal Saline Injections

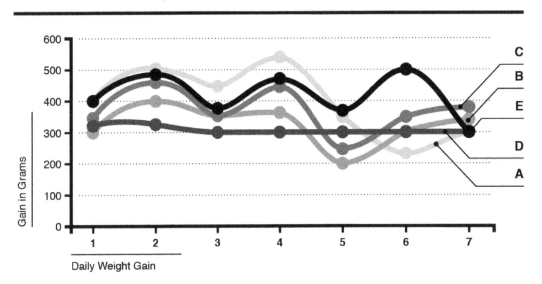

Figure 3 identifies the daily weight gain for participants receiving 2-AG injections.

Figure 3:

Daily Weight Gain for Participants Receiving Daily 2-AG Injections

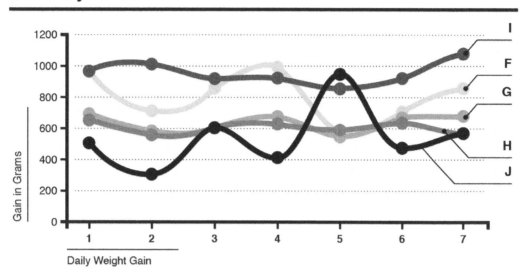

Daily Weight Gain

Figure 4 identifies the daily weight gain for participants receiving daily injections of 2-AG who were also limited to 4.5 hours sleep per night for 7 consecutive nights.

Figure 4:

Daily Weight Gain for Participants Receiving Daily 2-AG Injections Who Were Limited to 4.5 Hours of Sleep Per Night for 7 Consecutive Nights

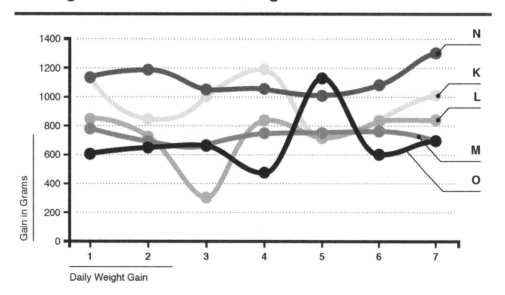

Daily Weight Gain

Figure 5 (below) identifies the participants' average daily weight gain by trial.

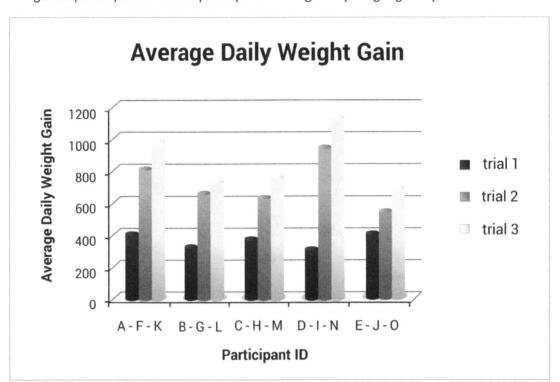

13. What was the main hypothesis for this study?
    a. 2-AG injections combined with sleep deprivation will result in weight gain.
    b. 2-AG injections will increase food intake beyond satiety.
    c. Sleep deprivation will result in weight gain.
    d. The placebo effect of the sterile normal saline will influence eating behavior.

14. Do the study results support the hypothesis? Choose the best answer.
    a. No, participants in trials 1 and 3 all gained weight.
    b. Yes, participants in trial 1 gained more weight daily than participants in trial 3.
    c. No, the average weight gain of participants in trial 2 and trial 3 was the same.
    d. Yes, all trial 3 participants gained more weight than trial 1 participants.

15. Describe the study results for participants D and H.
    a. Participant H gained more than one pound each day.
    b. Weight gain for each participant was inconsistent with the study hypothesis.
    c. There was significant fluctuation in the daily weight gain for both participants.
    d. Participant D's average daily weight was two times participant H's average daily weight gain.

16. According to the researchers, which of the following best describes the influence of sleep deprivation on eating behaviors?
    a. The total number of sleep hours is unrelated to the degree of body stress.
    b. Sleep deprivation stimulates the release of endogenous cannabinoids that may increase food intake.
    c. Deprivation of any variety triggers the hunger response.
    d. Sleep deprivation increases eating behaviors in the early morning hours.

17. According to the passage, how does 2-AG influence eating behaviors?
    a. Circadian fluctuations result in increased levels of 2-AG in the afternoon and evening.
    b. Endogenous cannabinoids like 2-AG increase gastric motility, which stimulates the hunger response.
    c. The sedation that results from the presence of 2-AG limits food intake.
    d. Endogenous cannabinoids block the opioid system, which decreases food-seeking behaviors.

Passage 4

Questions 18–22 pertain to the following passage:

A national wholesale nursery commissioned research to conduct a cost/benefit analysis of replacing existing fluorescent grow lighting systems with newer LED lighting systems. LEDs (light-emitting diodes) are composed of various semi-conductor materials that allow the flow of current in one direction. This means that LEDs emit light in a predictable range, unlike conventional lighting systems that give off heat and light in all directions. The wavelength of light of a single LED is determined by the properties of the specific semi-conductor. For instance, the indium gallium nitride system is used for blue, green, and cyan LEDs. As a result, growing systems can be individualized for the specific wavelength requirements for different plant species. In addition, LEDs don't emit significant amounts of heat compared to broadband systems, so plant hydration can be controlled more efficiently.

Figure 1 identifies the visible spectrum with the wavelength expressed in nanometers.

Figure 1:
The Visible Spectrum (Wavelength in Nanometers)

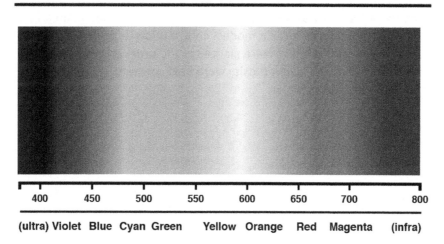

Figure 2 (below) identifies the absorption rates of different wavelengths of light.

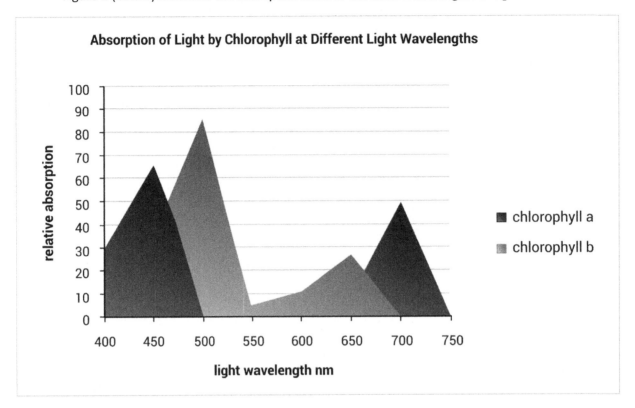

Researchers conducted three trials and hypothesized that LEDs would result in greater growth rates than conventional lighting or white light. They also hypothesized that using a combination of red, blue, green, and yellow wavelengths in the LED lighting system would result in a greater growth rate than using red or blue wavelengths alone. Although green and yellow wavelengths are largely reflected by the plant (Figure 2), the absorption rate is sufficient to make a modest contribution to plant growth. Fifteen Impatiens walleriana seed samples were planted in the same growing medium. Temperature, hydration, and light intensity were held constant. Plant height in millimeters was recorded as follows.

Figure 3 identifies the plant growth rate in millimeters with light wavelengths of 440 nanometers.

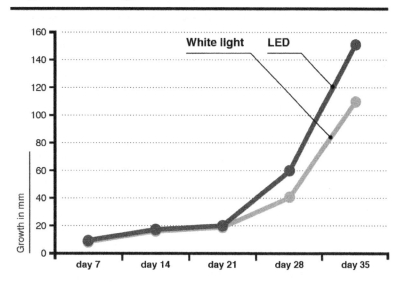

Figure 3:
Plant Growth Rate (mm) with Light wavelengths of 440 nm

Figure 4 (below) identifies the plant growth rate in mm with light wavelengths of 650 nanometers.

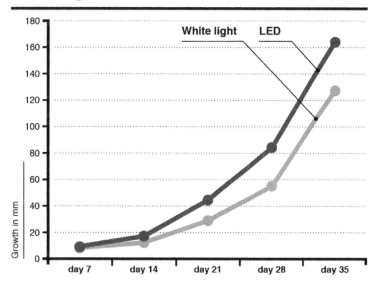

Figure 4:
Plant Growth Rate (mm) with Light wavelengths of 650 nm

Figure 5 (below) identifies the plant growth rate in millimeters with combined light wavelengths of 440, 550, and 650 nanometers.

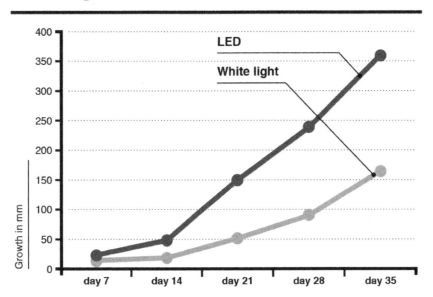

Figure 5:
Plant Growth Rate (mm) with Combined Light wavelengths of 440, 550, and 650 nm

Figure 6 (below) identifies average daily plant growth rate in millimeters.

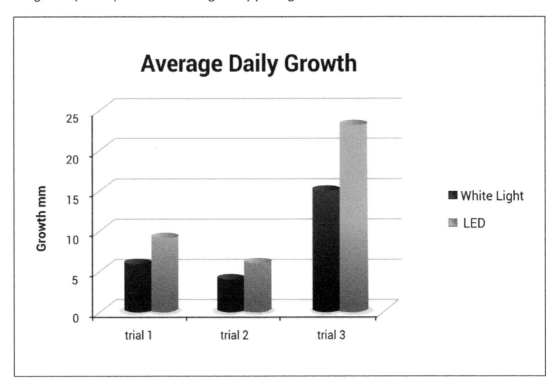

18. If the minimum plant height required for packaging a plant for sale is 150 millimeters, based on plant growth, how much sooner will the LED plants be packaged compared to the white light plants?
   - a. 14 days
   - b. 21 days
   - c. 35 days
   - d. 42 days

19. Plants reflect green and yellow light wavelengths. Do the results of the three trials support the view that plants also absorb and use green and yellow light wavelengths for growth?
   - a. Yes, green and yellow light wavelengths were responsible for plant growth in trial 3.
   - b. No, white light alone was responsible for measurable plant growth.
   - c. Yes, the growth rates in trial 3 were greater than the rates in trials 1 and 2.
   - d. No, only the red and blue wavelengths were effective in stimulating plant growth.

20. When did the greatest rate of growth occur for both groups in trial 1 and trial 2?
   - a. From 7 days to 14 days
   - b. From 28 days to 35 days
   - c. From 21 days to 28 days
   - d. From 14 days to 21 days

21. If an LED lighting system costs twice as much as a white light system, based only on the average daily growth rate as noted above, would it be a wise investment?
   - a. No, because multiple different semi-conductors would be necessary.
   - b. Yes, growth rates are better with LEDs.
   - c. No, the LED average daily growth rate was not two times greater than the white light rate.
   - d. Yes, LEDs use less electricity and water.

22. If the researchers conducted an additional trial, trial 4, to measure the effect of green and yellow wavelengths on plant growth, what would be the probable result?
   - a. The growth rate would exceed trial 1.
   - b. The growth rate would equal trial 3.
   - c. The growth rate would be the same as trial 2.
   - d. The growth rate would be less than trial 1 or trial 2.

Passage 5

Questions 23–28 pertain to the following passage:

Mangoes are a tropical fruit that grow on trees native to Southern Asia called the *Mangifera*. Mangoes are now grown in most frost-free tropical and subtropical locations around the world. India and China harvest the greatest numbers of mangoes. A major problem the mango industry faces each year is the destruction of fruit after harvest. This destruction is the result of spoilage or rotting that occurs during long shipping and storage times.

To prevent the spoilage of mangoes, fruits are stored and shipped in climate-controlled containers. Ideally, mangoes should be stored at around 5 °C, which is about the same temperature as a home refrigerator. Although storage at 5 °C is highly effective at preventing spoilage, the monetary costs associated with maintaining this temperature during long shipping times are prohibitive.

Fruit companies spend large amounts of money to learn about the underlying cause of spoilage and possible methods to prevent loss of their product. Anthracnose, an infection that causes mango decay, is caused by *Colletotrichum,* a type of fungus that has been identified as a major contributor to mango spoilage. This fungus, which may remain dormant on green fruit, grows on the surface of the mango and can penetrate the skin and cause spoilage. The infection first appears during the flowering period as small black dots that progress to dark brown or black areas as ripening occurs. Humidity and excessive rainfall increase the severity of this infection. Previous studies established that colony sizes smaller than 35 millimeters after 4 weeks of travel resulted in acceptable amounts of spoilage.

Currently, several additional pre-treatment measures aimed at prevention are employed to slow decay of the fruit from the harvest to the marketplace. Industry researchers examined the individual and collective benefits of two of these processes, including post-harvest hot water treatment and air cooling at varied transport temperatures in order to identify optimum post-harvest procedures.

Table 1 identifies the observed mango decay in millimeters at 5 °C, 7.5 °C, and 10 °C with two pre-treatment processes over time measured in days since harvest of the fruit.

Table 1: Days Since Harvest

	2	4	6	8	10	12	14	16	18	20	22	24	26	28
5° C														
Water	1	4	7	9	11	12	14	19	22	23	25	27	28	30
Air	0	2	3	6	8	9	11	12	13	15	16	17	18	19
7.5°C														
Water	2	3	4	5	6	8	9	11	12	13	14	15	16	27
Air	0	2	5	6	7	9	10	15	22	23	24	27	32	39
10°C														
Water	2	3	5	7	8	11	12	14	22	35	42	44	47	62
Air	1	2	4	6	7	9	10	15	19	23	27	29	35	44

Figure 1 (below) identifies the observed mango decay of fruit stored at 5 °C measured in millimeters, with two pretreatment processes, over time measured in days since harvest of the fruit.

Figure 1:
5 °C Mango Decay Rates

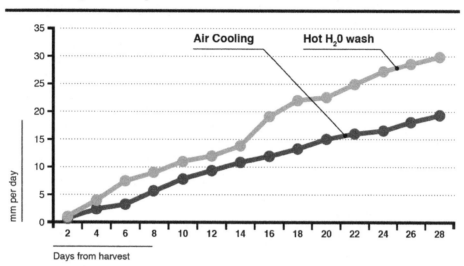

Figures 2 (below) identifies the observed mango decay of fruit stored at 7.5 °C, measured in millimeters, with two pretreatment processes, over time measured in days since harvest of the fruit.

Figure 2.
7.5 °C Mango Decay Rates

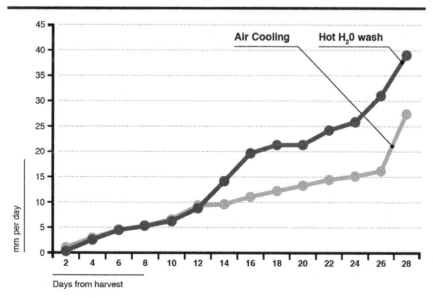

Figures 3 (below) identifies the observed mango decay of fruit stored at 10 °C measured in millimeters, with two pretreatment processes, over time measured in days since harvest of the fruit.

Figures 3:
10 °C Mango Decay Rates

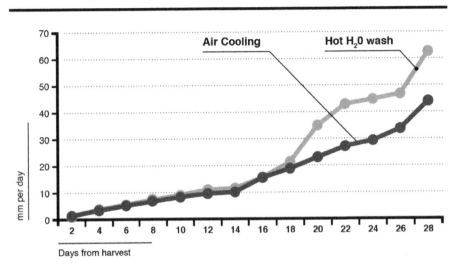

Figure 4 (below) identifies fruit decay measured in millimeters at 5 °C, 7.5 °C, and 10 °C with the combined pre-treatments over 28 days.

Figure 4:
Mango Decay Rates at 5 °C, 7.5 °C, and 10 °C with the Combined Pre-Treatments (Air Cooling & Water Bath)

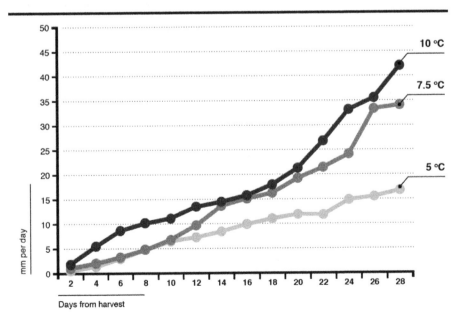

23. According to the passage above, which of the following statements is false?
    a. The optimal temperature for storing mangos is 5 °C.
    b. *Anacardiaceae Magnifera* is responsible for mango spoilage.
    c. Storing fruit at 5 °C is costly.
    d. Long distance shipping is a critical factor in mango spoilage.

24. If the mangoes were shipped from India to the U.S., and the trip was expected to take 20 days, which model would be best according to the data in Table 1?
    a. The 10 °C model, because fungal levels were acceptable for both pre-treatments.
    b. The 5 °C, model because it's more cost-effective.
    c. The 7.5 °C model, because this temperature is less expensive to maintain, and the fungal levels were acceptable.
    d. No single model is better than the other two models.

25. According to Figures 1–3 above, the largest one-day increase in fruit decay occurred under which conditions?
    a. Air cooling at 10 °C
    b. Hot water wash at 10 °C
    c. Air cooling at 7.5 °C
    d. Hot water wash at 7.5 °C

26. Which pre-treatment method reached unacceptable fungal levels first?
    a. Hot water wash at 7.5 °C
    b. Air cooling at 5 °C
    c. Hot water wash at 10 °C
    d. Air cooling at 10 °C

27. The researchers were attempting to identify the best shipping conditions for mangoes for a 28-day trip from harvest to market. Referencing Figures 1–4, which conditions would be the most cost-effective?
    a. Air cooling pre-treatment at 5 °C
    b. Air cooling and hot water wash pre-treatment at 5 °C
    c. Hot water wash pre-treatment at 7.5 °C
    d. Air cooling at 10 °C

28. Shipping mangoes at 5 °C is costly. According to the researchers' findings, is shipping mangoes at 5 °C more cost effective than 7.5 °C for trips lasting more than 28 days when combined air cooling and hot water wash treatments are applied?
    a. Yes, shipping at 7.5 °C combined with both pre-treatments resulted in an unacceptable fungal infection rate.
    b. Yes, fungal infection rates were below 35 mm for both pre-treatments 5 °C.
    c. No, air cooling pre-treatment was acceptable at 10 °C, and it's less expensive to ship fruit at 10 °C.
    d. No, hot water wash rates were lower than air cooling at 5 °C.

Passage 6

Questions 29–34 pertain to the following passage:

Scientists recently discovered that circadian rhythms help regulate sugar consumption by brown adipose tissue. The results of this study suggest that circadian rhythms and fat cells work together to warm the body in preparation for early morning activities involving cold weather. A circadian rhythm refers to life processes controlled by an internal "biological clock" that maintains a 24-hour rhythm. Sleep is controlled by one's circadian rhythm. To initiate sleep, the circadian rhythm stimulates the pineal gland to release the hormone melatonin, which causes sleepiness. Importantly, the circadian rhythm discerns when to begin the process of sleep based on the time of day. During the daytime, sunlight stimulates special cells within the eye, photosensitive retinal ganglion cells, which, in turn, allow the "biological clock" to keep track of how many hours of sunlight there are in a given day.

Brown adipose tissue (BAT) is a type of fat that plays an important role in thermogenesis, a process that generates heat. In humans and other mammals, there are two basic types of thermogenesis: shivering thermogenesis and non-shivering thermogenesis. Shivering thermogenesis involves physical movements, such as shaky hands or clattering teeth. Heat is produced as a result of energy being burned during physical activity. Non-shivering thermogenesis doesn't require physical activity; instead, it utilizes brown adipose tissue to generate heat. Brown fat cells appear dark because they contain large numbers of mitochondria, the organelles that burn sugar to produce energy and heat.

Researchers know that brown adipose tissue (BAT) is essential for maintaining body temperature. A new discovery in humans has shown that circadian rhythms cause BAT to consume more sugar in the early-morning hours. This spike in sugar consumption causes more heat to be produced in BAT. Scientists propose that our human ancestors could have benefited from extra body heat during cold hunts in the morning.

Perhaps more significantly, these new findings may suggest a role for BAT in the prevention of Type 2 Diabetes. Two important questions remain; to what degree does BAT affect blood glucose levels, and is it possible to increase BAT in a given individual? The demonstrated increase in sugar consumption and heat production of BAT is thought to be related to insulin-sensitivity. To examine the first question, researchers conducted three trials to examine the relationship between brown fat and blood glucose levels at different points in the day. PET scanning was used to estimate total body brown fat in 18 non-diabetic participants. Total body brown fat expressed as a proportion of total body fat (either 5%, 10%, or 20%) was the basis for group selection. The researchers hypothesized that the blood glucose levels would be inversely related to the percentage of BAT. Resulting data is included below.

Figure 1 (below) identifies the circadian cycle of blood glucose.

Figure 1:
Normal Circadian Plasma Glucose Levels

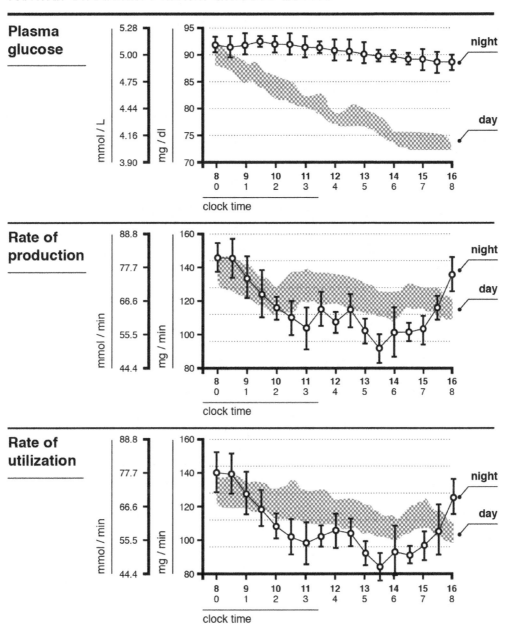

Figure 2 (below) identifies the resulting blood glucose measurements for participants with 5% total brown body fat.

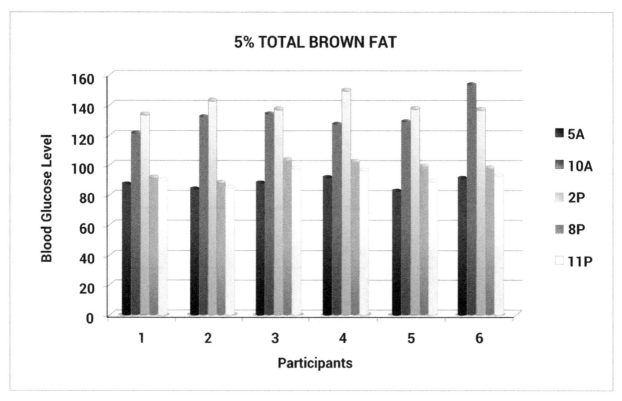

Figure 3 (below) identifies the resulting blood glucose measurements for participants with 10% total brown body fat.

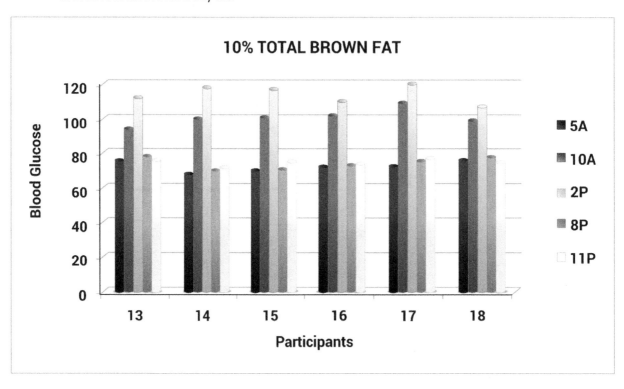

Figure 4 (below) identifies the resulting blood glucose measurements for participants with 20% total brown body fat.

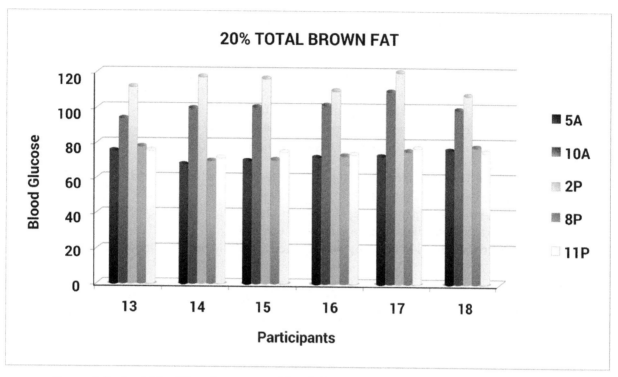

Figure 5 (below) identifies the average blood glucose measurements for the three trials.

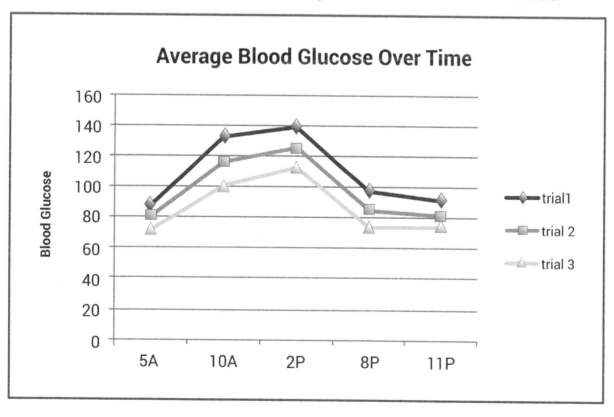

29. Which of the following describes the relationship of the research results in Figure 5?
    a. Positive correlation among the three trials
    b. Curvilinear relationship
    c. Weak negative relationship
    d. No demonstrated relationship

30. Which of the following statements concerning mitochondria is INCORRECT?
    a. Mitochondrial function is diminished in the presence of elevated blood glucose levels.
    b. Mitochondria are responsible for the color of brown fat.
    c. Mitochondria are capable of reproduction in response to energy needs.
    d. Mitochondria are responsible for binding oxygen in mature red blood cells.

31. According to Figure 5, participants' blood sugars were highest at what time of day?
    a. 5 a.m., because heat is generated early in the morning
    b. 8 p.m., because the participants ate less for dinner than lunch
    c. 11 p.m., because brown adipose tissue is not active at night
    d. 2 p.m., because the effects of the early-morning activity of the brown adipose tissue had diminished

32. Circadian rhythms control sleep by doing which of the following?
    a. Stimulating the pineal gland to release ganglia
    b. Stimulating the release of melatonin
    c. Suppressing shivering during cold mornings
    d. Instructing brown adipose tissue to release sugar

33. Which Participant in trial 1 had the highest average blood sugar for the group?
    a. 1
    b. 3
    c. 4
    d. 6

34. Is the data in Figure 5 consistent with the daytime plasma glucose trend in Figure 1?
    a. Yes, Figure 5 blood glucose readings declined from a morning to afternoon.
    b. No, blood glucose readings peaked at 2 p.m..
    c. Yes, morning glucose readings were higher in group 1.
    d. No, nighttime levels fluctuated between 100 and 110.

Passage 7

Questions 35–40 pertain to the following passage:

A biome is a major terrestrial or aquatic environment that supports diverse life forms. Freshwater biomes—including lakes, streams and rivers, and wetlands—account for 0.01% of the Earth's fresh water. Collectively, they are home to 6% of all recognized species. Standing water bodies may vary in size from small ponds to the Great Lakes. Plant life in lakes is specific to the zone of the lake that provides the optimal habitat for a specific species, based on the depth of the water as it relates to light. The photic layer is the shallower layer where light is available for photosynthesis. The aphotic layer is deeper, and the levels of sunlight are too low for photosynthesis. The benthic layer is the bottom-most layer, and its inhabitants are nourished by materials from the photic layer. Light-sensitive cyanobacteria and microscopic algae are two forms of phytoplankton that exist in lakes. As a result of nitrogen and phosphorous from agriculture and sewage run-off, algae residing near the surface can multiply abnormally so that available light is diminished to other species. Oxygen supplies may also be reduced when large numbers of algae die.

Recently, concerns have been raised about the effects of agriculture and commercial development on the quality of national freshwater bodies. In order to estimate the effect of human impact on freshwater, researchers examined plant life from the aphotic layer of three freshwater lakes of approximately the same size located in three different environments. Lake A was located in a remote forested area of western Montana. Lake B was located in central Kansas. Lake C was located in a medium-size city on the west coast of Florida. The researchers hypothesized that the microscopic algae and cyanobacteria populations from Lake A would approach appropriate levels for the size of the lake. They also hypothesized that the remaining two samples would reveal abnormal levels of the phytoplankton. In addition, the researchers measured the concentration of algae at different depths at four different times in another lake identified as having abnormal algae growth. These measurements attempted to identify the point at which light absorption in the photic layer was no longer sufficient for the growth of organisms in the aphotic layer. Resulting data is identified below.

Figure 1 (below) illustrates the zones of the freshwater lake.

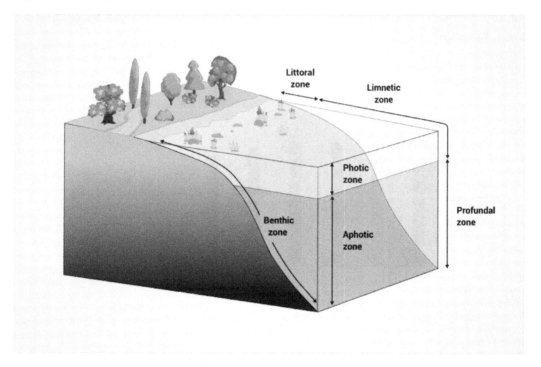

Figure 2 (below) identifies algae and cyanobacteria levels in parts per million for Lake A over six measurements.

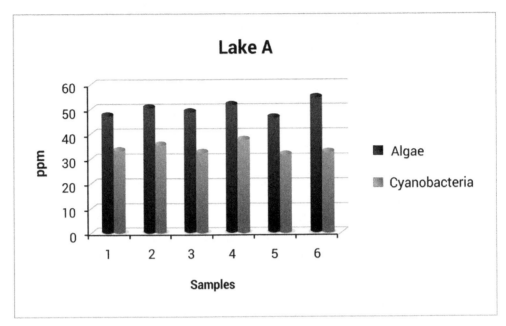

normal: Algae 50 p.p.m. Cyanobacteria 35 p.p.m.

Figure 3 (below) identifies algae and cyanobacteria levels in parts per million for Lake B over six measurements.

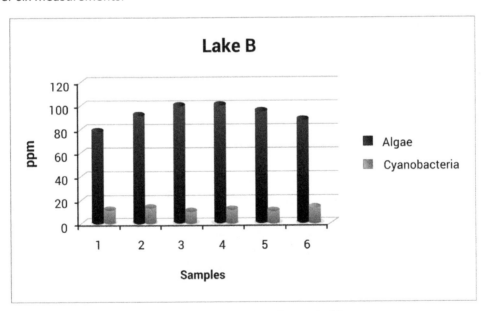

normal: Algae 50 p.p.m. Cyanobacteria 35 p.p.m.

Figure 4 (below) identifies algae and cyanobacteria levels in parts per million for Lake C over six measurements.

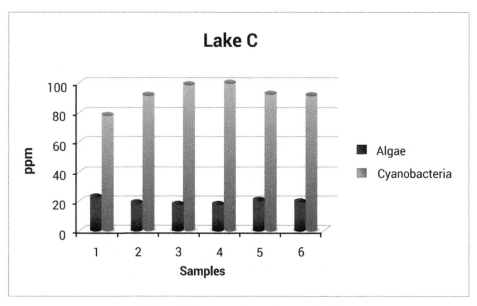

normal: Algae 50 p.p.m. Cyanobacteria 35 p.p.m.

Figure 5 (below) identifies cyanobacteria levels at different depths over time.

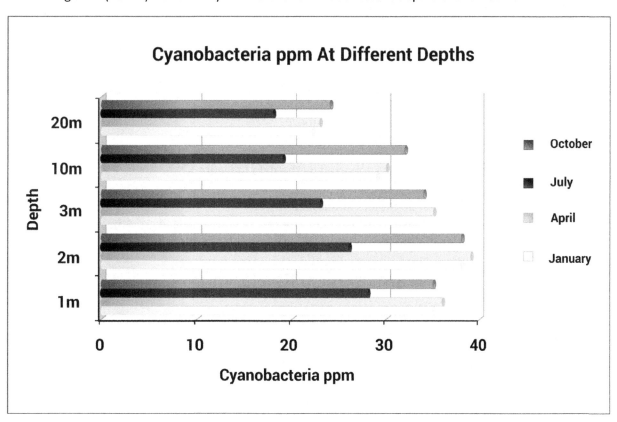

35. Based on Figure 2, was the researchers' hypothesis confirmed?
    a. No, the phytoplankton levels were not elevated in the first trial.
    b. Yes, the phytoplankton levels were raised above normal in each sample.
    c. No, the Lake A numbers were normal.
    d. Yes, algae levels were above normal in Lake C.

36. In Lake B, cyanobacteria were decreased and algae were increased. Which of the following is a possible explanation for this finding?
    a. The overgrowth of algae decreased the light energy available for cyanobacteria growth.
    b. Lake B experienced severe flooding, causing the water levels in the lake to rise above normal.
    c. Agricultural chemical residue depleted the food source for cyanobacteria.
    d. Cyanobacteria cannot survive in the cold winter weather in Lake B.

37. What common factor might explain the results for Lake B and Lake C?
    a. Population concentration
    b. Average humidity of the locations
    c. Average heat index
    d. Excess nitrogen and phosphorous in the ground water

38. As algae levels increase above normal, what happens to organisms in the aphotic level?
    a. Growth is limited but sustained.
    b. Species eventually die due to decreased oxygenation.
    c. Cyanobacteria increase to unsafe levels.
    d. Aerobic bacteria multiply.

39. Referencing Figures 2 and 3, which environment would favor organisms in the benthic layer of the corresponding lake?
    a. Figure 4, because the cyanobacteria are protective.
    b. Figure 3, because increased numbers of Algae provide more light.
    c. Figure 4, because cyanobacteria are able to survive.
    d. Figure 3, because the levels of both species are normal.

40. Which of the following statements is supported by the data in Figure 5?
    a. Algae growth is greater in July than April.
    b. Cyanobacteria can't exist at 20 meters in this lake.
    c. There's insufficient light in the aphotic layer at 3 meters to support algae growth.
    d. Cyanobacteria growth rates are independent of algae growth at 1 meter.

Mathematical Reasoning

1. Which of the following is the result of simplifying the expression: $\frac{4a^{-1}b^3}{a^4b^{-2}} \times \frac{3a}{b}$?
    a. $12a^3b^5$
    b. $12\frac{b^4}{a^4}$
    c. $\frac{12}{a^4}$
    d. $7\frac{b^4}{a}$

2. What is the product of two irrational numbers?
    a. Irrational
    b. Rational
    c. Contradictory
    d. Irrational or rational

3. The graph shows the position of a car over a 10-second time interval. Which of the following is the correct interpretation of the graph for the interval 1 to 3 seconds?

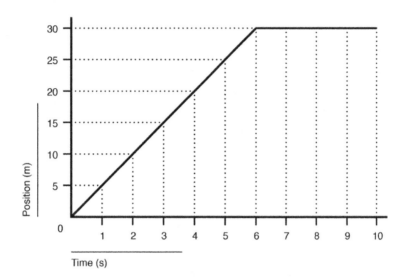

    a. The car remains in the same position.
    b. The car is traveling at a speed of 5m/s.
    c. The car is traveling up a hill.
    d. The car is traveling at 5mph.

4. How is the number -4 classified?
    a. Real, rational, integer, whole, natural
    b. Real, rational, integer, natural
    c. Real, rational, integer
    d. Real, irrational

5. In a statistical experiment, 29 college students are given an exam during week 11 of the semester, and 30 college students are given an exam during week 12 of the semester. Both groups are being tested to determine which exam week might result in a higher grade. What's the degree of freedom in this experiment?
    a. 29
    b. 30
    c. 59
    d. 28

6. What are the zeros of the function: $f(x) = x^3 + 4x^2 + 4x$?

    a. -2

    b. 0, -2

    c. 2

    d. 0, 2

7. If $g(x) = x^3 - 3x^2 - 2x + 6$ and $f(x) = 2$, then what is $g(f(x))$?

    a. -26

    b. 6

    c. $2x^3 - 6x^2 - 4x + 12$

    d. -2

8. $(2x - 4y)^2 =$

    a. $4x^2 - 16xy + 16y^2$

    b. $4x^2 - 8xy + 16y^2$

    c. $4x^2 - 16xy - 16y^2$

    d. $2x^2 - 8xy + 8y^2$

9. If x is not zero, then $\frac{3}{x} + \frac{5u}{2x} - \frac{u}{4} =$

    a. $\frac{12+10u-ux}{4x}$

    b. $\frac{3+5u-ux}{x}$

    c. $\frac{12x+10u+ux}{4x}$

    d. $\frac{12+10u-u}{4x}$

10. What is the product of the following expression?

$$(4x - 8)(5x^2 + x + 6)$$

    a. $20x^3 - 36x^2 + 16x - 48$

    b. $6x^3 - 41x^2 + 12x + 15$

    c. $204 + 11x^2 - 37x - 12$

    d. $2x^3 - 11x^2 - 32x + 20$

11. How could the following equation be factored to find the zeros?

$$y = x^3 - 3x^2 - 4x$$

    a. $0 = x^2(x - 4), x = 0, 4$

    b. $0 = 3x(x + 1)(x + 4), x = 0, -1, -4$

    c. $0 = x(x + 1)(x + 6), x = 0, -1, -6$

    d. $0 = x(x + 1)(x - 4), x = 0, -1, 4$

12. What is the simplified quotient of $\frac{5x^3}{3x^2y} \div \frac{25}{3y^9}$?

    a. $\frac{125x}{9y^{10}}$

    b. $\frac{x}{5y^8}$

    c. $\frac{5}{xy^8}$

    d. $\frac{xy^8}{5}$

13. What is the solution for the following equation?

$$\frac{x^2 + x - 30}{x - 5} = 11$$

    a. $x = -6$
    b. There is no solution.
    c. $x = 16$
    d. $x = 5$

14. Mom's car drove 72 miles in 90 minutes. How fast did she drive in feet per second?
    a. 0.8 feet per second
    b. 48.9 feet per second
    c. 0.009 feet per second
    d. 70. 4 feet per second

15. How do you solve $V = lwh$ for h?
    a. $lwV = h$

    b. $h = \frac{V}{lw}$

    c. $h = \frac{Vl}{w}$

    d. $h = \frac{Vw}{l}$

16. What is the domain for the function $y = \sqrt{x}$?
    a. All real numbers
    b. $x \geq 0$
    c. $x > 0$
    d. $y \geq 0$

17. If Sarah reads at an average rate of 21 pages in four nights, how long will it take her to read 140 pages?
    a. 6 nights
    b. 26 nights
    c. 8 nights
    d. 27 nights

18. The phone bill is calculated each month using the equation $c = 50g + 75$. The cost of the phone bill per month is represented by c, and g represents the gigabytes of data used that month. What is the value and interpretation of the slope of this equation?
 a. 75 dollars per day
 b. 75 gigabytes per day
 c. 50 dollars per day
 d. 50 dollars per gigabyte

19. What is the function that forms an equivalent graph to $y = \cos(x)$?
 a. $y = \tan(x)$

 b. $y = \csc(x)$

 c. $y = \sin(x + \frac{\pi}{2})$

 d. $y = \sin(x - \frac{\pi}{2})$

20. What is the solution for the equation $\tan(x) + 1 = 0$, where $0 \le x < 2\pi$?
 a. $x = \frac{3\pi}{4}, \frac{5\pi}{4}$

 b. $x = \frac{3\pi}{4}, \frac{\pi}{4}$

 c. $x = \frac{5\pi}{4}, \frac{7\pi}{4}$

 d. $x = \frac{3\pi}{4}, \frac{7\pi}{4}$

21. What is the inverse of the function $f(x) = 3x - 5$?
 a. $f^{-1}(x) = \frac{x}{3} + 5$

 b. $f^{-1}(x) = \frac{5x}{3}$

 c. $f^{-1}(x) = 3x + 5$

 d. $f^{-1}(x) = \frac{x+5}{3}$

22. What are the zeros of $f(x) = x^2 + 4$?
 a. $x = -4$
 b. $x = \pm 2i$
 c. $x = \pm 2$
 d. $x = \pm 4i$

23. Twenty is 40 percent of what number?
   a. 500
   b. 8
   c. 200
   d. 50

24. What is the simplified form of the expression $1.2 \times 10^{12} \div 3.0 \times 10^{8}$?
   a. 0.4×10^{4}
   b. 4.0×10^{4}
   c. 4.0×10^{3}
   d. 3.6×10^{20}

25. You measure the width of your door to be 36 inches. The true width of the door is 35.75 inches. What is the relative error in your measurement?
   a. 0.7%
   b. 0.007%
   c. 0.99%
   d. 0.1%

26. What are the y-intercept(s) for $y = x^2 + 3x - 4$?
   a. $y = 1$
   b. $y = -4$
   c. $y = 3$
   d. $y = 4$

27. Write the expression for three times the sum of twice a number and one minus 6.
   a. $2x + 1 - 6$
   b. $3x + 1 - 6$
   c. $3(x + 1) - 6$
   d. $3(2x + 1) - 6$

28. Which equation is not a function?
   a. $y = |x|$
   b. $y = \sqrt{x}$
   c. $x = 3$
   d. $y = 4$

29. How could the following function be rewritten to identify the zeros?

$$y = 3x^3 + 3x^2 - 18x$$

   a. $y = 3x(x + 3)(x - 2)$
   b. $y = x(x - 2)(x + 3)$
   c. $y = 3x(x - 3)(x + 2)$
   d. $y = (x + 3)(x - 2)$

30. What is the slope of the line tangent to the graph of $y = x^3 - 4$ at the point where $x = 2$?
    a. $3x^2$
    b. 4
    c. -4
    d. 12

31. Given the following triangle, what's the length of the missing side? Round the answer to the nearest tenth.

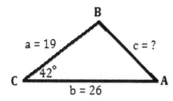

    a. 17.0
    b. 17.4
    c. 18.0
    d. 18.4

32. How many possible two-number combinations are there for the numbers 1, 2, 3, 4, and 5 if each number can only be used once in any combination and order DOES matter?
    a. 120
    b. 60
    c. 20
    d. 10

33. What are the first four terms of the series $\left\{ \frac{(-1)^{n+1}}{n^2+5} \right\}_{n=0}^{\infty}$?
    a. $\frac{1}{6}, \frac{1}{9}, \frac{1}{14}, \frac{1}{19}$

    b. $\frac{1}{6}, \frac{-1}{9}, \frac{1}{14}, \frac{-1}{19}$

    c. $\frac{-1}{5}, \frac{1}{6}, \frac{-1}{9}, \frac{1}{14}$

    d. $\frac{1}{5}, \frac{1}{6}, \frac{1}{9}, \frac{1}{14}$

34. A particle moves along the x-axis, so that at any time $t \geq 0$, its velocity is given by $v(t) = \frac{6}{t+3}$. What is the acceleration of the particle at time $t = 5$?
    a. $-\frac{2}{3}$

    b. $-\frac{3}{32}$

    c. $\frac{3}{4}$

    d. $\frac{2}{3}$

35. If the volume of a sphere is 288π cubic meters, what are the radius and surface area of the same sphere?

    a. Radius 6 meters and surface area 144π square meters

    b. Radius 36 meters and surface area 144π square meters

    c. Radius 6 meters and surface area 12π square meters

    d. Radius 36 meters and surface area 12π square meters

36. The triangle shown below is a right triangle. What's the value of x?

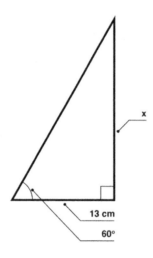

13 cm

60°

    a. $x = 1.73$

    b. $x = 0.57$

    c. $x = 13$

    d. $x = 22.49$

37. What's the midpoint of a line segment with endpoints $(-1, 2)$ and $(3, -6)$?

    a. $(1, 2)$

    b. $(1, 0)$

    c. $(-1, 2)$

    d. $(1, -2)$

38. What is the type of function that is modeled by the values in the following table?

X	f(x)
1	2
2	4
3	8
4	16
5	32

    a. Linear

    b. Exponential

    c. Quadratic

    d. Cubic

39. What is the simplified form of the following expression $\tan\theta\ \cos\theta$?

    a. $sin\theta$

    b. 1

    c. $csc\theta$

    d. $tan\theta$

40. A sample data set contains the following values: 1, 3, 5, 7. What's the standard deviation of the set?

    a. 2.58

    b. 4

    c. 6.23

    d. 1.1

41. A pair of dice is thrown, and the sum of the two scores is calculated. What's the expected value of the roll?

    a. 5

    b. 6

    c. 7

    d. 8

42. A ball is drawn at random from a ball pit containing 8 red balls, 7 yellow balls, 6 green balls, and 5 purple balls. What's the probability that the ball drawn is yellow?

    a. $\dfrac{1}{26}$

    b. $\dfrac{19}{26}$

    c. $\dfrac{7}{26}$

    d. 1

43. Two cards are drawn from a shuffled deck of 52 cards. What's the probability that both cards are Kings if the first card isn't replaced after it's drawn and is a King?

    a. $\dfrac{1}{169}$

    b. $\dfrac{1}{221}$

    c. $\dfrac{1}{13}$

    d. $\dfrac{4}{13}$

44. What's the probability of rolling a 6 at least once in two rolls of a die?

    a. $\dfrac{1}{3}$

    b. $\dfrac{1}{36}$

    c. $\dfrac{1}{6}$

    d. $\dfrac{11}{36}$

45. Given the set $A = \{1, 2, 3, 4, 5, 6, 7, 8, 9, 10\}$ and $B = \{1, 2, 3, 4, 5\}$, find $A - (A \cap B)$.
   a. $\{6, 7, 8, 9, 10\}$
   b. $\{1, 2, 3, 4, 5\}$
   c. $\{1, 2, 3, 4, 5, 6, 7, 8, 9, 10\}$
   d. $\emptyset$

46. Let p = "Alex is an engineering major," q = "Alex is not an English major," r = "Alex's sister is a history major," s = "Alex's sister has been to Germany," and t = "Alex's sister has been to Austria." Which of the following answers represents the statement "Alex is an engineering and English major, but his sister is a history major who hasn't been to either Germany or Austria."
   a. $p \wedge {\sim}q \wedge (r \vee ({\sim}s \vee {\sim}t))$
   b. $p \wedge q \wedge r \vee ({\sim}s \wedge {\sim}t)$
   c. $p \wedge {\sim}q \wedge r \wedge ({\sim}s \vee {\sim}t)$
   d. $p \wedge q \wedge (r \vee ({\sim}s \wedge {\sim}t))$

Social Studies

1. What is NOT a responsibility for citizens of democracy?
   a. To stay aware of current issues and history
   b. To avoid political action
   c. To actively vote in elections
   d. To understand and obey laws

2. Which of the following advancements was NOT invented by Greek culture?
   a. The alphabet
   b. The Hippocratic Oath
   c. Democratic government
   d. Theater

3. Which of the following was an important development in the twentieth century?
   a. The United States and the Soviet Union officially declared war on each other in the Cold War.
   b. The League of Nations signed the Kyoto Protocol.
   c. World War I ended when the United States defeated Japan.
   d. India violently partitioned into India and Pakistan after the end of colonialism.

4. What is NOT an effect of monopolies?
   a. Promote a diverse variety of independent businesses
   b. Inhibit developments that would be problematic for business
   c. Control the supply of resources
   d. Limit the degree of choice for consumers

5. Which method is NOT a way that governments manage economies in a market system?
   a. Laissez-faire
   b. Mercantilism
   c. Capitalism
   d. Self-interest

6. Which of the following nations did NOT establish colonies in what would become the United States?
    a. Italy
    b. England
    c. France
    d. Spain

7. Which of the following statements about the U.S. Constitution is true?
    a. It was signed on July 4, 1776.
    b. It was enacted at the end of the Revolutionary War.
    c. New York failed to ratify it, but it still passed by majority.
    d. It replaced the Articles of Confederation.

8. What is recognized as contributing to democratization after an authoritarian regime such as post-Communism?
    a. Independent media
    b. Corporatism
    c. Socialism
    d. Devolution effects

9. Which term is best defined as a group of people joined by a common culture, language, heritage, history, and religion?
    a. State
    b. Nation
    c. Regime
    d. Government

10. What has been described as the exercise of power to achieve a predetermined end?
    a. Sovereignty
    b. Authority
    c. Government
    d. Politics

11. The way or ways citizens are taught and encouraged to participate in the structures and processes of government is known as what?
    a. State Craft
    b. Nation Building
    c. Globalization
    d. Political Culture

12. Regime types fall along a continuum between which two extremes?
    a. Constitutional and non-constitutional
    b. Military and judicial
    c. Federal and communist
    d. Authoritarian and democratic

13. The European Union and United Nations are examples of what type of government?
    a. Regional
    b. Federal
    c. Supranational
    d. National

14. Which check does the legislative branch possess over the judicial branch?
    a. Appoint judges
    b. Call special sessions of Congress
    c. Rule legislation unconstitutional
    d. Determine the number of Supreme Court judges

15. Which of the following is NOT included in the Bill of Rights?
    a. Freedom to assemble
    b. Freedom against unlawful search
    c. Freedom to vote
    d. Reservation of non-enumerated powers to the states or the people

16. Which form of government divides power between a regional and central government?
    a. Democracy
    b. Constitutional monarchy
    c. Federalism
    d. Feudalism

17. Under Federalism, which is considered a concurrent power held by both the states and the federal government?
    a. Hold elections
    b. Regulate immigration
    c. Expand the territories of a state
    d. Pass and enforce laws

18. The United States elects the president by which of the following ways?
    a. Popular majority vote
    b. Plurality vote
    c. Electoral College
    d. Party list system

19. In the American election system, where do the candidates ultimately receive the nomination from their party?
    a. At the primary
    b. At the caucus
    c. At the debates
    d. At the party convention

20. Which of the following are reasons that geography is important to the examination of history?
    I. Historians make use of maps in their studies to get a clear picture of how history unfolded.
    II. Knowing the borders of different lands helps historians learn different cultures' interactions.
    III. Geography is closely linked with the flow of resources, technology, and population in societies.
    IV. Environmental factors, such as access to water and proximity of mountains, help shape the course of civilization.

    a. I, II, and III only
    b. II, III, and IV only
    c. I, II, and IV only
    d. I, III, and IV only

21. Which of the following was NOT an important invention in the twentieth century?
    a. Radio
    b. Telegraph
    c. Television
    d. Computers

22. What was a concern that George Washington warned of in his Farewell Address?
    a. The danger of political parties
    b. To be prepared to intervene in Europe's affairs
    c. The abolition of slavery
    d. To protect states' rights through sectionalism

23. The presidential and parliamentary systems differ in which of the following ways?
    a. The presidential system establishes a separation of powers.
    b. The legislature elects the chief executive in a presidential system.
    c. Voters directly elect the prime minister in a parliamentary system.
    d. The parliamentary system never includes a president.

24. Which political concept describes a ruling body's ability to influence the actions, behaviors, or attitudes of a person or community?
    a. Authority
    b. Sovereignty
    c. Power
    d. Legitimacy

25. Which part of the legislative process differs in the House and the Senate?
    a. Who may introduce the bill
    b. How debates about a bill are conducted
    c. Who may veto the bill
    d. What wording the bill contains

26. The Revolutionary War's final battle took place on October 19, 1781, when British General Lord Cornwallis surrendered to Washington's troops at what location?
    a. Yorktown, Virginia
    b. Valley Forge, Pennsylvania
    c. Trenton, New Jersey
    d. Saratoga, New York

27. What important U.S. structure was burned during the War of 1812?
    a. The Washington Monument
    b. Independence Hall
    c. The White House
    d. The Statue of Liberty

28. Who was elected President of the Confederate States of America during the Civil War?
    a. Robert E. Lee
    b. Jefferson Davis
    c. William T. Sherman
    d. Abraham Lincoln

29. The period of business and industrial growth from 1876 through the turn of the twentieth century was deemed by author Mark Twain as what?
   a. Manifest Destiny
   b. The Columbian Exchange
   c. The New Deal
   d. The Gilded Age

30. When did World War I begin?
   a. 1915
   b. 1917
   c. 1914
   d. 1918

31. Which of the following countries was a U.S. ally during World War II?
   a. The Soviet Union
   b. Italy
   c. Germany
   d. Japan

32. The North Atlantic Treaty Organization (NATO) was formed between which countries or regions?
   a. Canada, the U.S., and South America
   b. Western Europe, the U.S., and Canada
   c. The U.S., Western Europe, Canada, and the Soviet Union
   d. Asia, the U.S., and Western Europe

33. Which of these events was not a driving force for the passage of the Civil Rights Act in 1964?
   a. *Brown vs. the Board of Education*
   b. Freedom rides
   c. The G.I. Bill
   d. The Montgomery bus boycott

34. What program launched by the U.S. government under President Ronald Reagan was designed to shield the U.S. from nuclear attack by the Soviet Union?
   a. The Strategic Arms Limitation Talks (SALT I and II)
   b. The Strategic Defense Initiative (SDI)
   c. The Iran-Contra Affair
   d. *Glasnost*

35. After the terrorist attacks initiated by Islamic fundamentalist Osama bin Laden on September 11, 2001, President George W. Bush ordered bombing raids on various locations in what country in an attempt to bring down bin Laden and his al-Qaeda network?
   a. Afghanistan
   b. Iraq
   c. Kuwait
   d. Pakistan

Answer Explanations #1

Reading Comprehension

1. C: Gulliver becomes acquainted with the people and practices of his new surroundings. Choice *C* is the correct answer because it most extensively summarizes the entire passage. While Choices *A* and *B* are reasonable possibilities, they reference portions of Gulliver's experiences, not the whole. Choice *D* is incorrect because Gulliver doesn't express repentance or sorrow in this particular passage.

2. A: Principal refers to *chief* or *primary* within the context of this text. Choice *A* is the answer that most closely aligns with this answer. Choices *B* and *D* make reference to a helper or followers while Choice *C* doesn't meet the description of Gulliver from the passage.

3. C: One can reasonably infer that Gulliver is considerably larger than the children who were playing around him because multiple children could fit into his hand. Choice *B* is incorrect because there is no indication of stress in Gulliver's tone. Choices *A* and *D* aren't the best answer because though Gulliver seems fond of his new acquaintances, he didn't travel there with the intentions of meeting new people or to express a definite love for them in this particular portion of the text.

4. C: The emperor made a *definitive decision* to expose Gulliver to their native customs. In this instance, the word *mind* was not related to a vote, question, or cognitive ability.

5. A: Choice *A* is correct. This assertion does *not* support the fact that games are a commonplace event in this culture because it mentions conduct, not games. Choices *B*, *C*, and *D* are incorrect because these do support the fact that games were a commonplace event.

6. B: Choice *B* is the only option that mentions the correlation between physical ability and leadership positions. Choices *A* and *D* are unrelated to physical strength and leadership abilities. Choice *C* does not make a deduction that would lead to the correct answer—it only comments upon the abilities of common townspeople.

7. D: The use of "I" could have all of the effects for the reader; it could serve to have a "hedging" effect, allow the reader to connect with the author in a more personal way, and cause the reader to empathize more with the egrets. However, it doesn't distance the reader from the text, thus eliminating Choice *D*.

8. C: The quote provides an example of a warden protecting one of the colonies. Choice *A* is incorrect because the speaker of the quote is a warden, not a hunter. Choice B is incorrect because the quote does not lighten the mood but shows the danger of the situation between the wardens and the hunters. Choice *D* is incorrect because there is no humor found in the quote.

9. D: A *rookery* is a colony of breeding birds. Although *rookery* could mean Choice *A*, houses in a slum area, it does not make sense in this context. Choices *B* and *C* are both incorrect, as this is not a place for hunters to trade tools or for wardens to trade stories.

10. B: An important bird colony. The previous sentence is describing "twenty colonies" of birds, so what follows should be a bird colony. Choice *A* may be true, but we have no evidence of this in the text. Choice *C* does touch on the tension between the hunters and wardens, but there is no official "Bird Island Battle" mentioned in the text. Choice *D* does not exist in the text.

11. D: To demonstrate the success of the protective work of the Audubon Association. The text mentions several different times how and why the association has been successful and gives examples to back this fact. Choice *A* is incorrect because although the article, in some instances, calls certain people to act, it is not the purpose of the entire passage. There is no way to tell if Choices *B* and *C* are correct, as they are not mentioned in the text.

12. C: To have a better opportunity to hunt the birds. Choice *A* might be true in a general sense, but it is not relevant to the context of the text. Choice *B* is incorrect because the hunters are not studying lines of flight to help wardens, but to hunt birds. Choice *D* is incorrect because nothing in the text mentions that hunters are trying to build homes underneath lines of flight of birds for good luck.

13. A: It introduces certain insects that transition from water to air. Choice *B* is incorrect because although the passage talks about gills, it is not the central idea of the passage. Choices *C* and *D* are incorrect because the passage does not "define" or "invite," but only serves as an introduction to stoneflies, dragonflies, and mayflies and their transition from water to air.

14. C: The act of shedding part or all of the outer shell. Choices *A*, *B*, and *D* are incorrect.

15. B: The first paragraph serves as a contrast to the second. Notice how the first paragraph goes into detail describing how insects are able to breathe air. The second paragraph acts as a contrast to the first by stating "[i]t is of great interest to find that, nevertheless, a number of insects spend much of their time under water." Watch for transition words such as "nevertheless" to help find what type of passage you're dealing with.

16: C: The stage of preparation in between molting is acted out in the water, while the last stage is in the air. Choices *A, B,* and *D* are all incorrect. *Instars* is the phase between two periods of molting, and the text explains when these transitions occur.

17. C: The author's tone is informative and exhibits interest in the subject of the study. Overall, the author presents us with information on the subject. One moment where personal interest is depicted is when the author states, "It is of great interest to find that, nevertheless, a number of insects spend much of their time under water."

18. C: Their larva can breathe the air dissolved in water through gills of some kind. This is stated in the last paragraph. Choice *A* is incorrect because the text mentions this in a general way at the beginning of the passage concerning "insects as a whole." Choice *B* is incorrect because this is stated of beetles and water-bugs, and not the insects in question. Choice *D* is incorrect because this is the opposite of what the text says of instars.

19. A: Bring to light an alternative view on human perception by examining the role of technology in human understanding. This is a challenging question because the author's purpose is somewhat open-ended. The author concludes by stating that the questions regarding human perception and observation can be approached from many angles. Thus, they do not seem to be attempting to prove one thing or another. Choice *B* is incorrect because we cannot know for certain whether the electron experiment is the latest discovery in astroparticle physics because no date is given. Choice *C* is a broad generalization that does not reflect accurately on the writer's views. While the author does appear to reflect on opposing views of human understanding (Choice *D*), the best answer is Choice *A*.

20. C: It presents a problem, explains the details of that problem, and then ends with more inquiry. The beginning of this paragraph literally "presents a conundrum," explains the problem of partial understanding, and then ends with more questions, or inquiry. There is no solution offered in this paragraph, making Choices *A* and *B* incorrect. Choice *D* is incorrect because the paragraph does not begin with a definition.

21. D: Looking back in the text, the author describes that classical philosophy holds that understanding can be reached by careful observation. This will not work if they are overly invested or biased in their pursuit. Choices *A* and *C* are in no way related and are completely unnecessary. A specific theory is not necessary to understanding, according to classical philosophy mentioned by the author. Again, the key to understanding is observing the phenomena outside of it, without biased or predisposition. Thus, Choice *B* is wrong.

22. B: The electrons passed through both holes and then onto the plate. Choices *A* and *C* are wrong because such movement is not mentioned at all in the text. In the passage the author says that electrons that were physically observed appeared to pass through one hole or another. Remember, the electrons that were observed doing this were described as acting like particles. Therefore, Choice *D* is wrong. Recall that the plate actually recorded electrons passing through both holes simultaneously and hitting the plate This behavior, the electron activity that wasn't seen by humans, was characteristic of waves. Thus, Choice *B* is the right answer.

23. C: To demonstrate an example of natural phenomena humans discovered and understand without the use of tools or machines. Choice *A* mirrors the language in the beginning of the paragraph but is incorrect in its intent. Choice *B* is incorrect; the paragraph mentions nothing of "not knowing the true nature of gravity." Choice *D* is incorrect as well. There is no mention of an "alternative solution" in this paragraph.

24. A: The important thing to keep in mind is that we must choose a scenario that best parallels, or is most similar to, the discovery of the experiment mentioned in the passage. The important aspects of the experiment can be summed up like so: humans directly observed one behavior of electrons and then through analyzing a tool (the plate that recorded electron hits), discovered that there was another electron behavior that could not be physically seen by human eyes. This best parallels the scenario in Choice *A*. Like Feynman, the colorblind person is able to observe one aspect of the world but through the special goggles (a tool) he is able to see a natural phenomenon that he could not physically see on his own. While Choice *D* is compelling, the x-ray helps humans see the broken bone, not necessarily revealing that the bone is broken in the first place. The other choices do not parallel the scenario in question. Therefore, Choice *A* is the best choice.

25. B: The author would not agree that technology renders human observation irrelevant. Choice *A* is incorrect because much of the passage discusses how technology helps humans observe what cannot be seen with the naked eye, therefore the author would agree with this statement. This line of reasoning is also why the author would agree with Choice *D*, making it incorrect as well. As indicated in the second paragraph, the author seems to think that humans create inventions and tools with the goal of studying phenomena more precisely. This indicates increased understanding as people recognize limitations and develop items to help bypass the limitations and learn. Therefore, Choice *C* is incorrect as well. Again, the author doesn't attempt to disprove or dismiss classical philosophy.

26. A: The tone is exasperated. While contemplative is an option because of the inquisitive nature of the text, Choice *A* is correct because the speaker is annoyed by the thought of being included when he felt that the fellow members of his race were being excluded. The speaker is not nonchalant, nor accepting of the circumstances which he describes.

27. C: Choice C, *contented*, is the only word that has different meaning. Furthermore, the speaker expresses objection and disdain throughout the entire text.

28. B: To address the feelings of exclusion expressed by African Americans after the establishment of the Fourth of July holiday. While the speaker makes biblical references, it is not the main focus of the passage, thus eliminating Choice A as an answer. The passage also makes no mention of wealthy landowners and doesn't speak of any positive response to the historical events, so Choices C and D are not correct.

29. D: Choice D is the correct answer because it clearly makes reference to justice being denied.

30. D: Hyperbole. Choices A and B are unrelated. Assonance is the repetition of sounds and commonly occurs in poetry. Parallelism refers to two statements that correlate in some manner. Choice C is incorrect because amplification normally refers to clarification of meaning by broadening the sentence structure, while hyperbole refers to a phrase or statement that is being exaggerated.

31. C: Display the equivocation of the speaker and those that he represents. Choice C is correct because the speaker is clear about his intention and stance throughout the text. Choice A could be true, but the words "common text" is arguable. Choice B is also partially true, as another group of people affected by slavery are being referenced. However, the speaker is not trying to convince the audience that injustices have been committed, as it is already understood there have been injustices committed. Choice D is also close to the correct answer, but it is not the *best* answer choice possible.

32. C: We are looking for an inference—a conclusion that is reached on the basis of evidence and reasoning—from the passage that will likely explain why the famous children's author did not achieve her usual success with the new genre (despite the book's acclaim). Choice A is wrong because the statement is false according to the passage. Choice B is wrong because, although the passage says the author has a graduate degree on the subject, it would be an unrealistic leap to infer that she is the foremost expert on Antebellum America. Choice D is wrong because there is nothing in the passage to lead us to infer that people generally prefer a children's series to historical fiction. In contrast, Choice C can be logically inferred since the passage speaks of the great success of the children's series and the declaration that the fame of the author's name causes the children's books to "fly off the shelves." Thus, she did not receive any bump from her name since she published the historical novel under a pseudonym, and Choice C is correct.

33. C: The author contrasts two different viewpoints, then builds a case showing preference for one over the other. Choice A is incorrect because the introduction does not contain an impartial definition, but rather, an opinion. Choice B is incorrect. There is no puzzling phenomenon given, as the author doesn't mention any peculiar cause or effect that is in question regarding poetry. Choice D does contain another's viewpoint at the beginning of the passage; however, to say that the author has no stake in this argument is incorrect; the author uses personal experiences to build their case.

34. B: Choice B accurately describes the author's argument in the text: that poetry is not irrelevant. While the author does praise, and even value, Buddy Wakefield as a poet, the author never heralds him as a genius. Eliminate Choice A, as it is an exaggeration. Not only is Choice C an exaggerated statement, but the author never mentions spoken word poetry in the text. Choice D is wrong because this statement contradicts the writer's argument.

35. D: *Exiguously* means not occurring often, or occurring rarely, so Choice D would LEAST change the meaning of the sentence. Choice A, *indolently*, means unhurriedly, or slow, and does not fit the context of the sentence. Choice *B*, *inaudibly*, means quietly or silently. Choice *C*, *interminably*, means endlessly, or all the time, and is the opposite of the word *exiguously*.

36. D: A student's insistence that psychoanalysis is a subset of modern psychology is the most analogous option. The author of the passage tries to insist that performance poetry is a subset of modern poetry, and therefore, tries to prove that modern poetry is not "dying," but thriving on social media for the masses. Choice *A* is incorrect, as the author is not refusing any kind of validation. Choice *B* is incorrect; the author's insistence is that poetry will *not* lose popularity. Choice *C* mimics the topic but compares two different genres, while the author does no comparison in this passage.

37. B: The author's purpose is to disprove Gioia's article claiming that poetry is a dying art form that only survives in academic settings. In order to prove his argument, the author educates the reader about new developments in poetry (Choice *A*) and describes the brilliance of a specific modern poet (Choice *C*), but these serve as examples of a growing poetry trend that counters Gioia's argument. Choice *D* is incorrect because it contradicts the author's argument.

38. D: This question is difficult because the choices offer real reasons as to why the author includes the quote. However, the question specifically asks for the *main reason* for including the quote. The quote from a recently written poem shows that people are indeed writing, publishing, and performing poetry (Choice *B*). The quote also shows that people are still listening to poetry (Choice *C*). These things are true, and by their nature, serve to disprove Gioia's views (Choice *A*), which is the author's goal. However, Choice *D* is the most direct reason for including the quote, because the article analyzes the quote for its "complex themes" that "draws listeners and appreciation" right after it's given.

39. D: The author explains that Boethianism is a Medieval theological philosophy that attributes sin to temporary pleasure and righteousness with virtue and God's providence. Besides Choice *D,* the choices listed are all physical things. While these could still be divine rewards, Boethianism holds that the true reward for being virtuous is in God's favor. It is also stressed in the article that physical pleasures cannot be taken into the afterlife. Therefore, the best choice is *D*, God's favor.

40. C: *The Canterbury Tales* presents a manuscript written in the medieval period that can help illustrate Boethianism through stories and show how people of the time might have responded to the idea. Choices *A* and *B* are generalized statements, and we have no evidence to support Choice *B*. Choice *D* is very compelling, but it looks at Boethianism in a way that the author does not. The author does not mention "different levels of Boethianism" when discussing the tales, only that the concept appears differently in different tales. Boethianism also doesn't focus on enlightenment.

41. D: The author is referring to the principle that a desire for material goods leads to moral malfeasance punishable by a higher being. Choice *A* is incorrect; while the text does mention thieves ravaging others' possessions, it is only meant as an example and not as the principle itself. Choice *B* is incorrect for the same reason as A. Choice *C* is mentioned in the text and is part of the example that proves the principle, and also not the principle itself.

42. C: The word *avarice* most nearly means *parsimoniousness*, or an unwillingness to spend money. Choice *A* means *evil* or *mischief* and does not relate to the context of the sentence. Choice *B* is also incorrect, because *pithiness* means *shortness* or *conciseness*. Choice *D* is close because *precariousness* means dangerous or instability, which goes well with the context. However, we are told of the summoner's specific characteristic of greed, which makes Choice *C* the best answer.

43. D: Desire for pleasure can lead toward sin. Boethianism acknowledges desire as something that leads out of holiness, so Choice *A* is incorrect. Choice *B* is incorrect because in the passage, Boethianism is depicted as being wary of desire and anything that binds people to the physical world. Choice *C* can be eliminated because the author never says that desire indicates demonic.

44. B: Choice *A* uses similar language, but it is not the main point of disagreement. The reporter calls the loss devastating, and there's no reason to believe that the coach would disagree with this assessment. Eliminate this choice.

Choice *B* is strong since both passages mention the at-bats with runners in scoring position. The reporter asserts that the team lost due to the team failing to get such a hit. In contrast, the coach identifies several other reasons for the loss, including fielding and pitching errors. Additionally, the coach disagrees that the team even needed a hit in those situations.

Choice *C* is mentioned by the coach, but not by the reporter. It is unclear whether the reporter would agree with this assessment. Eliminate this choice.

Choice *D* is mentioned by the coach but not by the reporter. It is not stated whether the reporter believes that the team deserved to win. Eliminate this choice.

Therefore, Choice *B* is the correct answer.

45. C: Choice *A* is incorrect. The Conservative Politician definitely believes that spending on social welfare programs increases the national debt. However, the Liberal Politician does not address the cost of those programs. Choice *B* is a strong answer choice. The Liberal Politician explicitly agrees that certain classes of people rely on social welfare programs. The Conservative Politician actually agrees that people rely on the programs, but thinks this reliance is detrimental. This answer choice is slightly off base. Eliminate this choice. Choice *C* improves on Choice *B*. The Liberal Politician definitely believes that certain classes of people would be irreparably harmed. In contrast, the Conservative Politician asserts that the programs are actually harmful since people become dependent on the programs. The Conservative Politician concludes that people don't need the assistance and would be better off if left to fend for themselves. This is definitely the main point of disagreement. Choice *D* is not the main point of dispute. Neither of the politicians discusses whether *all* of the nation's leaders have bootstrapped their way to the top. Eliminate this choice.

Mathematical Reasoning

1. B: To simplify the given equation, the first step is to make all exponents positive by moving them to the opposite place in the fraction. This expression becomes $\frac{4b^3b^2}{a^1a^4} \times \frac{3a}{b}$. Then the rules for exponents can be used to simplify. Multiplying the same bases means the exponents can be added. Dividing the same bases means the exponents are subtracted.

2. D: The product of two irrational numbers can be rational or irrational. Sometimes, the irrational parts of the two numbers cancel each other out, leaving a rational number. For example, $\sqrt{2} * \sqrt{2} = 2$ because the roots cancel each other out. Technically, the product of two irrational numbers can be complex because complex numbers can have either the real or imaginary part (in this case, the imaginary part) equal zero and still be considered a complex number. However, Choice *D* is incorrect because the product of two irrational numbers is not an imaginary number so saying the product is complex *and* imaginary is incorrect.

3. B: The car is traveling at a speed of five meters per second. On the interval from one to three seconds, the position changes by fifteen meters. By making this change in position over time into a rate, the speed becomes ten meters in two seconds or five meters in one second.

4. C: The number negative four is classified as a real number because it exists and is not imaginary. It is rational because it does not have a decimal that never ends. It is an integer because it does not have a fractional component. The next classification would be whole numbers, for which negative four does not qualify because it is negative. Although -4 could technically be considered a complex number because complex numbers can have either the real or imaginary part equal zero and still be considered a complex number, Choice D is wrong because -4 is not considered an irrational number because it does not have a never-ending decimal component.

5. D: The degree of freedom for two samples is calculated as $df = \frac{(n_1-1)+(n_2-1)}{2}$ rounded to the lowest whole number. For this example, $df = \frac{(29-1)+(30-1)}{2} = \frac{28+29}{2} = 28.5$ which, rounded to the lowest whole number, is 28.

6. B: There are two zeros for the function $x = 0, -2$. The zeros can be found several ways, but this particular equation can be factored into $f(x) = x(x^2 + 4x + 4) = x(x + 2)(x + 2)$. By setting each factor equal to zero and solving for x, there are two solutions. On a graph, these zeros can be seen where the line crosses the x-axis.

7. D: This problem involves a composition function, where one function is plugged into the other function. In this case, the $f(x)$ function is plugged into the $g(x)$ function for each x-value. The composition equation becomes $g(f(x)) = 2^3 - 3(2^2) - 2(2) + 6$. Simplifying the equation gives the answer $g(f(x)) = 8 - 3(4) - 2(2) + 6 = 8 - 12 - 4 + 6 = -2$.

8. A: To expand a squared binomial, it's necessary use the *First, Inner, Outer, Last Method*.

$$(2x - 4y)^2$$

$$2x \cdot 2x + 2x(-4y) + (-4y)(2x) + (-4y)(-4y)$$

$$4x^2 - 8xy - 8xy + 16$$

$$y^2 4x^2 - 16xy + 16y^2$$

9. A: The common denominator here will be $4x$. Rewrite these fractions as

$$\frac{3}{x} + \frac{5u}{2x} - \frac{u}{4} = \frac{12}{4x} + \frac{10u}{4x} - \frac{ux}{4x} = \frac{12x+10u-ux}{4x}.$$

10. A: Finding the product means distributing one polynomial onto the other. Each term in the first must be multiplied by each term in the second. Then, like terms can be collected. Multiplying the factors yields the expression $20x^3 + 4x^2 + 24x - 40x^2 - 8x - 48$. Collecting like terms means adding the x^2 terms and adding the x terms. The final answer after simplifying the expression is $20x^3 - 36x^2 + 16x - 48$.

11. D: Finding the zeros for a function by factoring is done by setting the equation equal to zero, then completely factoring. Since there was a common x for each term in the provided equation, that would be factored out first. Then the quadratic that was left could be factored into two binomials $(x + 1)(x - 4)$. Setting each factor equation to zero and solving for x yields three zeros.

12. D: Dividing rational expressions follows the same rule as dividing fractions. The division is changed to multiplication, and the reciprocal is found in the second fraction. This turns the expression into $\frac{5x^3}{3x^2} \times \frac{3y^9}{25}$. Multiplying across and simplifying, the final expression is $\frac{xy^8}{5}$.

13. B: The equation can be solved by factoring the numerator into $(x + 6)(x - 5)$. Since that same factor exists on top and bottom, that factor $(x - 5)$ cancels. This leaves the equation $x + 6 = 11$. Solving the equation gives the answer $x = 5$. When this value is plugged into the equation, it yields a zero in the denominator of the fraction. Since this is undefined, there is no solution.

14. D: This problem can be solved by using unit conversion. The initial units are miles per minute. The final units need to be feet per second. Converting miles to feet uses the equivalence statement 1 mile=5,280 feet. Converting minutes to seconds uses the equivalence statement 1 minute=60 seconds. Setting up the ratios to convert the units is shown in the following equation $\frac{72\ miles}{90\ minutes} \times \frac{1\ minute}{60\ seconds} \times \frac{5280\ feet}{1\ mile} = 70.4$ feet per second. The initial units cancel out, and the new units are left.

15. B: The formula can be manipulated by dividing both the length, l, and the width, w, on both sides. The length and width will cancel on the right, leaving height by itself.

16. B: The domain is all possible input values, or x-values. For this equation, the domain is every number greater than or equal to zero. There are no negative numbers in the domain because taking the square root of a negative number results in an imaginary number.

17. D: This problem can be solved by setting up a proportion involving the given information and the unknown value. The proportion is $\frac{21\ pages}{4\ nights} = \frac{140\ pages}{x\ nights}$. Solving the proportion by cross-multiplying, the equation becomes $21x = 4 \times 140$, where $x = 26.67$. Since it is not an exact number of nights, the answer is rounded up to 27 nights. Twenty-six nights would not give Sarah enough time.

18. D: The slope from this equation is 50, and it is interpreted as the cost per gigabyte used. Since the g-value represents number of gigabytes and the equation is set equal to the cost in dollars, the slope relates these two values. For every gigabyte used on the phone, the bill goes up 50 dollars.

19. C: Graphing the function $y = \cos(x)$ shows that the curve starts at $(0, 1)$, has an amplitude of 2, and a period of 2π. This same curve can be constructed using the sine graph, by shifting the graph to the left $\frac{\pi}{2}$ units. This equation is in the form $y = \sin(x + \frac{\pi}{2})$.

20. D: Using SOHCAHTOA, tangent is $\frac{y}{x}$ for the special triangles. Since the value needs to be negative one, the angle must be some form of 45 degrees or $\frac{\pi}{4}$. The value is negative in the second and fourth quadrant, so that answer is $\frac{3\pi}{4}$ and $\frac{7\pi}{4}$.

21. A: This inverse of a function is found by switching the x and y in the equation and solving for y. In the given equation, solving for y is done by adding 5 to both sides, then dividing both sides by 3. This answer can be checked on the graph by verifying the lines are reflected over $y = x$.

22. B: The zeros of this function can be found by using the quadratic formula:

$$x = \frac{-b \pm \sqrt{b^2 - 4ac}}{2a}$$

Identifying a, b, and c can be done from the equation as well because it is in standard form. The formula becomes:

$$x = \frac{0 \pm \sqrt{0^2 - 4(1)(4)}}{2(1)} = \frac{\sqrt{-16}}{2}$$

Since there is a negative underneath the radical, the answer is a complex number.

23. D: Setting up a proportion is the easiest way to represent this situation. The proportion becomes $\frac{20}{x} = \frac{40}{100}$, where cross-multiplication can be used to solve for x. The answer can also be found by observing the two fractions as equivalent, knowing that twenty is half of forty, and fifty is half of one-hundred.

24. C: Scientific notation division can be solved by grouping the first terms together and grouping the tens together. The first terms can be divided, and the tens terms can be simplified using the rules for exponents. The initial expression becomes 0.4×10^4. This is not in scientific notation because the first number is not between 1 and 10. Shifting the decimal and subtracting one from the exponent, the answer becomes 4.0×10^3.

25. A: The relative error can be found by finding the absolute error and making it a percent of the true value. The absolute value is $36 - 35.75 = 0.25$. This error is then divided by 36—the true value—to find 0.7%.

26. B: The y-intercept of an equation is found where the x-value is zero. Plugging zero into the equation for x, the first two terms cancel out, leaving -4.

27. D: The expression is three times the sum of twice a number and 1, which is $3(2x + 1)$. Then, 6 is subtracted from this expression.

28. C: The equation $x = 3$ is not a function because it does not pass the vertical line test. This test is made from the definition of a function, where each x-value must be mapped to one and only one y-value. This equation is a vertical line, so the x-value of 3 is mapped with an infinite number of y-values.

29. A: The function can be factored to identify the zeros. First, the term $3x$ is factored out to the front because each term contains $3x$. Then, the quadratic is factored into $(x + 3)(x - 2)$.

30. D: Finding the slope of the line tangent to the given function involves taking the derivative twice. The first derivative gives the line tangent to the graph. The second derivative finds the slope of that line. The line tangent to the graph has an equation $y' = 3x^2$. The slope of this line at $x = 2$ is found by the second derivative, $y = 6x$ or $y = 6(2) = 12$.

31. B: Because this isn't a right triangle, SOHCAHTOA can't be used. However, the law of cosines can be used. Therefore, $c^2 = a^2 + b^2 - 2ab \cos C = 19^2 + 26^2 - 2 \times 19 \times 26 \times \cos 42° = 302.773$. Taking the square root and rounding to the nearest tenth results in $c = 17.4$.

32. C: Because order *does* matter, the total number of permutations needs to be computed.

$$P(5,2) = \frac{5!}{(5-2)!} = \frac{120}{6} = 20$$

represents the number of ways that two objects can be arranged from a set of five.

33. C: The numerator in the sequence $\left\{\frac{(-1)^{n+1}}{n^2+5}\right\}_{n=0}^{\infty}$ indicates that the sign of each term changes from term to term. The first term is negative because $n = 0$ and $-1^{n+1} = -1^1 = -1$. Therefore, the second term is positive. The third term is negative, etc. The denominator is evaluated like a function for plugging in the various n value. For example, the denominator of the first term, when n = 0, is $0^2 + 5 = 0$.

34. B: The acceleration of the particle can be found by taking the derivative of the velocity equation. This equation is:

$$v'(t) = \frac{0-6(1)}{(t+3)^2} = \frac{-6}{(t+3)^2}$$

Finding the acceleration at time $t = 5$ can be found by plugging five in for the variable t in the derivative. The equation and answer are:

$$v'(5) = \frac{-6}{(5+3)^2} = \frac{-6}{64} = \frac{-3}{32}$$

35. A: Because the volume of the given sphere is 288π cubic meters, this means $\frac{4}{3}\pi r^3 = 288\pi$. This equation is solved for r to obtain a radius of 6 meters. The formula for the surface area of a sphere is $4\pi r^2$, so if $r = 6$ in this formula, the surface area is 144π square meters.

36. D: SOHCAHTOA is used to find the missing side length. Because the angle and adjacent side are known, $\tan 60 = \frac{x}{13}$. Making sure to evaluate tangent with an argument in degrees, this equation gives $x = 13\tan 60 = 13 \times 1.73 = 22.49$.

37. D: The midpoint formula should be used.

$$M = \left(\frac{x_1 + x_2}{2}, \frac{y_1 + y_2}{2}\right) = \left(\frac{-1+3}{2}, \frac{2+(-6)}{2}\right) = (1, -2)$$

38. B: The table shows values that are increasing exponentially. The differences between the inputs are the same, while the differences in the outputs are changing by a factor of 2. The values in the table can be modeled by the equation $f(x) = 2^x$.

39. A: Using the trigonometric identity $\tan(\theta) = \frac{\sin(\theta)}{\cos(\theta)}$, the expression becomes $\frac{\sin\theta}{\cos\theta}\cos\theta$. The factors that are the same on the top and bottom cancel out, leaving the simplified expression $\sin\theta$.

40. A: First, the sample mean must be calculated. $\bar{x} = \frac{1}{4}(1+3+5+7) = 4$. The standard deviation of the data set is $\sigma = \sqrt{\frac{\Sigma(x-\bar{x})^2}{n-1}}$, and $n = 4$ represents the number of data points.

Therefore:

$$\sigma = \sqrt{\frac{1}{3}[(1-4)^2 + (3-4)^2 + (5-4)^2 + (7-4)^2]} = \sqrt{\frac{1}{3}(9+1+1+9)} = 2.58$$

41. C: The expected value is equal to the total sum of each product of individual score and probability. There are 36 possible rolls. The probability of rolling a 2 is $\frac{1}{36}$. The probability of rolling a 3 is $\frac{2}{36}$. The probability of rolling a 4 is $\frac{3}{36}$. The probability of rolling a 5 is $\frac{4}{36}$. The probability of rolling a 6 is $\frac{5}{36}$. The probability of rolling a 7 is $\frac{6}{36}$. The probability of rolling an 8 is $\frac{5}{36}$. The probability of rolling a 9 is $\frac{4}{36}$. The probability of rolling a 10 is $\frac{3}{36}$. The probability of rolling an 11 is $\frac{2}{36}$. Finally, the probability of rolling a 12 is $\frac{1}{36}$.

Each possible outcome is multiplied by the probability of it occurring. Like this:

$$2 \times \frac{1}{36} = a$$

$$3 \times \frac{2}{36} = b$$

$$4 \times \frac{3}{36} = c$$

And so forth.

Then all of those results are added together:

$$a + b + c \ldots = expected\ value$$

In this case, it equals 7.

42. C: The sample space is made up of $8 + 7 + 6 + 5 = 26$ balls. The probability of pulling each individual ball is $\frac{1}{26}$. Since there are 7 yellow balls, the probability of pulling a yellow ball is $\frac{7}{26}$.

43. B: For the first card drawn, the probability of a King being pulled is $\frac{4}{52}$. Since this card isn't replaced, if a King is drawn first the probability of a King being drawn second is $\frac{3}{51}$. The probability of a King being drawn in both the first and second draw is the product of the two probabilities: $\frac{4}{52} \times \frac{3}{51} = \frac{12}{2652}$ which, divided by 12, equals $\frac{1}{221}$.

44. D: The addition rule is necessary to determine the probability because a 6 can be rolled on either roll of the die. The rule used is $P(A\ or\ B) = P(A) + P(B) - P(A\ and\ B)$. The probability of a 6 being individually rolled is $\frac{1}{6}$ and the probability of a 6 being rolled twice is $\frac{1}{6} \times \frac{1}{6} = \frac{1}{36}$. Therefore, the probability that a 6 is rolled at least once is $\frac{1}{6} + \frac{1}{6} - \frac{1}{36} = \frac{11}{36}$.

45. A: $(A \cap B)$ is equal to the intersection of the two sets A and B, which is $\{1, 2, 3, 4, 5\}$. $A - (A \cap B)$ is equal to the elements of A that are <u>not</u> included in the set $(A \cap B)$. Therefore, $A - (A \cap B) = \{6, 7, 8, 9, 10\}$.

46. C: "Alex is an engineering and English major, but his sister is a history major who hasn't been to either Germany or Austria" can be rewritten as "p and not q and r and not s or not t." Using logical symbols, this is written as $p \wedge \sim q \wedge r \wedge (\sim s \vee \sim t)$.

Science

1. C: There is a 99% probability of PCR testing identifying *Histoplasma*. GM assay was more specific for identifying *Aspergillus,* 95% to 85%. True positive is defined by sensitivity. The sensitivity of GM assay testing is less than 70%.

2. D: *Histoplasma* is detectable 90 days from exposure. PCR testing is able to detect *Histoplasma* 91 days from exposure—one day after sufficient organisms exist for detection. *Candida* is detectable 45 days from exposure. PCR testing is able to detect *Candida* 72 days from exposure—27 days after a sufficient number of organisms exist for detection. *Aspergillus* is detectable 118 days from exposure. ELISA testing is able to detect *Aspergillus* 134 days from exposure—16 days after a sufficient number of organisms exist for detection. *Candida* is detectable 45 days from exposure. GM assay testing is able to detect *Candida* 56 days from exposure—11 days after a sufficient number of organisms exist for detection.

3. B: The probability that the GM assay will identify *Candida* is 69%. Therefore, there's a 31% probability that it won't be identified. ELISA sensitivity and specificity for *Histoplasma* are both greater than 80%. False-negative probabilities are represented by the specificity of a given testing method. The sensitivity and specificity for GM assay testing for *Aspergillus* is 9% and 96% respectively. All testing methods had greater than 90% specificity for the organisms.

4. C: The sensitivity of PCR testing for *Histoplasma* is 99%, and the test can identify the organism one day after it reaches a detectable colony size. The sensitivity for GM assay testing for *Histoplasma* is 65%. If physicians rely on GM assay testing, they may determine that the individual doesn't have the *Histoplasma* infection. Treatment will depend on the presence or absence of the infection as indicated by testing. Waiting for PCR testing is based on the sensitivity of the test, not the individual's current symptoms. The subclinical phase of *Histoplasma* is 28 days.

5. A: ELISA testing detects *Candida* three days after the organism is present in sufficient numbers to be recognized. PCR detects the organism more than three weeks after it is first detectable. ELISA testing sensitivity for *Candida* is 87% and PCR testing is 92%. However, the ability to identify the presence of the organism earlier in the process of infection (allowing early intervention) outweighs the differences in the probability of identifying the presence of the organism. There's a 92% probability that PCR testing will identify the presence of *Candida*. PCR testing is more sensitive than ELISA: 92% versus 87%.

6. D: The main difference in the scientists' opinions is related to the cause of mad cow disease. The existence of species-specific proteins was used by Scientist 2 to support viral infection as the cause of the disease. Transmission rates of the disease and the conversion of normal proteins to prions were not debated in the passage.

7. A: Scientist 2 proposed that viruses were the cause of mad cow disease because chemicals inactivated the viruses. The remaining choices are correct.

8. B: According to Scientist 1, abnormal prions are capable of "refolding" normal proteins in harmful prions. Abnormal proteins accumulate to produce the damaging conglomerations. Scientist 2 didn't find species-specific DNA and used this fact to support viruses as the cause of mad cow disease. According to Scientist 1, prions are located in the central nervous system, not the peripheral nervous system.

9. D: Mad cow disease can be spread between animal species and from animals to humans through consumption of diseased animal products. The resulting damage to the central nervous system is irreversible and will eventually cause the death of the animal. Scientist 2 would not agree that the infecting agent contained amino acids, as they form proteins, and Scientist 2 believes that a virus causes the disease. Scientist 2 demonstrated that the infected tissue of animals that were infected by a different species didn't contain species-specific DNA, which would have been the expected outcome if the infecting agent were a protein.

10. C: The accumulated masses of abnormal prions eventually form sponge-like holes in the brain and spinal cord that result in death. The passage doesn't mention the effects of the synapses, nerves, or blood supply.

11. D: The absence of disease resulting from the inactivated viral particles best supports the views of Scientist 2. There were no species-specific DNA sequences found in the infected particles. Scientist 2 didn't support the existence of prions as the cause of mad cow disease.

12. C: The actual process of "refolding" the normal protein into the abnormal protein isn't clear from this passage. Scientist 1 claims that prions cause the disease. Prions are an abnormal protein, not a virus. Scientist 1 claims that mad cow disease is caused by abnormal proteins.

13. C: The main hypothesis for this study involved the influence of 2-AG levels combined with sleep deprivation on eating behaviors. The combination of the two conditions, not each one separately, constitutes the main hypothesis. The passage didn't discuss a placebo effect in the normal saline injection group.

14. D: The study results support the hypothesis because the participants who received 1-AG injections and were sleep deprived gained more weight than participants who received sterile normal saline injections. The remaining choices do not support the hypothesis.

15. A: Participant H gained more than 1 pound (450g) per day. There was little fluctuation in the day-to-day weight gain for each participant. Participant H in trial 2 gained more weight than participant D in trial 1.

16. B: Sleep deprivation increases the levels and duration of action of 2-AG, an endogenous cannabinoid, especially in the late afternoon. The stress effect increases with the degree of sleep deprivation. The passage doesn't discuss a relationship between sleep deprivation and the hunger response. Eating behaviors are increased in late afternoon as a result of the extended duration of 2-AG action.

17. A: Circadian fluctuations increase the levels of 2-AG during the afternoon and evening. This increase is believed to stimulate food intake beyond the point of satiety. Endogenous cannabinoids decrease gastric motility. 2-AG may have a calming effect on mood, but food intake is still increased in the presence of afternoon and evening levels of 2-AG. Endogenous cannabinoids work with the opioid system to mediate the pain response, not food-seeking behaviors.

18. A: In trial 3, the plants grown with the combined-wavelength LED's reached 150 millimeters by day 21. The plants grown with white light reached 160 millimeters by day 35.

19. C: In trial 3, with LED lighting that included green and yellow wavelengths, plant growth was greater than trial 1 or trial 2 with either blue or red wavelengths. However, from the available information, it can only be said that green and yellow wavelengths *contributed to* plant growth in trial 3, but not that green and yellow wavelengths *alone* were responsible for plant growth in trial 3. There was plant growth in all lighting conditions.

20. B: In trial 1, from day 28 to day 35, white light growth increased by 71 millimeters, and red light increased by 78 millimeters. In trial 2, from day 28 to day 35, white light growth increased by 71 millimeters, and blue light increased by 78 millimeters.

21. C: The average daily growth with LED lighting was not twice the white light average daily growth. LED systems did result in better growth rates and they do require less water and electricity. However, the question is based on recorded average daily growth, and that rate was not double the white light rate.

22. D: The passage says that green and yellow wavelengths are reflected by the plant. Therefore, it's expected that those wavelengths would result in slower growth than the blue or red wavelengths, which are absorbed.

23. B: *Anacardiaceae Magnifera* is the genus and family name for the mango. The *Colletotrichum* fungus causes the spoilage. The remaining choices are correct.

24. C: According to Table 1, at 20 days, the fungal level at 7.5 °C was the same as the fungal level at 5 °C. Because the 7.5 °C temperature is less expensive than the 5 °C temperature, the 7.5 °C model is best. The 10 °C model is less expensive than the 7.5 °C, but fungal levels are greater. Only the 7.5 °C and 5 °C models had acceptable fungal levels at 20 days.

25. B: The hot water wash pre-treatment fungal level increased by 15 millimeters from day 26 to day 28 at 10 °C. It was the single largest one-day increase across the trials. Air cooling at 10 °C increased by 5 millimeters from day 14 to day 16. Air cooling at 7.5 °C increased by 7 millimeters from day 26 to day 28. Hot water wash at 7.5 °C increased 11 millimeters from day 26 to day 28.

26. C: The hot water wash fungal level at 10 °C reached 35 millimeters on day 20. The maximum fungal level for air cooling at 5 °C was 19 millimeters, and at 10 °C, 35 millimeters on day 26. The maximum fungal level for hot water at 7.5 °C was 36 millimeters on day 28.

27. C: The fungal levels were acceptable with the hot water wash at 7.5 °C, and the 7.5 °C temperature is less expensive to maintain. Air cooling and hot water wash pre-treatment at 5 °C resulted in acceptable fungal levels, but the 5 °C temperature is costlier. Fungal levels were not acceptable at 28 days at 10 °C.

28. B: Shipping mangoes at 5 °C is costly, but for the 28-day trip, the fungal levels were only acceptable in the 5 °C model. Air cooling fungal rates at 5 °C were lower than the hot water wash rates, but each was acceptable. Fungal rates at 7.5 °C and 10 °C were unacceptable.

29. A: The correlation was positive, because when one variable increased, the other increased, and when one variable decreased, the other decreased. There are two forms for a curvilinear relationship. In one curvilinear relationship, when variable 1 increases, a second variable increases as well, but only to a certain point, and then variable 2 decreases as variable 1 continues to increase. In the other form, variable 1 increases while variable 2 decreases to a certain point, after which both variables increase. In a negative relationship, high values for one variable are associated with low values for the second variable.

30. D: Mitochondrial activity is suppressed by elevated blood glucose levels. Mitochondria use sugar to produce cellular energy, and the presence of large numbers of mitochondria in BAT gives BAT a brownish color. Mitochondria contain DNA and can reproduce additional mitochondria when additional energy is required. In the body, mature red blood cells are the only cells that don't contain mitochondria.

31. D: Blood sugars for all groups identified in Figure 5 were highest at 2 p.m.

32. B: Circadian rhythms control sleep by stimulating the release of melatonin from the pineal gland. Ganglia are nerve cells, not hormones, that affect sleep. BAT doesn't release sugar; it utilizes sugar for heat production. Shivering on cold mornings is a desirable form of thermogenesis but isn't associated with sleep.

33. D: The average blood sugar for participant 6 was 115. Participant 1 was 105, participant 3 was 112, and participant 4 was 82.

34. B: The daytime blood glucose levels in Figure 1 decreased as the day progressed. The blood glucose levels in Figure 5 peaked for the day at 2 p.m. Night blood glucose levels didn't reach 100. Group I's levels are irrelevant to the question.

35. A: Based only on Figure 2, the researchers' hypothesis wasn't confirmed. Subsequent trials confirmed the hypothesis.

36. A: Increased algae levels can block sunlight, limiting growth of species inhabiting lower zones. The passage doesn't identify the effects of rainfall or cold temperatures on phytoplankton growth, so Choices *B* and *D* are incorrect. The passage identifies the effect of phosphorous and nitrogen residue on algae growth, but not as a food source for cyanobacteria.

37. D: The passage identifies freshwater contamination by phosphorous and nitrogen as the most common cause of algae overgrowth. Population density would be more common in Florida than Kansas.

38. B: As algae levels increase above normal, organisms in the aphotic level plants don't receive adequate light for normal growth and oxygen levels are decreased, resulting in the death of oxygen-dependent species.

39. C: Algae block the sunlight, which limits growth.

40. A: Algae growth was greater in July, which limited the amount of light reaching the lower zones of the lake, decreasing the levels of cyanobacteria. Cyanobacteria existed in less-than-normal concentrations at 20 meters, but there were measurable levels of the organisms. Algae growth at 3 meters wasn't measured. The passage states that cyanobacteria growth is associated with algae growth, not independent of algae growth.

Social Studies

1. B: To avoid involvement in political processes such as voting is antithetical to the principles of a democracy. Therefore, the principal responsibility of citizens is the opposite, and they should be steadily engaged in the political processes that determine the course of government.

2. A: Although Greeks used the alphabet as the basis for their written language, leading to a diverse array of literature, they learned about the alphabet from Phoenician traders. All the other options, in contrast, were invented in Greece.

3. D: It is important to realize that the Cold War was never an official war and that the United States and the Soviet Union instead funded proxy conflicts. The Kyoto Protocol was signed by members of the United Nations, as the League of Nations was long since defunct. While Japan was a minor participant in World War I, it was not defeated by America until World War II. The correct answer is *D:* India's partition between Hindu India and Islamic Pakistan led to large outbreaks of religious violence.

4. A: Rather than competition, a monopoly prevents other businesses from offering a certain product or service to consumers.

5. B: Mercantilism, which is built on the vision of full government control over the economy, is a hallmark of command system economies. Laissez-faire, capitalism, and self-interest, in contrast, are all fundamental concepts behind the market system.

6. A: England, France, and Spain all established North American colonies that would later be absorbed into the United States, but Italy, despite Christopher Columbus' role as an explorer, never established a colony in America.

7. D: The Constitution was signed in 1787; the Declaration of Independence was signed in 1776. It was successfully ratified by all the current states, including New York. Finally, the Articles of Confederation was established at the end of the American Revolution; the Constitution would replace the articles years later due to issues with the government's structure.

8. A: The media is tightly controlled and monitored in authoritarian regimes. Independent media is looked at as destabilizing to authoritarian regimes when there are reports on government abuse, corruption, and policy critiques. New information and views from other political parties can significantly impact the perceptions of local, national, and international publics. Independent media and media supported by the West helped to undermine the former USSR.

9. B: A Nation is defined as a group of people who have common traits, such as heritage, history, language, culture, and religion. It has nothing to do with borders, sovereignty, power, people in office, or the rules by which a government operates (all of which are found in the other answer terms of state, government, constitution, and regime).

10. D: Politics has been described by many as the exercise of power or use of force to achieve a particular end. Sovereignty is the ability of a particular government to gain and maintain the acquiescence of its populace. It exercises authority in this pursuit. If it fails, it may result in Regime change. However, it is politics that is used by governments in order to properly exercise Sovereignty and authority in meeting the needs of the people.

11. D: Political culture is the term used to describe the various ways a government seeks to encourage its people to participate in the political process. In liberal democracies, political culture encourages the free exchange of ideas, and high levels of education and input, including running for office. In authoritarian regimes, participation is discouraged apart from speaking well of the leader, the government, and its ideals. Some governments encourage direct participation, others discourage it based on the goals they have for their country and citizens.

12. D: Governmental regimes fall along a continuum between total authoritarianism and complete direct democracy. None of the countries studied in the AP course are totally authoritarian, nor a complete direct democracy. But they do all fall along this continuum with China and Iran towards the authoritarian end of the spectrum and the UK and Mexico towards the democratic end.

13. C: Supranational institutions are generally united over shared interests. As such, these institutions develop international laws, set international trade norms, and advocate for human rights and development.

14. D: The Constitution granted Congress the power to decide how many justices should be on the court, and Congress first decided on six judges in the Judiciary Act of 1789. The Constitution granted the power to appoint judges and to call special sessions of Congress to the president. Only the Supreme Court may interpret the laws enacted by Congress and rule a law unconstitutional and subsequently overturn the law.

15. C: The first ten amendments to the Constitution are collectively referred to as the Bill of Rights. The Founding Fathers did not support universal suffrage, and as such, the Bill of Rights did not encompass the freedom to vote. The Fifteenth Amendment provided that the right to vote shall not be denied on the basis of race, color, or previous condition of servitude, and women did not receive the right to vote until passage of the Nineteenth Amendment. The other three answer choices are included in the Bill of Rights—the freedom to assembly is established in the First Amendment; the freedom against unlawful search is established in the Fourth Amendment; and the reservation of non-enumerated powers to the states or the people is established in the Tenth Amendment.

16. C: Federalism divides power between regional and federal governments, and it is the form of government upon which the United States is structured, according to the Tenth Amendment. While a constitutional monarchy, Choice *B*, is typically divided between a monarch, the head of state, and a legislative body, usually a parliament, power is not reserved to the regional government. A democratic government, Choice *A*, is a government ruled by the people and does not specify division of powers. Feudalism, Choice *D*, is an economic system popular in medieval Europe where the monarchy granted the nobility land in exchange for military service, and the nobility allowed serfs to live on their land in exchange for labor or percentage of crops.

17. D: Both the states and the federal government may propose, enact, and enforce laws. States pass legislation that concerns the states in their state legislative houses, while the federal government passes federal laws in Congress. Only states may hold elections and determine voting procedures, even for federal offices such as the president of the United States, and only the federal government may expand any state territory, change state lines, admit new states into the nation, or regulate immigration and pass laws regarding naturalization of citizens.

18. C: The president of the United States is elected by the Electoral College. The number of electors for each state depends on the state's total number of senators and representatives. The president must receive a majority (270) of the electoral votes (538), and if this doesn't occur, the Twelfth Amendment empowers the House of Representatives to elect the president. Choices *A, B,* and *C* are different methods for electing candidates.

19. D: The two major political parties hold conventions to nominate their presidential candidate. The delegates are awarded based on candidates' performance in the primary elections or caucuses vote at the party convention to select the nominee. Primaries and caucuses are the democratic contests held by each state to award their delegates. The candidates participate in debates on the campaign issues, but they do not receive the nomination at debates.

20. C: I, II, and IV only. Historians make use of maps in their studies to get a clear picture of how history unfolded, knowing the borders of different lands helps historians learn different cultures' interactions, and environmental factors, such as access to water and the proximity of mountains, help determine the course of civilization. The phrase "Geography is closely linked with the flow of resources, technology, and population in societies" is a characteristic of economics.

21. B: Out of the four inventions mentioned, the first telegraphs were invented in the 1830s, not in the twentieth century. In contrast, the other inventions had considerable influence over the course of the twentieth century.

22. A: George Washington was a slave owner himself in life, so he did not make abolition a theme in his Farewell Address. On the other hand, he was concerned that sectionalism could potentially destroy the United States, and he warned against it. Furthermore, he believed that Americans should avoid getting involved in European affairs. However, one issue that he felt was especially problematic was the formation of political parties, and he urged against it in his farewell.

23. A: The presidential system establishes a separation of powers. In the presidential system, voters directly elect the chief executive, and the presidential system establishes a separation of powers between different branches of government. In contrast, the parliament elects the chief executive, and the increased collaboration and dependency creates a more responsive government. Choices *B* and *C* confuse how the executive is elected in each system. Choice *D* is incorrect because many parliamentary systems include a president, though the status of head of state is often purely ceremonial.

24. C: Power is the ability of a ruling body or political entity to influence the actions, behavior, and attitude of a person or group of people. Authority, Choice *A,* is the right and justification of the government to exercise power as recognized by the citizens or influential elites. Similarly, legitimacy, Choice *D,* is another way of expressing the concept of authority. Sovereignty, Choice *B,* refers to the ability of a state to determine and control their territory without foreign interference.

25. B: The process by which the House and Senate may debate a bill differs. In the House, how long a speaker may debate a bill is limited, while in the Senate, speakers may debate the bill indefinitely and delay voting on the bill by filibuster—a practice in which a speaker refuses to stop speaking until a majority vote stops the filibuster or the time for the vote passes. In both the House and the Senate, anyone may introduce a bill. Only the president of the United States may veto the bill, so neither the House nor Senate holds that power. Before the bill may be presented to the president to be signed, the wording of the bill must be identical in both houses. Another procedural difference is that the number of amendments is limited in the House but not the Senate; however, this does not appear as an answer choice.

26. A: British General Lord Cornwallis surrendered to Washington's troops at Yorktown, Virginia. No battles occurred at Valley Forge, but Washington's troops suffered major losses as a result of starvation, disease, and exposure to the cold, making Choice *B* incorrect. Choice *C* is incorrect because the Battle of Trenton was the first major battle of the Revolution, which occurred when Washington led his troops across the Delaware River to wage a surprise attack on British and Hessian soldiers stationed in Trenton on December 25, 1776. Choice *D*, Saratoga, New York, was the site of a major victory by General John Burgoyne in October 1777 and prompted European countries to help support the American cause.

27. C: British soldiers burned the White House during the War of 1812. Neither the Washington Monument nor the Statue of Liberty – Choices *A* and *D* – were built at the time, and Philadelphia's Independence Hall, Choice *B*, escaped conflict during this war.

28. B: Jefferson Davis was elected president of the Confederate States of America in November 1861. Choice *A*, General Robert E. Lee, was the leader of the Confederate Army. Choice *C*, William T. Sherman, was a union general famous for his march through Georgia and the burning of Atlanta in 1864. Choice *D*, Abraham Lincoln, was President of the U.S. during the Civil War.

29. D: This period was called the Gilded Age since it appeared shiny and golden on the surface, but was fueled by undercurrents of corruption led by big businessmen known as robber barons. Choice *A*, Manifest Destiny, is the concept referring to the pursuit and acquisition of new lands by the U.S., which led to the purchase of Alaska from Russia in 1867 and the annexation of Hawaii in 1898. The Columbian Exchange, Choice *B*, was an era of discovery, conquest, and colonization of the Americas by the Europeans. The New Deal, Choice *C*, was a plan launched by President Franklin Delano Roosevelt to help rebuild America's economy after the Great Depression.

30. C: World War I began in 1914 when a Serbian assassin killed Archduke Franz Ferdinand of Austria and prompted Austria-Hungary to declare war on Serbia. 1915, Choice *A*, is the year when German submarines sank the passenger ship *Lusitania*, killing 128 Americans and leading many to support U.S. efforts to enter the war. 1917, Choice *B*, is the year the U.S. entered World War I, declaring war on Germany. 1918, Choice *D*, signaled the end of the war when American troops helped defeat the German army that September. Fighting ended in November after Germany signed a peace agreement.

31. A: The Soviet Union was invaded by Germany in 1941 and allied with Britain and subsequently the U.S. President Roosevelt, British Prime Minister Winston Churchill, and Soviet director Joseph Stalin met in 1945 to plan their final assault on Germany and discuss postwar strategies. Germany aligned with Italy and Japan in 1940 to form the Axis Alliance. Their goal was to establish a German empire in Europe and place Japan in control over Asia. Thus, Choices *B*, *C*, and *D* are incorrect.

32. B: The North Atlantic Treaty Organization (NATO) was formed between Western Europe, Canada, and the U.S. in defense of Soviet hostility after the Soviet Union introduced Communism into Eastern Europe. The Soviet Union countered by creating the Warsaw Pact.

33. C: The G.I. Bill was a government program started in the 1950s that gave military veterans a free education. In the revolutionary 1954 case, *Brown vs. the Board of Education*, the Supreme Court ruled that school segregation was illegal, thereby setting the Civil Rights Movement in motion, making Choice *A* incorrect. *Freedom Rides*, Choice *B*, and the Montgomery bus boycott, Choice *D*, were among the non-violent protests against segregation that took place in the U.S. in the 1960s.

34. B: President Reagan advocated *peace through strength*, building up the U.S. military and launching the Strategic Defense Initiative (SDI), also called *Star Wars*. Choice *A*, the Strategic Arms Limitation Talks (SALT I and II), negotiated between 1972 and 1979, resulted in limits on nuclear weapons for both the U.S. and Russia. Choice *C*, the Iran-Contra Affair, was a scandal involving the secret sale of weapons to

Iran in exchange for American hostages. Choice *D*, *Glasnost*, was a policy of political openness launched by Soviet leader Mikhail Gorbachev.

35. A: Afghanistan was the site of the bombing raids. Bush invaded Iraq, Choice *B*, in 2003 when Iraqi dictator Saddam Hussein defied the terms of the truce agreed upon in 1991 after the Gulf War. Kuwait, Choice *C*, was invaded by Iraq in 1990, sparking the Gulf War. Pakistan, Choice *D*, is where Osama bin Laden was killed by a group of Navy SEALs under orders from President Obama.

GED Practice Test #2

Reading Comprehension

Questions 1–6 are based upon the following passage:

What is the working man?

My Good Friends,—When I first imparted to the committee of the projected Institute my particular wish that on one of the evenings of my readings here the main body of my audience should be composed of working men and their families, I was animated by two desires; first, by the wish to have the great pleasure of meeting you face to face at this Christmas time, and accompany you myself through one of my little Christmas books; and second, by the wish to have an opportunity of stating publicly in your presence, and in the presence of the committee, my earnest hope that the Institute will, from the beginning, recognise one great principle—strong in reason and justice—which I believe to be essential to the very life of such an Institution. It is, that the working man shall, from the first unto the last, have a share in the management of an Institution which is designed for his benefit, and which calls itself by his name.

I have no fear here of being misunderstood—of being supposed to mean too much in this. If there ever was a time when any one class could of itself do much for its own good, and for the welfare of society—which I greatly doubt—that time is unquestionably past. It is in the fusion of different classes, without confusion; in the bringing together of employers and employed; in the creating of a better common understanding among those whose interests are identical, who depend upon each other, who are vitally essential to each other, and who never can be in unnatural antagonism without deplorable results, that one of the chief principles of a Mechanics' Institution should consist. In this world, a great deal of the bitterness among us arises from an imperfect understanding of one another. Erect in Birmingham a great Educational Institution, properly educational; educational of the feelings as well as of the reason; to which all orders of Birmingham men contribute; in which all orders of Birmingham men meet; wherein all orders of Birmingham men are faithfully represented—and you will erect a Temple of Concord here which will be a model edifice to the whole of England.

Contemplating as I do the existence of the Artisans' Committee, which not long ago considered the establishment of the Institute so sensibly, and supported it so heartily, I earnestly entreat the gentlemen—earnest I know in the good work, and who are now among us—by all means to avoid the great shortcoming of similar institutions; and in asking the working man for his confidence, to set him the great example and give him theirs in return. You will judge for yourselves if I promise too much for the working man, when I say that he will stand by such an enterprise with the utmost of his patience, his perseverance, sense, and support; that I am sure he will need no charitable aid or condescending patronage; but will readily and cheerfully pay for the advantages which it confers; that he will prepare himself in individual cases where he feels that the adverse circumstances around him have rendered it necessary; in a word, that he will feel his responsibility like an honest man, and will most honestly and manfully discharge it. I now proceed to the pleasant task to which I assure you I have looked forward for a long time.

from Charles Dickens' speech in Birmingham in England on December 30, 1853 on behalf of the Birmingham and Midland Institute.

1. Which word is most closely synonymous with the word *patronage* as it appears in the following statement?

...that I am sure he will need no charitable aid or condescending patronage

a. Auspices
b. Aberration
c. Acerbic
d. Adulation

2. Which term is most closely aligned with the definition of the term *working man* as it is defined in the following passage?

You will judge for yourselves if I promise too much for the working man, when I say that he will stand by such an enterprise with the utmost of his patience, his perseverance, sense, and support...

a. Plebian
b. Viscount
c. Entrepreneur
d. Bourgeois

3. Which of the following statements most closely correlates with the definition of the term *working man* as it is defined in Question 41?

a. A working man is not someone who works for institutions or corporations, but someone who is well-versed in the workings of the soul.
b. A working man is someone who is probably not involved in social activities because the physical demand for work is too high.
c. A working man is someone who works for wages among the middle class.
d. The working man has historically taken to the field, to the factory, and now to the screen.

4. Based upon the contextual evidence provided in the passage above, what is the meaning of the term *enterprise* in the third paragraph?

a. Company
b. Courage
c. Game
d. Cause

5. The speaker addresses his audience as *My Good Friends.* What kind of credibility does this salutation give to the speaker?

    a. The speaker is an employer addressing his employees, so the salutation is a way for the boss to bridge the gap between himself and his employees.

    b. The speaker's salutation is one from an entertainer to his audience, and uses the friendly language to connect to his audience before a serious speech.

    c. The salutation is used ironically to give a somber tone to the serious speech that follows.

    d. The speech is one from a politician to the public, so the salutation is used to grab the audience's attention.

6. According to the passage, what is the speaker's second desire for his time in front of the audience?

    a. To read a Christmas story

    b. For the working man to have a say in his institution, which is designed for his benefit.

    c. To have an opportunity to stand in their presence

    d. For the life of the institution to be essential to the audience as a whole

Questions 7–12 are based upon the following passage:

How do we use our common sense in politics?

"MANKIND being originally equals in the order of creation, the equality could only be destroyed by some subsequent circumstance; the distinctions of rich, and poor, may in a great measure be accounted for, and that without having recourse to the harsh ill sounding names of oppression and avarice. Oppression is often the consequence, but seldom or never the means of riches; and though avarice will preserve a man from being necessitously poor, it generally makes him too timorous to be wealthy.

But there is another and greater distinction for which no truly natural or religious reason can be assigned, and that is, the distinction of men into KINGS and SUBJECTS. Male and female are the distinctions of nature, good and bad the distinctions of heaven; but how a race of men came into the world so exalted above the rest, and distinguished like some new species, is worth enquiring into, and whether they are the means of happiness or of misery to mankind.

In the early ages of the world, according to the scripture chronology, there were no kings; the consequence of which was there were no wars; it is the pride of kings which throw mankind into confusion Holland without a king hath enjoyed more peace for this last century than any of the monarchical governments in Europe. Antiquity favors the same remark; for the quiet and rural lives of the first patriarchs hath a happy something in them, which vanishes away when we come to the history of Jewish royalty.

Government by kings was first introduced into the world by the Heathens, from whom the children of Israel copied the custom. It was the most prosperous invention the Devil ever set on foot for the promotion of idolatry. The Heathens paid divine honors to their deceased kings, and the Christian world hath improved on the plan by doing the same to their living ones. How impious is the title of sacred majesty applied to a worm, who in the midst of his splendor is crumbling into dust!

As the exalting one man so greatly above the rest cannot be justified on the equal rights of nature, so neither can it be defended on the authority of scripture; for the will of the

Almighty, as declared by Gideon and the prophet Samuel, expressly disapproves of government by kings. All anti-monarchical parts of scripture have been very smoothly glossed over in monarchical governments, but they undoubtedly merit the attention of countries, which have their governments yet to form. "Render unto Caesar the things which are Caesar's" is the scripture doctrine of courts, yet it is no support of monarchical government, for the Jews at that time were without a king, and in a state of vassalage to the Romans.

Near three thousand years passed away from the Mosaic account of the creation, till the Jews under a national delusion requested a king. Till then their form of government (except in extraordinary cases, where the Almighty interposed) was a kind of republic administered by a judge and the elders of the tribes. Kings they had none, and it was held sinful to acknowledge any being under that title but the Lord of Hosts. And when a man seriously reflects on the idolatrous homage which is paid to the persons of Kings, he need not wonder, that the Almighty ever jealous of his honor, should disapprove of a form of government which so impiously invades the prerogative of heaven.

from Thomas Pain, "Common Sense"

7. According to passage, what role does avarice, or greed, play in poverty?
   a. It can make a man very wealthy
   b. It is the consequence of wealth
   c. Avarice can prevent a man from being poor, but too fearful to be very wealthy
   d. Avarice is what drives a person to be very wealthy

8. Of these distinctions, which does the author believe to be beyond natural or religious reason?
   a. Good and bad
   b. Male and female
   c. Human and animal
   d. King and subjects

9. According to the passage, what are the Heathens responsible for?
   a. Government by kings
   b. Quiet and rural lives of patriarchs
   c. Paying divine honors to their living kings
   d. Equal rights of nature

10. Which of the following best states Paine's rationale for the denouncement of monarchy?
    a. It is against the laws of nature
    b. It is against the equal rights of nature and is denounced in scripture
    c. Despite scripture, a monarchal government is unlawful
    d. Neither the law nor scripture denounce monarchy

11. Based on the passage, what is the best definition of the word *idolatrous*?
    a. Worshipping heroes
    b. Being deceitful
    c. Sinfulness
    d. Engaging in illegal activities

12. What is the essential meaning of lines 41-44?

> And when a man seriously reflects on the idolatrous homage which is paid to the persons of Kings, he need not wonder, that the Almighty ever jealous of his honor, should disapprove of a form of government which so impiously invades the prerogative of heaven.

    a. God would disapprove of the irreverence of a monarchical government.
    b. With careful reflection, men should realize that heaven is not promised.
    c. God will punish those that follow a monarchical government.
    d. Belief in a monarchical government cannot coexist with belief in God.

Questions 13–18 are based on the following passage:

Where is the traveler going?

When I got on the coach the driver had not taken his seat, and I saw him talking with the landlady. They were evidently talking of me, for every now and then they looked at me, and some of the people who were sitting on the bench outside the door came and listened, and then looked at me, most of them pityingly. I could hear a lot of words often repeated, queer words, for there were many nationalities in the crowd; so I quietly got my polyglot dictionary from my bag and looked them out. I must say they weren't cheering to me, for amongst them were "Ordog"—Satan, "pokol"—hell, "stregoica"—witch, "vrolok" and "vlkoslak"—both of which mean the same thing, one being Slovak and the other Servian for something that is either were-wolf or vampire.

When we started, the crowd round the inn door, which had by this time swelled to a considerable size, all made the sign of the cross and pointed two fingers towards me. With some difficulty I got a fellow-passenger to tell me what they meant; he wouldn't answer at first, but on learning that I was English, he explained that it was a charm or guard against the evil eye. This was not very pleasant for me, just starting for an unknown place to meet an unknown man; but everyone seemed so kind-hearted, and so sorrowful, and so sympathetic that I couldn't but be touched. I shall never forget the last glimpse which I had of the inn-yard and its crowd of picturesque figures, all crossing themselves, as they stood round the wide archway, with its background of rich foliage of oleander and orange trees in green tubs clustered in the centre of the yard. Then our driver cracked his big whip over his four small horses, which ran abreast, and we set off on our journey.

I soon lost sight and recollection of ghostly fears in the beauty of the scene as we drove along, although had I known the language, or rather languages, which my fellow-passengers were speaking, I might not have been able to throw them off so easily. Before us lay a green sloping land full of forests and woods, with here and there steep hills, crowned with clumps of trees or with farmhouses, the blank gable end to the road. There was everywhere a bewildering mass of fruit blossom—apple, plum, pear, cherry; and as we drove by I could see the green grass under the trees spangled with the fallen petals. In and out amongst these green hills of what they call here the "Mittel Land" ran the road, losing itself as it swept round the grassy curve, or was shut out by the straggling ends of pine woods, which here and there ran down the hillsides like tongues of flame. The road was rugged, but still we seemed to fly over it with a feverish haste. I couldn't understand then what the haste meant, but the driver was evidently bent on losing no time in reaching Borgo Prund.

13. What type of narrator is found in this passage?
    a. First person
    b. Second person
    c. Third-person limited
    d. Third-person omniscient

14. Which of the following is true of the traveler?
    a. He wishes the driver would go faster.
    b. He's returning to the country of his birth.
    c. He has some familiarity with the local customs.
    d. He doesn't understand all of the languages being used.

15. How does the traveler's mood change between the second and third paragraphs?
    a. From relaxed to rushed
    b. From fearful to charmed
    c. From confused to enlightened
    d. From comfortable to exhausted

16. Who is the traveler going to meet?
    a. A kind landlady
    b. A distant relative
    c. A friendly villager
    d. A complete stranger

17. Based on the details in this passage, what can readers probably expect to happen in the story?
    a. The traveler will become a farmer.
    b. The traveler will arrive late at his destination.
    c. The traveler will soon encounter danger or evil.
    d. The traveler will have a pleasant journey and make many new friends.

18. Which sentence from the passage provides a clue for question 39?
    a. "I must say they weren't cheering to me, for amongst them were "Ordog"—Satan, "pokol"—hell, "stregoica"—witch, "vrolok" and "vlkoslak"—both of which mean the same thing, one being Slovak and the other Servian for something that is either were-wolf or vampire."
    b. "When I got on the coach the driver had not taken his seat, and I saw him talking with the landlady."
    c. "Then our driver cracked his big whip over his four small horses, which ran abreast, and we set off on our journey."
    d. "There was everywhere a bewildering mass of fruit blossom—apple, plum, pear, cherry; and as we drove by I could see the green grass under the trees spangled with the fallen petals."

Questions 19–24 are based on the following passage:

What part should the government play?

I heartily accept the motto, "that government is best which governs least," and I should like to see it acted up to more rapidly and systematically. Carried out, it finally amounts to this, which also I believe—"that government is best which governs not at all," and when men are prepared for it, that will be the kind of government which they will have. Government is at best but an expedient; but most governments are usually, and all governments are sometimes, inexpedient.

The objections which have been brought against a standing army, and they are many and weighty, and deserve to prevail, may also at last be brought against a standing government. The standing army is only an arm of the standing government. The government itself, which is only the mode which the people have chosen to execute their will, is equally liable to be abused and perverted before the people can act through it. Witness the present Mexican war, the work of comparatively a few individuals using the standing government as their tool; for, in the outset, the people would not have consented to this measure.

This American government—what is it but a tradition, though a recent one, endeavoring to transmit itself unimpaired to posterity, but each instant losing some of its integrity? It has not the vitality and force of a single living man; for a single man can bend it to his will. It is a sort of wooden gun to the people themselves. But it is not the less necessary for this; for the people must have some complicated machinery or other, and hear its din, to satisfy that idea of government which they have. Governments show thus how successfully men can be imposed on, even impose on themselves, for their own advantage. It is excellent, we must all allow. Yet this government never of itself furthered any enterprise, but by the alacrity with which it got out of its way. It does not keep the country free. It does not settle the West. It does not educate. The character inherent in the American people has done all that has been accomplished; and it would have done somewhat more, if the government had not sometimes got in its way. For government is an expedient by which men would fain succeed in letting one another alone; and, as has been said, when it is most expedient, the governed are most let alone by it. Trade and commerce, if they were not made of india-rubber, would never manage to bounce over the obstacles which legislators are continually putting in their way; and, if one were to judge these men wholly by the effects of their actions and not partly by their intentions, they would deserve to be classed and punished with those mischievous persons who put obstructions on the railroads.

But, to speak practically and as a citizen, unlike those who call themselves no-government men, I ask for, not at once no government, but at once a better government. Let every man make known what kind of government would command his respect, and that will be one step toward obtaining it.

The following passage is an excerpt from Civil Disobedience, *by Henry David Thoreau*

19. Which phrase best encapsulates Thoreau's use of the term *expedient* in the first paragraph?
    a. A dead end
    b. A state of order
    c. A means to an end
    d. Rushed construction

20. Which best describes Thoreau's view on the Mexican War?
    a. Government is inherently corrupt because it must wage war.
    b. Government can easily be manipulated by a few individuals for their own agenda.
    c. Government is a tool for the people, but it can also act against their interest.
    d. The Mexican War was a necessary action, but not all the people believed this.

21. What is Thoreau's purpose for writing?
    a. His goal is to illustrate how government can function if ideals are maintained.
    b. He wants to prove that true democracy is the best government, but it can be corrupted easily.
    c. Thoreau reflects on the stages of government abuses.
    d. He is seeking to prove that government is easily corruptible and inherently restrictive of individual freedoms that can simultaneously affect the whole state.

22. Which example best supports Thoreau's argument?
    a. A vote carries in the Senate to create a new road tax.
    b. The president vetoes the new FARM bill.
    c. Prohibition is passed to outlaw alcohol.
    d. Trade is opened between the United States and Iceland.

23. Which best summarizes this section from the following passage?
    "This American government—what is it but a tradition, though a recent one, endeavoring to transmit itself unimpaired to posterity, but each instant losing some of its integrity? It has not the vitality and force of a single living man; for a single man can bend it to his will. It is a sort of wooden gun to the people themselves."

    a. The government may be instituted to ensure the protections of freedoms, but this is weakened by the fact that it is easily manipulated by individuals.
    b. Unlike an individual, government is uncaring.
    c. Unlike an individual, government has no will, making it more prone to be used as a weapon against the people.
    d. American government is modeled after other traditions but actually has greater potential to be used to control people.

24. According to Thoreau, what's the main reason why government eventually fails to achieve progress?
    a. There are too many rules.
    b. Legislation eventually becomes a hindrance to the lives and work of everyday people.
    c. Trade and wealth eventually become the driving factor of those in government.
    d. Government doesn't separate religion and state.

Questions 25–30 are based on the following passage:

In this excerpt from a novel set in nineteenth-century France, two friends, Albert de Morcef and the Count of Monte Cristo, discuss Parisian social life. Read it and answer questions 118-124.

> "Mademoiselle Eugénie is pretty—I think I remember that to be her name."

> "Very pretty, or rather, very beautiful," replied Albert, "but of that style of beauty which I don't appreciate; I am an ungrateful fellow."

> "Really," said Monte Cristo, lowering his voice, "you don't appear to me to be very enthusiastic on the subject of this marriage."

> "Mademoiselle Danglars is too rich for me," replied Morcerf, "and that frightens me."

> "Bah," exclaimed Monte Cristo, "that's a fine reason to give. Are you not rich yourself?"

"My father's income is about 50,000 francs per annum; and he will give me, perhaps, ten or twelve thousand when I marry."

"That, perhaps, might not be considered a large sum, in Paris especially," said the count; "but everything doesn't depend on wealth, and it's a fine thing to have a good name, and to occupy a high station in society. Your name is celebrated, your position magnificent; and then the Comte de Morcerf is a soldier, and it's pleasing to see the integrity of a Bayard united to the poverty of a Duguesclin; disinterestedness is the brightest ray in which a noble sword can shine. As for me, I consider the union with Mademoiselle Danglars a most suitable one; she will enrich you, and you will ennoble her."

Albert shook his head, and looked thoughtful. "There is still something else," said he.

"I confess," observed Monte Cristo, "that I have some difficulty in comprehending your objection to a young lady who is both rich and beautiful."

"Oh," said Morcerf, "this repugnance, if repugnance it may be called, isn't all on my side."

"Whence can it arise, then? for you told me your father desired the marriage."

"It's my mother who dissents; she has a clear and penetrating judgment, and doesn't smile on the proposed union. I cannot account for it, but she seems to entertain some prejudice against the Danglars."

"Ah," said the count, in a somewhat forced tone, "that may be easily explained; the Comtesse de Morcerf, who is aristocracy and refinement itself, doesn't relish the idea of being allied by your marriage with one of ignoble birth; that is natural enough."

25. The meaning of the word "repugnance" is closest to:
    a. Strong resemblance
    b. Strong dislike
    c. Extreme shyness
    d. Extreme dissimilarity

26. What can be inferred about Albert's family?
    a. Their finances are uncertain.
    b. Albert is the only son in his family.
    c. Their name is more respected than the Danglars'.
    d. Albert's mother and father both agree on their decisions.

27. What is Albert's attitude towards his impending marriage?
    a. Pragmatic
    b. Romantic
    c. Indifferent
    d. Apprehensive

28. What is the best description of the Count's relationship with Albert?
    a. He's like a strict parent, criticizing Albert's choices.
    b. He's like a wise uncle, giving practical advice to Albert.
    c. He's like a close friend, supporting all of Albert's opinions.
    d. He's like a suspicious investigator, asking many probing questions.

29. Which sentence is true of Albert's mother?
    a. She belongs to a noble family.
    b. She often makes poor choices.
    c. She is primarily occupied with money.
    d. She is unconcerned about her son's future.

30. Based on this passage, what is probably NOT true about French society in the 1800s?
    a. Children often received money from their parents.
    b. Marriages were sometimes arranged between families.
    c. The richest people in society were also the most respected.
    d. People were often expected to marry within their same social class.

Questions 31–36 are based on the following passage:

What is the trial of the Lancashire witches?

Four hundred years ago, in 1612, the north-west of England was the scene of England's biggest peacetime witch trial: the trial of the Lancashire witches. Twenty people, mostly from the Pendle area of Lancashire, were imprisoned in the castle as witches. Ten were hanged, one died in gaol, one was sentenced to stand in the pillory, and eight were acquitted. The 2012 anniversary sees a small flood of commemorative events, including works of fiction by Blake Morrison, Carol Ann Duffy, and Jeanette Winterson. How did this witch trial come about, and what accounts for its enduring fame?

We know so much about the Lancashire Witches because the trial was recorded in unique detail by the clerk of the court, Thomas Potts, who published his account soon afterwards as *The Wonderful Discovery of Witches in the County of Lancaster*. I have recently published a modern-English edition of this book, together with an essay piecing together what we know of the events of 1612. It has been a fascinating exercise, revealing how Potts carefully edited the evidence, and also how the case against the "witches" was constructed and manipulated to bring about a spectacular show trial. It all began in mid-March when a pedlar from Halifax named John Law had a frightening encounter with a poor young woman, Alizon Device, in a field near Colne. He refused her request for pins and there was a brief argument during which he was seized by a fit that left him with "his head … drawn awry, his eyes and face deformed, his speech not well to be understood; his thighs and legs stark lame." We can now recognize this as a stroke, perhaps triggered by the stressful encounter. Alizon Device was sent for and surprised all by confessing to the bewitching of John Law and then begged for forgiveness.

When Alizon Device was unable to cure the pedlar, the local magistrate, Roger Nowell was called in. Characterized by Thomas Potts as "God's justice" he was alert to instances of witchcraft, which were regarded by the Lancashire's puritan-inclined authorities as part of the cultural rubble of "popery"—Roman Catholicism—long overdue to be swept away at the end of the county's very slow protestant reformation. "With weeping tears" Alizon explained that she had been led astray by her grandmother, "old Demdike," well-known in the district for her knowledge of old Catholic prayers, charms, cures, magic, and curses. Nowell quickly interviewed Alizon's grandmother and mother, as well as Demdike's supposed rival, "old Chattox" and her daughter Anne. Their panicky attempts to explain themselves and shift the blame to others eventually only ended up incriminating them, and the four were sent to Lancaster gaol in early April to await trial at the summer assizes. The initial picture revealed was of a couple of poor, marginal local families in the forest of Pendle with a longstanding reputation for magical powers, which they had occasionally used at the request of their wealthier neighbours. There had been disputes but none of these were part of ordinary village life. Not until 1612 did any of this come to the attention of the authorities.

The net was widened still further at the end of April when Alizon's younger brother James and younger sister Jennet, only nine years old, came up between them with a story about a "great meeting of witches" at their grandmother's house, known as Malkin Tower. This meeting was presumably to discuss the plight of those arrested and the threat of further arrests, but according to the evidence extracted from the children by the magistrates, a plot was hatched to blow up Lancaster castle with gunpowder, kill the gaoler, and rescue the imprisoned witches. It was, in short, a conspiracy against royal authority to rival the gunpowder plot of 1605—something to be expected in a county known for its particularly strong underground Roman Catholic presence.

Those present at the meeting were mostly family members and neighbours, but they also included Alice Nutter, described by Potts as "a rich woman [who] had a great estate, and children of good hope: in the common opinion of the world, of good temper, free from envy or malice." Her part in the affair remains mysterious, but she seems to have had Catholic family connections, and may have been one herself, providing an added motive for her to be prosecuted.

31. What's the point of this passage, and why did the author write it?
    a. The author is documenting a historic witchcraft trial while uncovering/investigating the role of suspicion and anti-Catholicism in the events.
    b. The author seeks long-overdue reparations for the ancestors of those accused and executed for witchcraft in Lancashire.
    c. The author is educating the reader about actual occult practices of the 1600s.
    d. The author argues that the Lancashire witch trials were more brutal than the infamous Salem trials.

32. Which term best captures the meaning of the author's use of "enduring" in the first paragraph?
    a. Un-original
    b. Popular
    c. Wicked
    d. Circumstantial

33. What textual information is present within the passage that most lends itself to the author's credibility?
    a. His prose is consistent with the time.
    b. This is a reflective passage; the author doesn't need to establish credibility.
    c. The author cites specific quotes.
    d. The author has published a modern account of the case and has written on the subject before.

34. What might the following excerpt suggest about the trial or, at the very least, Thomas Potts' account of the trial(s)?

"It has been a fascinating exercise, revealing how Potts carefully edited the evidence, and also how the case against the 'witches' was constructed and manipulated to bring about a spectacular show trial."

a. The events were so grand that the public was allowed access to such a spectacular set of cases.
b. Sections may have been exaggerated or stretched to create notoriety on an extraordinary case.
c. Evidence was faked, making the trial a total farce.
d. The trial was corrupt from the beginning.

35. Which statement best describes the political atmosphere of the 1600s that influenced the Alizon Device witch trial/case?
a. Fear of witches was prevalent during this period.
b. Magistrates were seeking ways to cement their power during this period of unrest.
c. In a highly superstitious culture, the Protestant church and government were highly motivated to root out any potential sources that could undermine the current regime.
d. Lancashire was originally a prominent area for pagan celebration, making the modern Protestants very weary of whispers of witchcraft and open to witch trials to resolve any potential threats to Christianity.

36. Which best describes the strongest "evidence" used in the case against Alizon and the witches?
a. Knowledge of the occult and witchcraft
b. "Spectral evidence"
c. Popular rumors of witchcraft and Catholic association
d. Self-incriminating speech

Questions 37–42 are based on the following passage:

What kinds of myths did they use?

The prominent civilized nations—the Babylonians and Egyptians, the Hebrews and Hindus, the Persians, the Greeks and the Romans, as well as the Teutons and others—all began at an early stage to glorify their national heroes—mythical princes and kings, founders of religions, dynasties, empires, or cities—in a number of poetic tales and legends. The history of the birth and of the early life of these personalities came to be especially invested with fantastic features, which in different nations—even though widely separated by space and entirely independent of each other—present a baffling similarity or, in part, a literal correspondence. Many investigators have long been impressed with this fact, and one of the chief problems of mythological research still consists in the elucidation of the reason for the extensive analogies in the fundamental outlines of mythical tales, which are rendered still more puzzling by the unanimity in certain details and their reappearance in most of the mythical groupings.

The mythological theories, aiming at the explanation of these remarkable phenomena, are, in a general way, as follows:

1. The "Idea of the People," propounded by Adolf Bastian. This theory assumes the existence of elemental ideas, so that the unanimity of the myths is a necessary sequence of the uniform disposition of the human mind and the manner of its manifestation, which within certain limits

is identical at all times and in all places. This interpretation was urgently advocated by Adolf Bauer as accounting for the wide distribution of the hero myths.

2. The explanation by original community, first applied by Theodor Benfey to the widely distributed parallel forms of folklore and fairy tales. Originating in a favorable locality (India), these tales were first accepted by the primarily related (Indo-Germanic) peoples, then continued to grow while retaining the common primary traits, and ultimately radiated over the entire earth. This mode of explanation was first adapted to the wide distribution of the hero myths by Rudolf Schubert.

3. The modern theory of migration, or borrowing, according to which individual myths originate from definite peoples (especially the Babylonians) and are accepted by other peoples through oral tradition (commerce and traffic) or through literary influences. The modern theory of migration and borrowing can be readily shown to be merely a modification of Benfey's theory, necessitated by newly discovered and irreconcilable material. This profound and extensive research of modern investigations has shown that India, rather than Babylonia, may be regarded as the first home of the myths. Moreover, the tales presumably did not radiate from a single point, but traveled over and across the entire inhabited globe. This brings into prominence the idea of the interdependence of mythological structures, an idea which was generalized by Braun as the basic law of the nature of the human mind: Nothing new is ever discovered as long as it is possible to copy. The theory of elemental ideas, so strenuously advocated by Bauer over a quarter of a century ago, is unconditionally declined by the most recent investigators (Winckler, Stucken), who maintain the migration theory.

There is really no such sharp contrast between the various theories or their advocates, for the concept of elemental ideas does not interfere with the claims of primary common possession or of migration. Furthermore, the ultimate problem is not whence and how the material reached a certain people; the question is: Where did it come from to begin with? All these theories would explain only the variability and distribution of the myths, but not their origin. Even Schubert, the most inveterate opponent of Bauer's view, acknowledges this truth, by stating that all these manifold sagas date back to a single very ancient prototype. But he is unable to tell us anything of the origin of this prototype. Bauer likewise inclines to this mediating view; he points out repeatedly that in spite of the multiple origin of independent tales, it is necessary to concede a most extensive and ramified borrowing, as well as an original community of the concepts in related peoples.

from *The Myth of the Birth of the Hero, A Psychological Interpretation of Mythology*, by Otto Rank

37. Which term best defines *elucidation* as it's used in the first paragraph of the passage?
    a. Definition
    b. Specification
    c. Ramification
    d. Explanation

38. Based on the title of his work and the context of the selected passage, which statement may serve as the best explanation for why Rank is studying mythology?

   a. Psychologist Carl Jung proved the concept of archetypes seems to suggest universal concepts and ideas.

   b. The proliferation of common mythic structures around the world and cultures suggest shared, fundamental human ideas and values. To study these myths is to study the core of human thought.

   c. The study of the mythic hero may uncover the true origins of the first leaders.

   d. Studying mythology enables Rank to analyze how conflicts can be mitigated across various cultures, helping him develop new psychological analysis strategies and therapies.

39. Which statement provides an example that would correlate the following theory from the main passage?

   "The 'Idea of the People,' propounded by Adolf Bastian. This theory assumes the existence of elemental ideas, so that the unanimity of the myths is a necessary sequence of the uniform disposition of the human mind and the manner of its manifestation, which within certain limits is identical at all times and in all places."

   a. Human beings have the need to understand their origins, hence the presence of creation myths.

   b. The idea of winter as a cold season needed explanation; therefore, myths developed to analyze and interpret the natural phenomena, creating stories that account for seasonal change.

   c. Heroes exemplify power and strength.

   d. The Germanic and Nordic people wanted to understand why chaos exists in the world; the giants, beings of chaos and destruction, explained how natural phenomena occurred.

40. Reading through the body of the text, why is it appropriate that the mentioned theories are in fact called *theories*?

   a. They are scientific explanations.

   b. There is no reason; this was an artistic choice.

   c. While very insightful, these theories as of yet cannot be officially proven; however, they are likely.

   d. These are all competing ideas.

41. What are some insights that can be drawn from the following description of the third theory of mythic origins statement that can also relate to the rest of the passage?

   "This brings into prominence the idea of the interdependence of mythological structures, an idea which was generalized by Braun as the basic law of the nature of the human mind: Nothing new is ever discovered as long as it is possible to copy."

   a. Humans lack originality; there are no new ideas.

   b. The cultural minds of human beings evolved from a set of basic ideas.

   c. Human culture is interdependent on one another; there is no unique culture but a sundered mythic cycle that once was universal.

   d. Recurring mythic structures seem to be reiterations of shared human experiences/stories, used over and over but modified throughout various cultures.

42. Which answer best exemplifies the mentioned theory/explanation in the following description of the second theory of mythic origins?

> "The explanation by original community, first applied by Theodor Benfey to the widely distributed parallel forms of folklore and fairy tales. Originating in a favorable locality (India), these tales were first accepted by the primarily related (Indo-Germanic) peoples, then continued to grow while retaining the common primary traits, and ultimately radiated over the entire earth."

a. A tribe begins trading with another tribe. Through this interaction, different myths are shared, including the story of the hero.
b. A tribe has a legend of how the sky was formed. At some point, the tribe splits into different tribes, and each retains the myth. Some of the newer tribes attribute sky creation to different gods or tricksters.
c. The myth of Aeneas and Dido explains the ancient rivalry between Carthage and Rome.
d. There is a myth of a world flood in many cultures.

Questions 43–45 are based on the following passage:

How did the history museums come to be?

A desire to preserve objects of nature which aroused special interest or possessed unusual powers may be presumed to have been an instinct of the earliest man. We may imagine the cave man storing in his cave the bright gem, or curious seed, or rare animal skin which attracted his attention and, perchance, urging upon his descendants the desirability of preserving it. Such instincts are undoubtedly possessed by barbarous tribes. But such hoards have no permanent value or maintenance as long as there is a lack of a fixed habitation or of a social organization sufficiently strong to pass them from one generation to another. Hence, it may be noted in passing, an essential condition for the existence of museums is a sufficiently civilized and permanent state of society to preserve objects from generation to generation.

In the life of the ancient Egyptians conditions making toward the preservation of natural objects doubtless became more favorable than had previously been the case, since there are preserved to us from their time many objects of their art which were originally objects of nature. While material which they prized now occupies an honored place in our museums and their civilization was instrumental in preserving it to us, there is no evidence, so far as I know, that they undertook the collection and preservation of natural objects for their own sake.

The Greeks gave us the word museum, but that they ever established a museum in the modern sense seems very unlikely. Whatever their practice may have been regarding the preservation and exhibition of works of art, it seems quite certain that they carried on little, if any, effort of this kind with regard to nature. Alexander the Great, about 325 BC, is said to have gathered together many animals and plants in order that they might be studied by Aristotle, "the father of natural history," but so far as we know no effort was made to preserve these specimens to later times. The first record of placing natural history specimens on exhibition is said to be made when Hanno, a Carthaginian, somewhat before Alexander's time, procured skins of gorillas in Africa and put them in the temple of Astarte. We also know that the monstrous horns of wild bulls which had occasioned great devastation in Macedonia were hung in the temple of Hercules by order of King Philip.

The Romans seem, like the Greeks, not to have taken much interest in the preservation of natural objects, at least as far as any record has reached the present time. We know that emperors and other individuals possessed collections of statues and other works of art, and among these we find occasional mention of the preservation of so-called "natural curiosities," such as bones of giants or peculiar human skeletons, but that any broad interest in nature existed which led to efforts to preserve and study its forms we have no record. Stray sources of information tell us of a crocodile, found in attempting to discover the sources of the Nile, being preserved in the temple of Isis at Cesarea, also that a large piece of the root of the cinnamon tree was kept in a golden vessel in one of the temples at Rome. Pliny relates that the bones of a sea monster, probably a whale, "to which Andromeda was exposed," were preserved at Joppa and afterwards brought to Rome. Suetonious says that the Emperor Augustus had a collection of natural curiosities in his palace.

One reason suggested by Beckmann for the rarity of collections of natural objects among ancient peoples was the lack of knowledge of satisfactory means of preserving such as were perishable. The preservative virtues of what was then called "spirit of wine," but which we now know as alcohol, seem to have been but little known, and only immersion in salt brine or a covering with wax or honey served at that time for the preservation of perishable materials.

The great institute of Alexandria in Egypt, founded in the third century BC, is generally spoken of as being the first natural-history museum of antiquity, but while this had botanical and zoological gardens, there is little reason to suppose that it was a museum of nature in the modern sense. The name museum in that institution was applied to a portion set apart for the study of sciences, and indicated rather a place of study than one for exhibition of objects.

from "The Rise of Natural History Museums," by Oliver Cummings Farrington

43. Which statement best captures the goal of this excerpt?
   a. The author argues that the ancient Greeks, not the Egyptians, invented museums.
   b. The author is reflecting on the history of museums while detailing his own visits to museums.
   c. The author seeks to sketch the history behind modern museums by discussing ancient roots.
   d. The author wants to prove that actual museums didn't evolve until the 1850s.

44. Which best encapsulates the core reasoning behind the author's idea, "Hence, it may be noted in passing, an essential condition for the existence of museums is a sufficiently civilized and permanent state of society to preserve objects from generation to generation"?
   a. A refined level of sophistication is needed to understand and pass down the knowledge of artifacts within a museum.
   b. Stable civil conditions and a learned society are key for museum preservation and education; if the city is unstable, museum interest and artifacts are threatened.
   c. Museums can't exist as a nomadic, or traveling practice; the artifacts won't be preserved.
   d. The continuation of museums relies on educating future generations.

45. What seems to be the main criteria for a site to be considered a museum in the modern sense?
   a. A location that contain artifacts that are archaic in nature and significant to specific events
   b. A central location that houses artifacts
   c. The wealth to purchase items and display them safely without risk of damage or theft
   d. A central location that displays artifacts for the general public to learn and enjoy

Extended Response

There are two passages below. Read both of the passages carefully all the way through. Then, choose which passage you think is better supported by evidence. In your response, be sure to use your own evidence from the passages. You will have forty-five minutes to plan, write, and edit your response. Your essay should be around 500 words.

Passage I

Shakespeare and His Plays

People who argue that William Shakespeare is not responsible for the plays attributed to his name are known as anti-Stratfordians (from the name of Shakespeare's birthplace, Stratford-upon-Avon). The most common anti-Stratfordian claim is that William Shakespeare simply was not educated enough or from a high enough social class to have written plays overflowing with references to such a wide range of subjects like history, the classics, religion, and international culture. William Shakespeare was the son of a glove-maker, he only had a basic grade school education, and he never set foot outside of England—so how could he have produced plays of such sophistication and imagination? How could he have written in such detail about historical figures and events, or about different cultures and locations around Europe? According to anti-Stratfordians, the depth of knowledge contained in Shakespeare's plays suggests a well-traveled writer from a wealthy background with a university education, not a countryside writer like Shakespeare. But in fact, there is not much substance to such speculation, and most anti-Stratfordian arguments can be refuted with a little background about Shakespeare's time and upbringing.

First of all, those who doubt Shakespeare's authorship often point to his common birth and brief education as stumbling blocks to his writerly genius. Although it is true that Shakespeare did not come from a noble class, his father was a very *successful* glove-maker and his mother was from a very wealthy land-owning family—so while Shakespeare may have had a country upbringing, he was certainly from a well-off family and would have been educated accordingly. Also, even though he did not attend university, grade school education in Shakespeare's time was actually quite rigorous and exposed students to classic drama through writers like Seneca and Ovid. It is not unreasonable to believe that Shakespeare received a very solid foundation in poetry and literature from his early schooling.

Next, anti-Stratfordians tend to question how Shakespeare could write so extensively about countries and cultures he had never visited before (for instance, several of his most famous works like *Romeo and Juliet* and *The Merchant of Venice* were set in Italy, on the opposite side of Europe!). But again, this criticism does not hold up under scrutiny. For one thing, Shakespeare was living in London, a bustling metropolis of international trade, the most populous city in England, and a political and cultural hub of Europe. In the daily crowds of people, Shakespeare would certainly have been able to meet travelers from other countries and hear firsthand accounts of life in their home country. And, in addition to the influx of information from world travelers, this was also the age of the printing press, a jump in technology that made it possible to print and circulate books much more easily than in the past. This also allowed for a freer flow of information across different countries, allowing people to read about life and ideas from throughout Europe. One needn't travel the continent in order to learn and write about its culture.

Passage II

The following passage is from The Shakespeare Problem Restated *by G.G. Greenwood*

Now there is very good authority for saying, and I think the truth is so, that at least two of the plays published among the works of Shakespeare are not his at all; that at least three others contain very little, if any, of his writing; and that of the remainder, many contain long passages that are non-Shakespearean. But when we have submitted them all the crucible of criticism we have a magnificent residuum of the purest gold. Here is the true Shakespeare; here is the great magician who, by a wave of his wand, could transmute brass into gold, or make dry bones live and move and have immortal being. Who was this great magician—this mighty dramatist who was "not of an age, but for all time"? Who was the writer of *Venus* and *Lucrece* and the *Sonnets* and *Lear* and *Hamlet*? Was it William Shakespeare of Stratford, the Player? So it is generally believed, and that hypothesis I had accepted in unquestioning faith till my love of the works naturally led me to an examination of the life of the supposed author of them. Then I found that as I read my faith melted away "into thin air." It was not, certainly, that I had (nor have I now) any wish to disbelieve. I was, and I am, altogether willing to accept the Player as the immortal poet if only my reason would allow me to do so. Why not? . . . But the question of authorship is, nevertheless, a most fascinating one. If it be true, as the Rev. Leonard Bacon wrote that "The great world does not care sixpence who wrote *Hamlet,*" the great world must, at the same time, be a very small world, and many of us must be content to be outside it. Having given, then, the best attention I was able to give to the question, and more time, I fear, than I ought to have devoted to it, I was brought to the conclusion, as many others have been, that the man who is, truly enough, designated by Messrs. Garnett and Gosse as a "Stratford rustic" is not the true Shakespeare. . .

That Shakespeare the "Stratford rustic and London actor" should have acquired this learning, this culture, and this polish; that *he* should have travelled into foreign lands, studied the life and topography of foreign cities, and the manners and customs of all sorts and conditions of men; that *he* should have written some half-dozen dramas . . . besides qualifying himself as a professional actor; that *he* should have done all this and a good deal more between 1587 and 1592 is a supposition so wild that it can only be entertained by those who are prepared to accept it as a miracle. "And miracles do not happen!"

Mathematical Reasoning

1. Which of the following is largest?
    a. 0.45
    b. 0.096
    c. 0.3
    d. 0.313

2. Which of the following is NOT a way to write 40 percent of N?

    a. $(0.4)N$

    b. $\frac{2}{5}N$

    c. $40N$

    d. $\frac{4N}{10}$

3. Which is closest to 17.8×9.9?

    a. 140
    b. 180
    c. 200
    d. 350

4. Five of six numbers have a sum of 25. The average of all six numbers is 6. What is the sixth number?

    a. 8
    b. 10
    c. 11
    d. 12

5. If $\frac{5}{2} \div \frac{1}{3} = n$, then n is between:

    a. 5 and 7
    b. 7 and 9
    c. 9 and 11
    d. 3 and 5

6. A closet is filled with red, blue, and green shirts. If $\frac{1}{3}$ of the shirts are green and $\frac{2}{5}$ are red, what fraction of the shirts are blue?

    a. $\frac{4}{15}$

    b. $\frac{1}{5}$

    c. $\frac{7}{15}$

    d. $\frac{1}{2}$

7. Shawna buys $2\frac{1}{2}$ gallons of paint. If she uses $\frac{1}{3}$ of it on the first day, how much does she have left?

    a. $1\frac{5}{6}$ gallons

    b. $1\frac{1}{2}$ gallons

    c. $1\frac{2}{3}$ gallons

    d. 2 gallons

8. On Monday, Robert mopped the floor in 4 hours. On Tuesday, he did it in 3 hours. If on Monday, his average rate of mopping was p sq. ft. per hour, what was his average rate on Tuesday?

a. $\frac{4}{3}p$ sq. ft. per hour

b. $\frac{3}{4}p$ sq. ft. per hour

c. $\frac{5}{4}p$ sq. ft. per hour

d. $p + 1$ sq. ft. per hour

9. The variable y is directly proportional to x. If $y = 3$ when $x = 5$, then what is y when $x = 20$?
  a. 10
  b. 12
  c. 14
  d. 16

10. There are $4x + 1$ treats in each party favor bag. If a total of $60x + 15$ treats are distributed, how many bags are given out?
  a. 15
  b. 16
  c. 20
  d. 22

11. A rectangle has a length that is 5 feet longer than three times its width. If the perimeter is 90 feet, what is the length in feet?
  a. 10
  b. 20
  c. 25
  d. 35

12. In an office, there are 50 workers. A total of 60% of the workers are women, and the chances of a woman wearing a skirt is 50%. If no men wear skirts, how many workers are wearing skirts?
  a. 12
  b. 15
  c. 16
  d. 20

13. What is the volume of a cube with the side equal to 3 inches?
  a. 6 in³
  b. 27 in³
  c. 9 in³
  d. 3 in³

14. What is the volume of a cube with the side equal to 5 centimeters?
  a. 10 cm³
  b. 15 cm³
  c. 50 cm³
  d. 125 cm³

15. What is the length of the hypotenuse of a right triangle with one leg equal to 3 centimeters and the other leg equal to 4 centimeters?

    a. 7 cm

    b. 5 cm

    c. 25 cm

    d. 12 cm

16. What is the length of the other leg of a right triangle with a hypotenuse of 10 inches and a leg of 8 inches?

    a. 6 in

    b. 18 in

    c. 80 in

    d. 13 in

17. What is the answer to $(2 + 2i)(2 - 2i)$?

    a. 8

    b. $8i$

    c. 4

    d. $4i$

18. What is the answer to $(3 + 3i)(3 - 3i)$?

    a. 18

    b. $18i$

    c. 9

    d. $9i$

19. What is the answer to $\frac{2+2i}{2-2i}$?

    a. 8

    b. $8i$

    c. $2i$

    d. i

20. What is the answer to $\frac{3+3i}{3-3i}$?

    a. 18

    b. $18i$

    c. i

    d. $9i$

21. According to building code regulations, the roof of a house has to be set at a minimum angle of 39° up to a maximum angle of 48° to ensure snow and rain will properly slide off it. What is the maximum incline in terms of radians?

    a. $\frac{\pi}{4}$

    b. $\frac{\pi}{15}$

    c. $\frac{4\pi}{15}$

    d. $\frac{3\pi}{4}$

22. Two chords intersect inside of a circle. The segments of one chord have lengths 3 and $x + 2$. The segments of the other chord have lengths x and $3x + 2$. What are the lengths of these chords?
   a. 1 units
   b. 2 units
   c. 3 units
   d. 6 units

23. Two chords intersect inside of a circle. The segments of one chord have the lengths 4 and $2x + 2$. The segments of the other chord have lengths x and $3x + 2$. What are the lengths of these chords?
   a. 10 units
   b. 2 units
   c. 1 units
   d. 3 units

24. Which of the following numbers has the greatest value?
   a. 1.4378
   b. 1.07548
   c. 1.43592
   d. 0.89409

25. The value of 6 x 12 is the same as:
   a. 2 x 4 x 4 x 2
   b. 7 x 4 x 3
   c. 6 x 6 x 3
   d. 3 x 3 x 4 x 2

26. This chart indicates how many sales of CDs, vinyl records, and MP3 downloads occurred over the last year. Approximately what percentage of the total sales was from CDs?

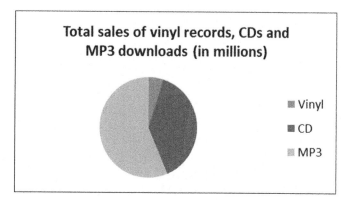

   a. 55%
   b. 25%
   c. 40%
   d. 5%

27. After a 20% sale discount, Frank purchased a new refrigerator for $850. How much did he save from the original price?

    a. $170

    b. $212.50

    c. $105.75

    d. $200

28. What is the value of *b* in this equation?

$$5b - 4 = 2b + 17$$

    a. 13

    b. 24

    c. 7

    d. 21

29. A school has 15 teachers and 20 teaching assistants. They have 200 students. What is the ratio of faculty to students?

    a. 3:20

    b. 4:17

    c. 3:2

    d. 7:40

30. Express the solution to the following problem in decimal form:

$$\frac{3}{5} \times \frac{7}{10} \div \frac{1}{2}$$

    a. 0.042

    b. 84%

    c. 0.84

    d. 0.42

31. Alan currently weighs 200 pounds, but he wants to lose weight to get down to 175 pounds. What is this difference in kilograms? (1 pound is approximately equal to 0.45 kilograms.)

    a. 9 kg

    b. 11.25 kg

    c. 78.75 kg

    d. 90 kg

32. Johnny earns $2334.50 from his job each month. He pays $1437 for monthly expenses. Johnny is planning a vacation in 3 months' time that he estimates will cost $1750 total. How much will Johnny have left over from three months' of saving once he pays for his vacation?

    a. $948.50

    b. $584.50

    c. $852.50

    d. $942.50

33. Solve the following:

$$4 \times 7 + (25 - 21)^2 \div 2$$

   a. 512
   b. 36
   c. 60.5
   d. 22

34. The total perimeter of a rectangle is 36 cm. If the length of each side is 12 cm, what is the width?
   a. 3 cm
   b. 12 cm
   c. 6 cm
   d. 8 cm

35. Dwayne has received the following scores on his math tests: 78, 92, 83, 97. What score must Dwayne get on his next math test to have an overall average of at least 90?
   a. 89
   b. 98
   c. 95
   d. 100

36. What is the overall median of Dwayne's current scores: 78, 92, 83, 97?
   a. 19
   b. 85
   c. 83
   d. 87.5

37. In Jim's school, there are 3 girls for every 2 boys. There are 650 students in total. Using this information, how many students are girls?
   a. 260
   b. 130
   c. 65
   d. 390

38. Kimberley earns $10 an hour babysitting, and after 10 p.m., she earns $12 an hour, with the amount paid being rounded to the nearest hour accordingly. On her last job, she worked from 5:30 p.m. to 11 p.m. In total, how much did Kimberley earn on her last job?
   a. $45
   b. $57
   c. $62
   d. $42

39. Solve this equation:

$$9x + x - 7 = 16 + 2x$$

    a. $x = -4$

    b. $x = 3$

    c. $x = \dfrac{9}{8}$

    d. $x = \dfrac{23}{8}$

40. Arrange the following numbers from least to greatest value:
$0.85, \dfrac{4}{5}, \dfrac{2}{3}, \dfrac{91}{100}$

    a. $0.85, \dfrac{4}{5}, \dfrac{2}{3}, \dfrac{91}{100}$

    b. $\dfrac{4}{5}, 0.85, \dfrac{91}{100}, \dfrac{2}{3}$

    c. $\dfrac{2}{3}, \dfrac{4}{5}, 0.85, \dfrac{91}{100}$

    d. $0.85, \dfrac{91}{100}, \dfrac{4}{5}, \dfrac{2}{3}$

41. Keith's bakery had 252 customers go through its doors last week. This week, that number increased to 378. Express this increase as a percentage.

    a. 26%

    b. 50%

    c. 35%

    d. 12%

42. If $4x - 3 = 5$, then $x =$

    a. 1

    b. 2

    c. 3

    d. 4

43. Simplify the following fraction:

$$\dfrac{\frac{5}{7}}{\frac{9}{11}}$$

    a. $\dfrac{55}{63}$

    b. $\dfrac{7}{1000}$

    c. $\dfrac{13}{15}$

    d. $\dfrac{5}{11}$

44. The following graph compares the various test scores of the top three students in each of these teacher's classes. Based on the graph, which teacher's students had the lowest range of test scores?

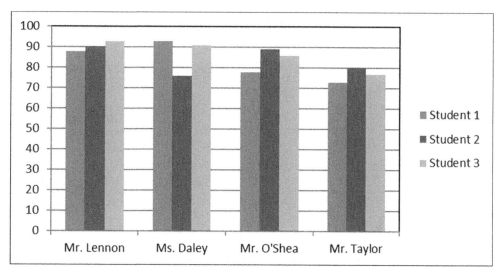

    a. Mr. Lennon
    b. Mr. O'Shea
    c. Mr. Taylor
    d. Ms. Daley

45. Bernard can make $80 per day. If he needs to make $300 and only works full days, how many days will this take?
    a. 2
    b. 3
    c. 4
    d. 5

46. Which measure for the center of a small sample set would be most affected by outliers?
    a. Mean
    b. Median
    c. Mode
    d. None of the above

Science

Passage 1

Questions 1–5 pertain to Passage 1:

Predators are animals that eat other animals. Prey are animals that are eaten by a predator. Predators and prey have a distinct relationship. Predators rely on the prey population for food and nutrition. They evolve physically to catch their prey. For example, they develop a keen sense of sight, smell, or hearing. They may also be able to run very fast or camouflage to their environment in order to sneak up on their prey. Likewise, the prey population may develop these features to escape and hide from their predators. As predators catch more prey, the prey population dwindles. With fewer prey to catch, the predator population also dwindles. This happens in a cyclical manner over time.

Figure 1 below shows the cyclical population growth in a predator-prey relationship.

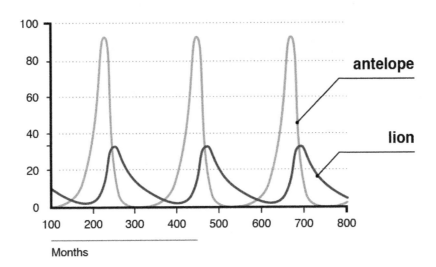

Figure 2 below shows a predator-prey cycle in a circular picture diagram

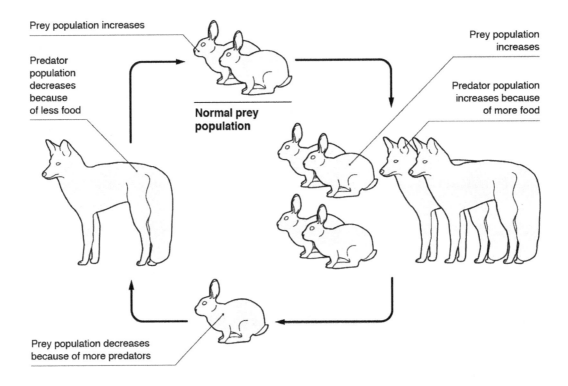

1. Looking at Figure 1, approximately how long is one cycle of the prey population, which includes the population being low, reaching a peak, and then becoming low again?
   a. 200 months
   b. 100 months
   c. 800 months
   d. 400 months

2. In Figure 2, which animal is the predator?
   a. Both the fox and rabbit
   b. Fox only
   c. Rabbit only
   d. Neither the fox nor the rabbit

3. What causes the predator population to decrease?
   a. When there's an increase in the prey population
   b. When winter arrives
   c. When the prey start attacking the predators
   d. When there are fewer prey to find

4. What causes the prey population to increase?
   a. When the predator population decreases, so more prey survive and reproduce.
   b. When there's an increase in the predator population
   c. When there's more sunlight
   d. The prey population always remains the same size.

5. Which is NOT a feature that a prey population can develop to hide from their predator?
   a. Keen sense of smell
   b. Camouflage ability
   c. A loud voice
   d. Keen sense of hearing

Passage 2

Questions 6–10 pertain to Passage 2:

Greenhouses are glass structures that people grow plants in. They allow plants to survive and grow even in the cold winter months by providing light and trapping warm air inside. Light is allowed in through the clear glass walls and roof. Warm air comes in as sunlight through the glass roof. The sunlight is converted into heat, or infrared energy, by the surfaces inside the greenhouse. This heat energy then takes longer to pass back through the glass surfaces and causes the interior of the greenhouse to feel warmer than the outside climate.

Plants may grow better inside a greenhouse versus outside for several reasons. There is more control of the temperature and humidity of the environment inside the greenhouse. The carbon dioxide produced by plants is trapped inside the greenhouse and can increase the rate of photosynthesis of the plants. There are also fewer pests and diseases inside the greenhouse.

Figure 1 below shows how a greenhouse works.

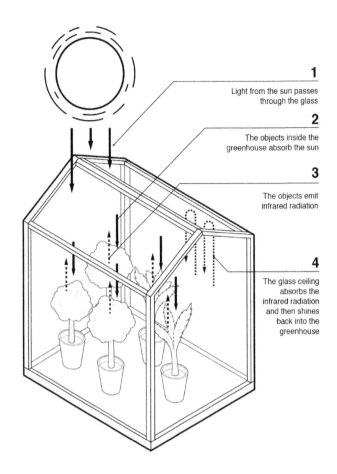

1
Light from the sun passes
through the glass

2
The objects inside the
greenhouse absorb the sun

3
The objects emit
infrared radiation

4
The glass ceiling
absorbs the
infrared radiation
and then shines
back into the
greenhouse

Scientist A wants to compare how a tomato plant grows inside a greenhouse versus outside a greenhouse.

Figure 2 below shows a graph of her results over 3 months.

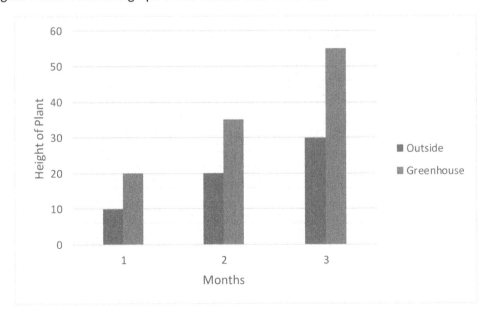

6. Looking at Figure 1, what gets trapped inside the greenhouse that helps plants grow?
   a. Short-wavelength IR
   b. Long-wavelength IR
   c. Cold air
   d. Water

7. Which plant grew taller from Scientist A's experiment?
   a. Outside
   b. Both grew to the same height.
   c. They both remained the same height for 3 months.
   d. Greenhouse

8. What gets converted to heat inside a greenhouse?
   a. Water
   b. Sunlight
   c. Plants
   d. Oxygen

9. What type of wavelength moves through the greenhouse glass easily according to Figure 1?
   a. Short-wavelength IR
   b. Oxygen
   c. Carbon dioxide
   d. Long-wavelength IR

10. What is one reason that plants may grow better inside a greenhouse?
    a. Colder air
    b. Less photosynthesis occurs in the greenhouse
    c. Fewer pests
    d. Less sunlight comes into the greenhouse

Passage 3

Questions 11–15 pertain to Passage 3:

In chemistry, a titration is a method that is used to determine the concentration of an unknown solution. Generally, a known volume of a solution of known concentration is mixed with the unknown solution. Once the reaction of the two solutions has been completed, the concentration of the unknown solution can be calculated. When acids and bases are titrated, the progress of the reaction is monitored by changes in the pH of the known solution. The equivalence point is when just enough of the unknown solution has been added to neutralize the known solution. A color reaction may also occur so that with the drop of solution that causes complete neutralization, the solution turns bright pink, for example. For acids that only have one proton, usually a hydrogen atom, the halfway point between the beginning of the curve and the equivalence point is where the amount of acid and base are equal in the solution. At this point, the pH is equal to the pK_a, or the acid dissociation constant.

Figure 1 below shows a general titration curve of a strong acid with a strong base.

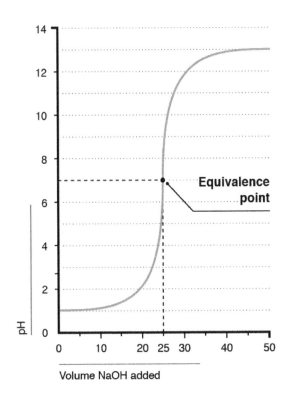

Figure 2 below shows the chemical reaction of a strong acid with a strong base.

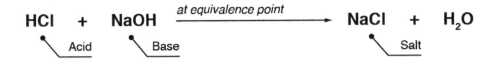

Figure 3 shows the titration curve for acetic acid.

Titration Curve of Acetic Acid

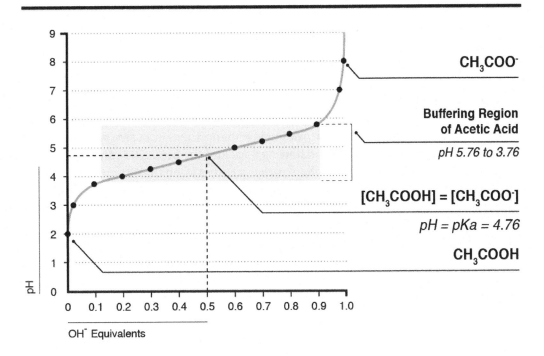

11. How much NaOH is added to the HCl solution to reach the equivalence point in Figure 1?
    a. 10
    b. 40
    c. 50
    d. 25

12. What is the acid dissociation constant of the titration curve in the Figure 3?
    a. 4.21
    b. 3.50
    c. 4.76
    d. 6.52

13. What is the pH of the acetic acid before the titration has started in Figure 3?
    a. 1
    b. 4.76
    c. 7
    d. 6

14. What is one of the products of the chemical equation in Figure 2?
    a. HCl
    b. NaCl
    c. NaOH
    d. Cl⁻

15. How would you describe the solution at the equivalence point in Figure 1?
    a. Neutral
    b. Acidic
    c. Basic
    d. Unknown

Passage 4

Questions 16–20 pertain to Passage 4:

The heart is a muscle that is responsible for pumping blood through the body. It is divided into four chambers: the right atrium, right ventricle, left atrium, and left ventricle. Blood enters the atria and is then pumped into the ventricles below them. There is a valve between the atria and ventricles that prevents the blood from flowing back into the atria. The valve between the right atrium and ventricle has three folds whereas the valve between the left atrium and ventricle has two folds. Arteries carry oxygen-rich blood away from the heart to the body. Veins carry oxygen-poor blood from the body back to the heart. From there, the blood gets pumped to the lungs to get re-oxygenated and then back to the heart before circulating to the body. The heart beats every second of the day. For an adult, the normal heartrate is between 60 and 100 beats per minute. For a child, a normal heartrate is between 90 and 120 beats per minute.

Figure 1 below shows how blood gets pumped through the body.

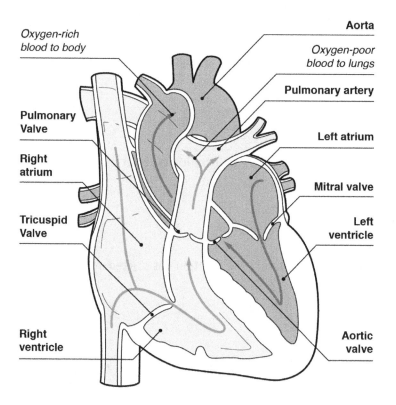

16. Where is the oxygen-poor blood pumped to before returning to the heart to get circulated to the rest of the body?
   a. Lungs
   b. Brain
   c. Stomach
   d. Kidney

17. Which heart valve has two folds?
   a. Pulmonary artery
   b. Tricuspid valve
   c. Mitral valve
   d. Aorta

18. If the aorta contains oxygen-rich blood, what type of vessel is it?
   a. Vein
   b. Pulmonary
   c. Airway
   d. Artery

19. Which heartrate (beats per minute) would be considered abnormal for a child?
   a. 85
   b. 90
   c. 100
   d. 60

20. The aorta is the artery that breaks into smaller vessels to transport blood to the rest of the body. Looking at the figure, which is the final chamber that the blood flows through before entering the aorta?
   a. Right ventricle
   b. Left ventricle
   c. Right atrium
   d. Left atrium

Passage 5

Questions 21–25 pertain to Passage 5:

There are three types of rocks: sedimentary, metamorphic, and igneous. Sedimentary rock is formed from sediment, such as sand, shells, and pebbles. The sediment gathers together and hardens over time. It is generally soft and breaks apart easily. This is the only type of rock that contains fossils, which are the remains of animals and plants that lived a long time ago. Metamorphic rock forms under the surface of the earth due to changes in heat and pressure. These rocks usually have ribbon-like layers and may contain shiny crystals. Igneous rock forms when molten rock, or magma, cools and hardens. An example of molten rock is lava, which escapes from an erupting volcano. This type of rock looks shiny and glasslike.

Figure 1 below is a chart of different types of rocks.

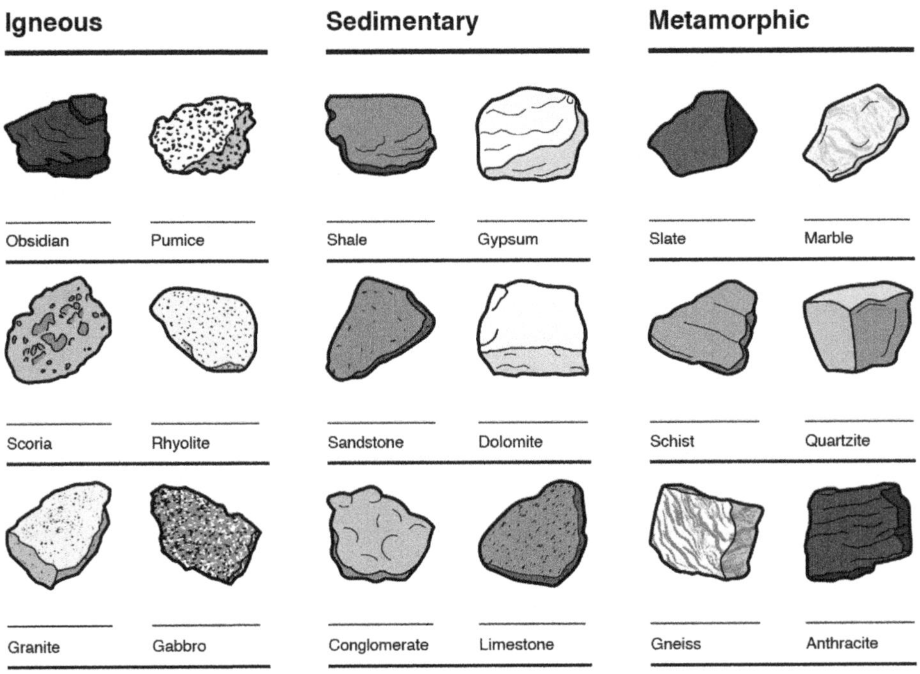

21. A volcano erupts and lava comes out and hardens once it is cooled. What type of rock is formed?
    A. Sedimentary
    B. Metamorphic
    C. Igneous
    D. Lava does not cool

22. Scientist A found a piece of granite rock, as seen in Figure 1. What type of rock is it?
    a. Igneous
    b. Metamorphic
    c. Sedimentary
    d. Fossil

23. Which type of rock could a fossil be found in?
    a. Igneous
    b. Bone
    c. Metamorphic
    d. Sedimentary

24. Which is an example of a metamorphic rock in the figure?
    a. Sandstone
    b. Slate
    c. Granite
    d. Limestone

25. What type of rock would most likely be formed at and found on the beach?
    a. Sedimentary
    b. Shells
    c. Igneous
    d. Metamorphic

Passage 6

Questions 26–30 pertain to Passage 6:

The greenhouse effect is a natural process that warms the Earth's surface, similar to what occurs in a greenhouse meant to grow plants. Solar energy reaches the Earth's atmosphere and warms the air and land. Some of the energy is absorbed by the greenhouse gases found in the Earth's atmosphere and by the land, and the rest is reflected back into space. Greenhouse gases include water vapor, carbon dioxide, methane, nitrous oxide, and chlorofluorocarbons. In recent decades, human activity has increased the amount of greenhouse gases present in the Earth's atmosphere, which has created a warmer atmosphere than normal and increased the Earth's temperature.

Figure 1 below shows the process of the greenhouse effect.

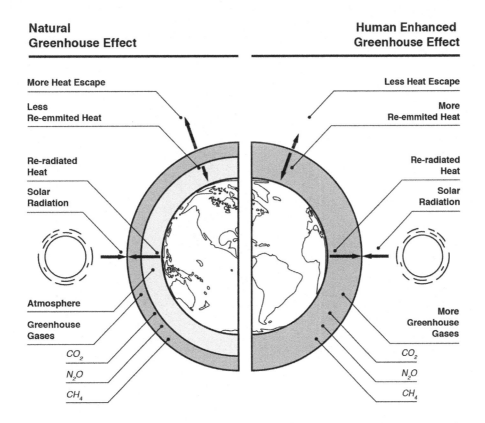

Figure 2 below describes the greenhouse gases that are produced from human activity.

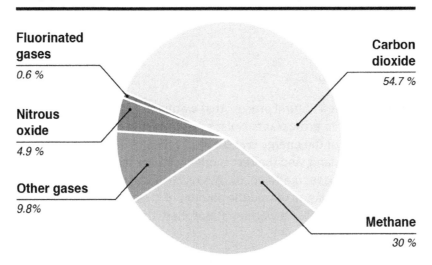

Major Greenhouse Gases from People's Activities

Fluorinated gases
0.6 %

Nitrous oxide
4.9 %

Other gases
9.8%

Carbon dioxide
54.7 %

Methane
30 %

Figure 3 below describes the human activities that produce carbon dioxide.

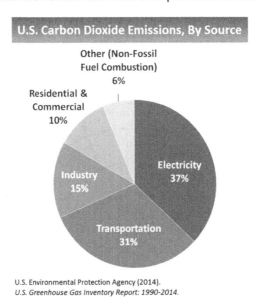

U.S. Carbon Dioxide Emissions, By Source

Other (Non-Fossil Fuel Combustion)
6%

Residential & Commercial
10%

Industry
15%

Electricity
37%

Transportation
31%

U.S. Environmental Protection Agency (2014).
U.S. Greenhouse Gas Inventory Report: 1990-2014.

26. Which is not an example of a greenhouse gas?
    a. Methane
    b. Carbon dioxide
    c. Nitrous oxide
    d. Water vapor

27. Looking at Figure 3, what could a person do to decrease how much carbon dioxide they produce?
    a. Leave lights on all the time
    b. Walk instead of drive a car
    c. Always drive in their own car everywhere
    d. Leave the television on all the time

28. Looking at Figure 1, which is the second highest greenhouse gas produced by human activity?
    a. Methane
    b. Fluorinated gases
    c. Nitrous oxide
    d. Carbon dioxide

29. Looking at Figure 1, what gets increasingly trapped in the Earth's atmosphere with increased human activity?
    a. Space
    b. The Sun
    c. Heat
    d. Water vapor

30. What type of charts are found in Figures 2 and 3?
    a. Scatter plots
    b. Line graphs
    c. Bar graphs
    d. Pie charts

Passage 7

Questions 31–35 pertain to Passage 7:

A meteorologist uses many different tools to predict the weather. They study the atmosphere and changes that are occurring to predict what the weather will be like in the future. Listed below are some of the tools that a meteorologist uses:

- Thermometer: measures air temperature
- Barometer: measures air pressure
- Rain gauge: measures rainfall over a specific time
- Anemometer: measures air speed
- Wind vane: shows which direction the wind is blowing

Figure 1 below shows data that is collected by a meteorologist.

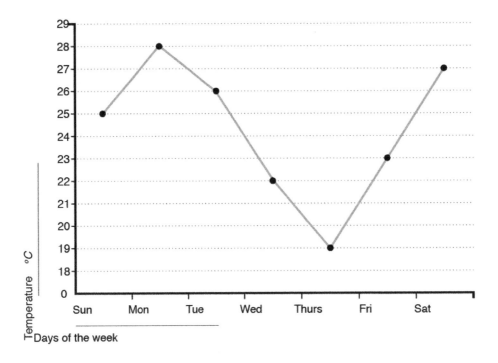

Figure 2 below shows data collected from a rain gauge.

Rainfall

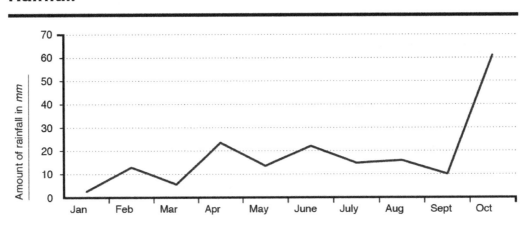

31. What tool would a meteorologist use to find out how fast the wind is blowing?
    a. Anemometer
    b. Barometer
    c. Thermometer
    d. Wind vane

32. What tool was used to collect the data shown in Figure 1?
    a. Rain gauge
    b. Thermometer
    c. Barometer
    d. Anemometer

33. The wind vane is pointing north. What does this tell us?
    a. Wind is blowing in an eastern direction.
    b. A storm is coming.
    c. The wind is blowing in a northern direction.
    d. The wind is blowing in a southern direction.

34. Looking at Figure 2, which month had the lowest rainfall?
    a. January
    b. April
    c. September
    d. October

35. Looking at Figure 2, what was the approximate amount of rain that fell in June?
    a. 0 mm
    b. 10 mm
    c. 50 mm
    d. 20 mm

Passage 8

Questions 36–40 pertain to Passage 8:

Cells are the smallest functional unit of living organisms. Organisms can be single-celled or multicellular. Each cell contains organelles that are responsible for distinct functions and are essential for the organism's life. Plants and animals have different necessities for generating energy and nutrients. Their cells are similar but also have unique features.

Figure 1 below is a depiction of the organelles in an animal cell.

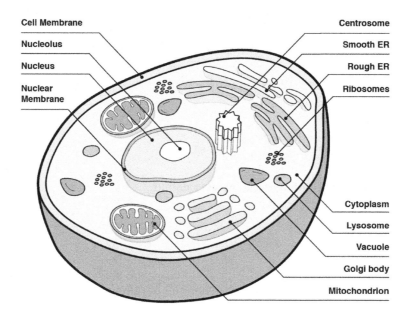

Figure 2 below depicts the organelles of a plant cell.

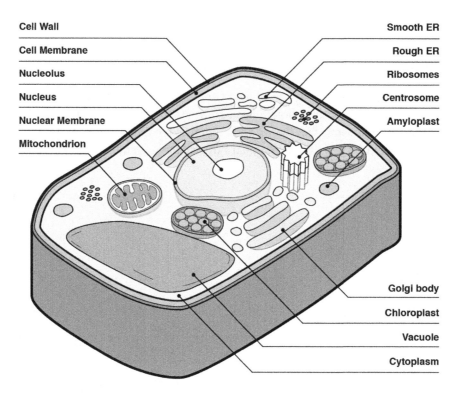

Figure 3 below describes the function of many important organelles.

Cell Organelle	Function
Cell wall	*(Plants only)* Maintains the shape of the cell and is a protective barrier for the internal contents of the cell.
Chloroplasts	*(Plants only)* Site of photosynthesis, which converts sunlight energy to glucose storage energy.
Nucleus	*(Plants and Animals)* Contains the cell's DNA.
Ribosomes	*(Plants and Animals)* Puts together long chains of amino acids to build proteins. Smallest organelle in the cell.
Mitochondria	*(Plants and Animals)* The powerhouse of the cell. Converts the stored glucose energy to ATP energy, which drives forward almost all of the cell's reactions.
Cell membrane	*(Plants and Animals)* Regulates what molecules can move in and out of the cell. Made of a phospholipid bilayer.
Cytoplasm	*(Plants and Animals)* The liquid that fills the inside of the cell.
Vacuole	*(Plants and Animals)* A membranous sac that encloses anything in the cell that needs to be kept separate, such as food and water.
Golgi Body	*(Plants and Animals)* Receives products produced by the endoplasmic reticulum (ER) and adds final changes to them.
Lysosomes	*(Plants and Animals)* A membranous sac that is full of digestive juices. Breaks down larger molecules into smaller parts so that they can be used to build new parts of the cell.
Rough endoplasmic reticulum (ER)	*(Plants and Animals)* A large folded membrane that is covered with ribosomes. Helps fold and modify the proteins built by the ribosomes before sending them to the Golgi body.
Smooth endoplasmic reticulum (ER)	*(Plants and Animals)* A large folded membrane that puts together lipids.
Microtubules and microfilaments	*(Plants and Animals)* Long tubes that allow the cell to move and provide an internal structure of support for the cell.

36. Which is an organelle found in a plant cell but not an animal cell?
    a. Mitochondria
    b. Chloroplast
    c. Golgi body
    d. Nucleus

37. Where is the nucleolus located in both plant and animal cells?
    a. Near the chloroplast
    b. Inside the mitochondria
    c. Inside the nucleus
    d. Attached to the cell membrane

38. Which organelle is responsible for generating energy for the cell and is referred to as the powerhouse of the cell?
   a. Mitochondria
   b. Nucleus
   c. Ribosomes
   d. Cell wall

39. What does the cell membrane do?
   a. Builds proteins
   b. Breaks down large molecules
   c. Contains the cell's DNA
   d. Controls which molecules are allowed in and out of the cell

40. What are chloroplasts responsible for in plant cells?
   a. Maintaining the cell's shape
   b. Containing the cell's DNA
   c. Converting energy from sunlight to glucose
   d. Building proteins

Social Studies

1. Which of the following is the primary problem with map projections?
   a. They are not detailed.
   b. They do not include physical features.
   c. They distort areas near the poles.
   d. They only focus on the Northern Hemisphere.

2. Which type of map illustrates the world's climatological regions?
   a. Topographic Map
   b. Conformal Projection
   c. Isoline Map
   d. Thematic Map

3. Latitudinal lines are used to measure distance in which direction?
   a. East to west
   b. North to south
   c. Between two sets of coordinates
   d. In an inexact manner

4. Literacy rates are more likely to be higher in which area?
   a. Developing nations
   b. Northern Hemispherical Nations
   c. Developed Nations
   d. Near centers of trade

5. All of the following are negative demographic indicators EXCEPT which of the following?
    a. High Infant Mortality Rates
    b. Low Literacy Rates
    c. High Population Density
    d. Low Life Expectancy

6. Which of the following is NOT a factor in a location's climate?
    a. Latitudinal position
    b. Elevation
    c. Longitudinal position
    d. Proximity to mountains

7. A developing nation is more likely to have which of the following?
    a. Complex highway networks
    b. Higher rates of subsistence farmers
    c. Stable government systems
    d. Little economic instability

8. A developing nation is more likely to have which of the following?
    a. Complex highway networks
    b. Higher rates of subsistence farmers
    c. Stable government systems
    d. Little economic instability

9. Which best describes ethnic groups?
    a. Subgroups within a population who share a common history, language, or religion
    b. Divisive groups within a nation's boundaries seeking independence
    c. People who choose to leave a location
    d. Any minority group within a nation's boundaries

10. Which of the following could be considered a pull factor for a particular area?
    a. High rates of unemployment
    b. Low GDP
    c. Educational opportunity
    d. High population density

11. In recent years, agricultural production has been affected by which of the following?
    a. The prevalence of biotechnology and GMOs
    b. Weaker crop yields due to poor soil
    c. Plagues of pests, which have limited food production
    d. Revolutions in irrigation, which utilize salinated water

12. Which of the following is true of political boundaries?
    a. They have remained static for centuries.
    b. They are generally visible on Earth.
    c. They are constantly changing.
    d. They are never disputed among nations.

13. Which of the following is the subgroup of economics that studies large-scale economic issues such as unemployment, interest rates, price levels, and national income?
   a. Microeconomics
   b. Macroeconomics
   c. Scarcity
   d. Supply and demand

14. A homeowner hires a landscape company to mow the grass because he or she would like to use that time to do something else. The trade-off of paying someone to do a job to make more valuable use of time is an example of what?
   a. Economic systems
   b. Supply and demand
   c. Opportunity cost
   d. Inflation

15. Which kind of market does not involve government interventions or monopolies while trades are made between suppliers and buyers?
   a. Free
   b. Command
   c. Gross
   d. Exchange

16. Which is NOT an indicator of economic growth?
   a. GDP (Gross Domestic Product)
   b. Unemployment
   c. Inflation
   d. Theory of The Firm

17. In a business cycle, a recession occurs between which cycles?
   a. Expansion, peak
   b. Peak, contraction
   c. Contraction, trough
   d. Trough, expansion

18. What is the name of the central bank that controls the value of money in the United States?
   a. Commodity Reserve
   b. Central Reserve
   c. Federal Reserve
   d. Bank Reserve

19. Which option does NOT sustain monetary policies?
   a. Closed market operations
   b. Open market operations
   c. Assuring bank reserves
   d. Adjusting interest rates

20. What determines the exchange rate in a "floating" or "flexible" exchange?
    a. The government
    b. Taxes
    c. The Federal Reserve
    d. The market

21. Which statement is true about inflation and purchasing power?
    a. As inflation decreases, purchasing power increases.
    b. As inflation increases, purchasing power decreases.
    c. As inflation increases, purchasing power increases.
    d. As inflation decreases, purchasing power decreases.

22. Which statement is true about goods and services?
    a. The quantity of goods and services matters more than their value.
    b. The value of goods and services matters more than their quantity.
    c. The quality of goods and services matters more than their production.
    d. The production of goods and services matters more than their quality.

23. What caused the end of the Western Roman Empire in 476 CE?
    a. Invasions by Germanic tribes
    b. The Mongol invasion
    c. The assassination of Julius Caesar
    d. Introduction of Taoism in Rome

24. Which of the following statements best describes King Louis XIV of France?
    a. He abdicated his throne during the French Revolution.
    b. He supported the American Revolution.
    c. He was the ultimate example of an absolute monarch.
    d. He created the concept of the Mandate of Heaven.

25. Which of the following consequences did NOT result from the discovery of the New World in 1492 CE?
    a. Proof that the world was round instead of flat
    b. The deaths of millions of Native Americans
    c. Biological exchange between Europe and the New World
    d. The creation of new syncretic religions

26. Which of the following statements best describes the relationship, if any, between the revolutions in America and France?
    a. The French Revolution inspired the American Revolution.
    b. The American Revolution inspired the French Revolution.
    c. They both occurred simultaneously.
    d. There was no connection between the French and American revolutions.

27. Which of the following was a consequence of industrialization in Europe during the 1800s?
    a. The birth of the working class
    b. The expansion of European empires in Africa and Asia
    c. Improved transportation and economic efficiency
    d. All of the above

28. Which of the following military technologies did NOT play a role in World War I from 1914 to 1918?
    a. The atomic bomb
    b. Poison gas
    c. Armored tanks
    d. Aircraft

29. Which of the following statements best describes international affairs between World War I and World War II?
    a. A lenient World War I peace treaty for Germany delayed the start of World War II.
    b. The policy of appeasement only encouraged further aggression by Hitler.
    c. A powerful League of Nations fostered increased cooperation and negotiation.
    d. Tensions grew between Germany and Japan.

30. Which of the following trends did NOT occur after the end of the Cold War in 1991?
    a. A decrease in nationalistic tension
    b. An increase in cultural and economic globalization
    c. An increase in religious fundamentalism
    d. An increase in environmentalism

31. Which of the following correctly lists the Thirteen Colonies?
    a. Connecticut, Delaware, Georgia, Maryland, Massachusetts, New Hampshire, New Jersey, New York, North Carolina, Pennsylvania, Rhode Island, South Carolina, Virginia
    b. Carolina, Connecticut, Delaware, Maryland, Massachusetts, New Hampshire, New Jersey, New York, Ohio, Pennsylvania, Rhode Island, Virginia, West Virginia
    c. Connecticut, Delaware, Georgia, Maine, Massachusetts, New Hampshire, New Jersey, New York, North Carolina, South Carolina, Pennsylvania, Vermont, Virginia
    d. Canada, Connecticut, Delaware, Georgia, Florida, Maryland, Massachusetts, New Hampshire, New York, North Carolina, Rhode Island, South Carolina, Virginia

32. Which of the following was NOT an issue contributing to the American Revolution?
    a. Increased taxes on the colonies
    b. Britain's defeat in the French and Indian War
    c. The stationing of British soldiers in colonists' homes
    d. Changes in class relations

33. The election of a presidential candidate from which party led to the Civil War?
    a. Democrat
    b. Whig
    c. Republican
    d. Federalist

34. Which of the following sets comprises a primary cause and effect of the American Revolution?
    a. A cause was the taxation of the colonies, and an effect was the civil rights movement.
    b. A cause was the Declaration of Independence, and an effect was the Constitution.
    c. A cause was the French and Indian War, and an effect was the Bill of Rights.
    d. A cause was the debate over slavery, and an effect was the Seven Years' War.

35. What are the two main parts of the federal legislative branch?
    a. President and vice president
    b. Federal and state
    c. District court and court of appeals
    d. Senate and House of Representatives

Answer Explanations #2

Reading Comprehension

1. A: The word *patronage* most nearly means *auspices*, which means *protection* or *support*. Choice *B*, *aberration*, means *deformity* and does not make sense within the context of the sentence. Choice *C*, *acerbic*, means *bitter* and also does not make sense in the sentence. Choice *D*, *adulation*, is a positive word meaning *praise*, and thus does not fit with the word *condescending* in the sentence.

2. D: *Working man* is most closely aligned with Choice *D*, *bourgeois*. In the context of the speech, the word *bourgeois* means *working* or *middle class*. Choice *A*, *plebian*, does suggest *common people*; however, this is a term that is specific to ancient Rome. Choice *B*, *viscount*, is a European title used to describe a specific degree of nobility. Choice *C*, *entrepreneur*, is a person who operates their own business.

3. C: In the context of the speech, the term *working man* most closely correlates with Choice *C*, *working man is someone who works for wages among the middle class.* Choice *A* is not mentioned in the passage and is off-topic. Choice *B* may be true in some cases, but it does not reflect the sentiment described for the term *working man* in the passage. Choice *D* may also be arguably true. However, it is not given as a definition but as *acts* of the working man, and the topics of *field, factory,* and *screen* are not mentioned in the passage.

4. D: *Enterprise* most closely means *cause*. Choices *A, B,* and *C* are all related to the term *enterprise*. However, Dickens speaks of a *cause* here, not a company, courage, or a game. *He will stand by such an enterprise* is a call to stand by a cause to enable the working man to have a certain autonomy over his own economic standing. The very first paragraph ends with the statement that the working man *shall . . . have a share in the management of an institution which is designed for his benefit.*

5. B: The speaker's salutation is one from an entertainer to his audience and uses the friendly language to connect to his audience before a serious speech. Recall in the first paragraph that the speaker is there to "accompany [the audience] . . . through one of my little Christmas books," making him an author there to entertain the crowd with his own writing. The speech preceding the reading is the passage itself, and, as the tone indicates, a serious speech addressing the "working man." Although the passage speaks of employers and employees, the speaker himself is not an employer of the audience, so Choice *A* is incorrect. Choice *C* is also incorrect, as the salutation is not used ironically, but sincerely, as the speech addresses the well-being of the crowd. Choice *D* is incorrect because the speech is not given by a politician, but by a writer.

6: B: Choice *A* is incorrect because that is the speaker's *first* desire, not his second. Choices *C* and *D* are tricky because the language of both of these is mentioned after the word *second*. However, the speaker doesn't get to the second wish until the next sentence. Choices *C* and *D* are merely prepositions preparing for the statement of the main clause, Choice *B,* for the working man to have a say in his institution which is designed for his benefit.

7. C: In lines 6 and 7, it is stated that avarice can prevent a man from being necessitously poor, but too timorous, or fearful, to achieve real wealth. According to the passage, avarice does tend to make a person very wealthy. The passage states that oppression, not avarice, is the consequence of wealth. The passage does not state that avarice drives a person's desire to be wealthy.

8. D: Paine believes that the distinction that is beyond a natural or religious reason is between king and subjects. He states that the distinction between good and bad is made in heaven. The distinction between male and female is natural. He does not mention anything about the distinction between humans and animals.

9. A: The passage states that the Heathens were the first to introduce government by kings into the world. The quiet lives of patriarchs came before the Heathens introduced this type of government. It was Christians, not Heathens, who paid divine honors to living kings. Heathens honored deceased kings. Equal rights of nature are mentioned in the paragraph, but not in relation to the Heathens.

10. B: Paine asserts that a monarchy is against the equal rights of nature and cites several parts of scripture that also denounce it. He doesn't say it is against the laws of nature. Because he uses scripture to further his argument, it is not despite scripture that he denounces the monarchy. Paine addresses the law by saying the courts also do not support a monarchical government.

11. A: To be *idolatrous* is to worship idols or heroes, in this case, kings. It is not defined as being deceitful. While idolatry is considered a sin, it is an example of a sin, not a synonym for it. Idolatry may have been considered illegal in some cultures, but it is not a definition for the term.

12. A: The essential meaning of the passage is that the Almighty, God, would disapprove of this type of government. While heaven is mentioned, it is done so to suggest that the monarchical government is irreverent, not that heaven isn't promised. God's disapproval is mentioned, not his punishment. The passage refers to the Jewish monarchy, which required both belief in God and kings.

13. A: First person. This is a straightforward question that requires readers to know that a first-person narrator speaks from an "I" point of view.

14. D: He doesn't understand all of the languages being used. This can be inferred from the fact that the traveler must refer to his dictionary to understand those around him. Choice *A* isn't a good choice because the traveler seems to wonder why the driver needs to drive so fast. Choice B isn't mentioned in the passage and doesn't seem like a good answer choice because he seems wholly unfamiliar with his surroundings. This is why Choice C can also be eliminated.

15. B: From fearful to charmed. This can be found in the first sentence of the third paragraph, which states, "I soon lost sight and recollection of ghostly fears in the beauty of the scene as we drove along." Also, readers should get a sense of foreboding from the first two paragraphs, where superstitious villagers seem frightened on the traveler's behalf. However, the final paragraph changes to delighted descriptions of the landscape's natural beauty. Choices *A* and *D* can be eliminated because the traveler is anxious, not relaxed or comfortable at the beginning of the passage. Choice *C* can also be eliminated because the traveler doesn't gain any particular insights in the last paragraph, and in fact continues to lament that he cannot understand the speech of those around him.

16. D: A complete stranger. The answer to this reading comprehension question can be found in the second paragraph, when the traveler is "just starting for an unknown place to meet an unknown man"—in other words, a complete stranger.

17. C: The traveler will soon encounter danger or evil. Answering this prediction question requires readers to understand foreshadowing, or hints that the author gives about what will happen next. There are numerous hints scattered throughout this passage: the villager's sorrow and sympathy for the traveler and their superstitious actions; the spooky words that the traveler overhears; the driver's unexplained haste. All of these point to a danger that awaits the protagonist.

18. A: "I must say they weren't cheering to me, for amongst them were "Ordog"—Satan, "pokol"—hell, "stregoica"—witch, "vrolok" and "vlkoslak"—both of which mean the same thing, one being Slovak and the other Servian for something that is either were-wolf or vampire." As mentioned in question 39, this sentence is an example of how the author hints at evil to come for the traveler. The other answer choices aren't related to the passage's grim foreshadowing.

19. C: This is a tricky question, but it can be solved through careful context analysis and vocabulary knowledge. One can infer that the use of "expedient," while not necessarily very positive, isn't inherently bad in this context either. Note how in the next line, he says, "but most governments are usually, and all governments are sometimes, inexpedient." This use of "inexpedient" indicates that a government becomes a hindrance rather than a solution; it slows progress rather than helps facilitate progress. Thus, Choice *A* and Choice *D* can be ruled out because these are more of the result of government, not the intention or initial design. Choice *B* makes no logical sense. Therefore, Choice *C* is the best description of *expedient*. Essentially, Thoreau is saying that government is constructed as a way of developing order and people's rights, but the rigidness of government soon inhibits justice and human rights.

20. B: While Choice *D* is the only answer that mentions the Mexican War directly, Thoreau clearly thinks the war is unnecessary because the people generally didn't consent to the war. Choices *A*, *B*, and *C* are all correct to a degree, but the answer asks for the best description. Therefore, Choice *B* is the most accurate representation of Thoreau's views. Essentially, Thoreau brings to light the fact that the few people in power can twist government and policy for their own needs.

21. D: Choice *C* and Choice *B* are completely incorrect. Thoreau is not defending government in any way. His views are set against government. As mentioned in the text, he appreciates little government but favors having no government structure at all. The text is reflective by nature, but what makes Choice *D* a more appropriate answer is the presence of evidence in the text. Thoreau cites current events and uses them to illustrate the point he's trying to make.

22. C: One of Thoreau's biggest criticisms of government is its capacity to impose on the people's freedoms and liberties, enacting rules that the people don't want and removing power from the individual. None of the scenarios directly impose specific regulations or restrictions on the people, except Prohibition. Prohibition removed the choice to consume alcohol in favor of abstinence, which was favored by the religious conservatives of the time. Thus, Thoreau would point out that this is a clear violation of free choice and an example of government meddling.

23. A: Choice *B* is totally irrelevant. Choice *C* is also incorrect; Thoreau never personifies government. Also, this doesn't coincide with his wooden gun analogy. Choice *D* is compelling because of its language but doesn't define the statement. Choice *A* is the most accurate summary of the main point of Thoreau's statement.

24. B: Thoreau specifically cites that legislators "are continually putting in their way." This reflects his suspicion and concern of government intervention. Recall that Thoreau continually mentions that government, while meant as a way to establish freedom, is easily used to suppress freedom, piling on regulations and rules that inhibit progress. Choice *B* is the answer that most directly states how Thoreau sees government getting in the way of freedom.

25. B: Strong dislike. This vocabulary question can be answered using context clues and common sense. Based on the rest of the conversation, the reader can gather that Albert isn't looking forward to his marriage. As the Count notes that "you don't appear to me to be very enthusiastic on the subject of this marriage," and also remarks on Albert's "objection to a young lady who is both rich and beautiful," readers can guess Albert's feelings. The answer choice that most closely matches "objection" and "not . . . very enthusiastic" is B, "strong dislike."

26. C: Their name is more respected than the Danglars'. This inference question can be answered by eliminating incorrect answers. Choice A is tempting, considering that Albert mentions money as a concern in his marriage. However, although he may not be as rich as his fiancée, his father still has a stable income of 50,000 francs a year. Choice B isn't mentioned at all in the passage, so it's impossible to make an inference. Finally, Choice D is clearly false because Albert's father arranged his marriage but his mother doesn't approve of it. Evidence for Choice C can be found in the Count's comparison of Albert and Eugénie: "she will enrich you, and you will ennoble her." In other words, the Danglars are wealthier but the Morcef family has a more noble background.

27. D: Apprehensive. As in question 7, there are many clues in the passage that indicate Albert's attitude towards his marriage—far from enthusiastic, he has many reservations. This question requires test takers to understand the vocabulary in the answer choices. "Pragmatic" is closest in meaning to "realistic," and "indifferent" means "uninterested." The only word related to feeling worried, uncertain, or unfavorable about the future is "apprehensive."

28. B: He is like a wise uncle, giving practical advice to Albert. Choice A is incorrect because the Count's tone is friendly and conversational. Choice C is also incorrect because the Count questions why Albert doesn't want to marry a young, beautiful, and rich girl. While the Count asks many questions, he isn't particularly "probing" or "suspicious"—instead, he's asking to find out more about Albert's situation and then give him advice about marriage.

29. A: She belongs to a noble family. Though Albert's mother doesn't appear in the scene, there's more than enough information to answer this question. More than once is his family's noble background mentioned (not to mention that Albert's mother is the Comtess de Morcef, a noble title). The other answer choices can be eliminated—she is obviously deeply concerned about her son's future; money isn't her highest priority because otherwise she would favor a marriage with the wealthy Danglars; and Albert describes her "clear and penetrating judgment," meaning she makes good decisions.

30. C: The richest people in society were also the most respected. The Danglars family is wealthier but the Morcef family has a more aristocratic name, which gives them a higher social standing. Evidence for the other answer choices can be found throughout the passage: Albert mentioned receiving money from his father's fortune after his marriage; Albert's father has arranged this marriage for him; and the Count speculates that Albert's mother disapproves of this marriage because Eugénie isn't from a noble background like the Morcef family, implying that she would prefer a match with a girl from aristocratic society.

31. A: Choice D can be eliminated because the Salem witch trials aren't even mentioned. While sympathetic to the plight of the accused, the author doesn't demand or urge the reader to demand reparations to the descendants; therefore, Choice B can also be ruled out. It's clear that the author's main goal is to educate the reader and shed light on the facts and hidden details behind the case. However, his focus isn't on the occult, but the specific Lancashire case itself. He goes into detail about suspects' histories and ties to Catholicism, revealing how the fears of the English people at the time sealed the fate of the accused witches. Choice A is correct.

32. B: It's important to note that these terms may not be an exact analog for *enduring*. However, through knowledge of the definition of *enduring*, as well as the context in which it's used, an appropriate synonym can be found. Plugging "circumstantial" into the passage in place of "enduring" doesn't make sense. Nor does "un-original," this particular case of witchcraft, stand out in history. "Wicked" is very descriptive, but this is an attribute applied to people, not events; therefore, this is an inappropriate choice as well. *Enduring* literally means long lasting, referring to the continued interest in this particular case of witchcraft. Therefore, it's a popular topic of 1600s witch trials, making "popular," Choice B, the best choice.

33. D: Choices A and B are irrelevant. The use of quotes lends credibility to the author. However, the presence of quotes alone doesn't necessarily mean that the author has a qualified perspective. What establishes the writer as a reliable voice is that the author's previous writing on the subject has been published before. This qualification greatly establishes the author's credentials as a historical writer, making Choice D the correct answer.

34. B: Choice A is incorrect, clearly taking the statement somewhat literally. The remaining three choices appear somewhat interconnected, and though they may be proven at some point later in the article, the focus must remain on the given excerpt. It's very possible that evidence was tampered with or even falsified, but this statement doesn't refer to this. While the author alludes that there may have been evidence tampering and potentially corruption, what the writer is directly saying is that the documentation of the court indicates an elaborate trial. It's clear that exaggerations may have taken place both during the case and in the written account. The reasoning behind this was to gain the attention of the people and even the crown. Choice B is the best answer because it not only aligns with the above statement, but ultimately encompasses the potentiality of Choices C and D as well.

35. C: Several of these answers could have contributed to the fear and political motivations around the Lancashire witch trials. What this answer's looking for is very specific: political motivations and issues that played a major role in the case. Choice C clearly outlines the public fears of the time. It also describes how the government can use this fear to weed out and eliminate traces of Catholicism (and witchcraft too). Catholicism and witchcraft were seen as dangerous and undermining to English Protestantism and governance. Choice D can be eliminated; while this information may have some truth and is certainly consistent with the general fear of witchcraft, the details about Lancashire's ancient history aren't mentioned in the text. Choice A is true but not necessarily political in nature. Choice B is very promising, though not outright mentioned.

36. D: The best evidence comes from Alizon herself. The text mentions that she confessed to bewitching John Law, thinking that she did him harm. From here she names her grandmother, who she believes corrupted her. Choice B can be ruled out; spectral evidence isn't mentioned. The case draws on knowledge of superstition of witchcraft, but this in itself can't be considered evidence, so Choice A is incorrect. Choice C isn't evidence in a modern sense; rumors have no weight in court and therefore are not evidence. While this is used as evidence to some degree, this still isn't the bestevidence against Alizon and the witches.

37. D: If unfamiliar with this term, plugging each term into the sentence in place of "elucidation" will help rule out answers that don't make sense. Using this method, Choices B and C can be ruled out because they don't fit the sentence. "Definition" looks promising, but this term isn't as comprehensive an explanation. After all, the author is seeking to uncover why myths are the way they are—the reason why there are so many shared concepts. "Rank" is looking for an explanation for why myths appear as they do. In fact, *explanation* is a synonym for *elucidation*. Choice *D* is correct.

38. B: The title and general focus of the passage reveal a lot about the motivations and interests of the writer. This is a study in psychology, so the author's main area of interest is the study of how humans think and process the world. Choice *A* can be eliminated easily. While Rank was in fact a contemporary of Jung, this information is neither relevant nor even mentioned in the text. The other answers are very compelling, but in this case, one must look at what the author already sees in mythology. The reach and similarities in various mythologies suggest a common source—a common humanity. While he doesn't explicitly want to use this knowledge to develop new analysis strategies and therapies (Choice *D*), this does seem to hint to a common human mind-set that would be crucial for his work. Thus, Choice *B* is the best answer. Also, Choice *C* is too narrow and of less interest to the author.

39. A: The key to understanding this theory lies in "the existence of elemental ideas, so that the unanimity of the myths is a necessary sequence of the uniform disposition of the human mind and the manner of its manifestation." In other words, elemental ideas are core questions or ideas that apply to everyone. Choice *B* is compelling, but the idea of winter, and cold climate, doesn't necessarily apply to cultures in climates with mild winters, like in Africa. Choice *C* doesn't offer a lot to consider. Choice *D* is focused on Germanic and Nordic peoples. The best answer will address overarching ideas and concepts that exist throughout the world cultures: elemental ideas. The idea that best exemplifies the Idea of the People theory is Choice *A* because it hints to innate human curiosity and the drive to define the world. Choice *C* can then be ruled out entirely.

40. C: Choice *A* is incorrect; these are not scientific explanations. Choice *B* is incorrect; these are appropriately labeled as "theories, and there is a reason behind this choice. Choice *D* is incorrect and actually a major clue. The author doesn't say that these are competing ideas; rather, he directly says they don't conflict. In truth, all these theories could have a basis in historical fact. However, these can't be proven by physical means. It would be virtually impossible to track, and therefore prove, the exact reason why mythology resonates throughout various cultures and its exact origin. There simply isn't physical evidence. Therefore, these ideas are called *theories* because, while they hold probable truth, they cannot be tested or proven. Choice *C* is correct.

41. D: This can be a very deceptive description, even pessimistic sounding if not considered with the context of the rest of the passage. Choice *A* is incorrect; this takes too rigid a stance on the lines. The quote doesn't condemn people to unoriginality, merely that ideas can be used over and over again, even adapted or copied. Choice *B* looks compelling but doesn't take the rest of the reading into account. Choice *C* is very tempting; it uses similar language to the selection, but note the use of "sundered." Nowhere in the text (both the main passage and the selected quote) is there a mention of sundering or a breakaway from a single culture, but rather the spreading and sharing of ideas. Again, there is also this hint of a lack of originality that isn't necessarily true. Choice *D*, however, is a phrase that perfectly ties the presented quote with the rest of the passage, a kind of bridge that adds another layer to mythology's origins.

42. B: Choice *A* is compelling, but this statement relates more to the migration theory of spreading mythology. It's a little too broad and less focused on community relations. Choice *D* is compelling and might be the best answer without the presence of Choice *B*. Choice *B* clearly displays what the "explanation by original community idea" focuses on. Note how this theory is centered on a central community (or communities) that expands into different areas. Another key point is that the stories "continued to grow while retaining the common primary traits." In other words, the stories might have grown or changed in some ways, but they still retained core aspects in the narrative. This theory is best exemplified in Choice *B*.

43. C: It's very clear that the author is chronicling the development of museums, but is there a defined viewpoint that he is trying to impress upon the reader? No. The author presents facts, and even inferences, but he is clearly not trying to claim something new. Instead, he's simply providing details about the rise of museums by describing the first examples of people collecting and displaying items. This makes Choice *A* and Choice *D* incorrect. Also, the 1850s weren't even mentioned in this excerpt. The author doesn't insert himself into the piece; there's no use of "I." There also isn't any mention of his own experiences. This also means that Choice *B* is incorrect. Clearly, the author is documenting the development of museums by focusing on collections that, while not conforming to modern museums, would give rise to the idea later on. Choice *C* is correct.

44. B: Generally, all the questions seem to hold some truth, but the goal is to find the answer that best explains the excerpt. Choice *C* can be eliminated first. It doesn't address the statement directly; besides, there are traveling exhibits. Choice *D* is very true, but this doesn't provide the reasoning behind the statement. Choice *A* is very strong, but Choice *B* is actually stronger. Choice *B* addresses the fact that a stable society enables the museum to be maintained and visitors to actively visit the museum. Thus, Choice *B* is correct.

45. D: Recall that the text illustrates that initially it was primarily royalty that owned collections and displayed them, but this didn't necessarily mean that these artifacts made up a museum. This eliminates Choice *A*. The author goes on to reflect on how the great institute of Alexandria wouldn't really be considered a museum because "the name museum in that institution was applied to a portion set apart for the study of sciences, and indicated rather a place of study than one for exhibition of objects." While a museum is a place of study, it's clear that the modern museum is primarily geared for exhibition. With this in mind, Choice *B* simply falls short and can be eliminated. The answer that sums up the core criteria for a modern museum is Choice *D*. The purpose of a modern museum is not just to house artifacts but to display them for the public. With this in mind, Choice *C* falls short by not addressing the core role of a museum.

Mathematical Reasoning

1. A: Figure out which is largest by looking at the first non-zero digits. Choice *B*'s first non-zero digit is in the hundredths place. The other three all have non-zero digits in the tenths place, so it must be *A*, *C*, or *D*. Of these, *A* has the largest first non-zero digit.

2. C: 40*N* would be 4000% of *N*. It's possible to check that each of the others is actually 40% of *N*.

3. B: Instead of multiplying these out, the product can be estimated by using $18 \times 10 = 180$. The error here should be lower than 15, since it is rounded to the nearest integer, and the numbers add to something less than 30.

4. C: The average is calculated by adding all six numbers, then dividing by 6. The first five numbers have a sum of 25. If the total divided by 6 is equal to 6, then the total itself must be 36. The sixth number must be $36 - 25 = 11$.

5. B: $\frac{5}{2} \div \frac{1}{3} = \frac{5}{2} \times \frac{3}{1} = \frac{15}{2} = 7.5$.

6. A: The total fraction taken up by green and red shirts will be $\frac{1}{3} + \frac{2}{5} = \frac{5}{15} + \frac{6}{15} = \frac{11}{15}$. The remaining fraction is $1 - \frac{11}{15} = \frac{15}{15} - \frac{11}{15} = \frac{4}{15}$.

7. C: If she has used $\frac{1}{3}$ of the paint, she has $\frac{2}{3}$ remaining. $2\frac{1}{2}$ gallons are the same as $\frac{5}{2}$ gallons. The calculation is $\frac{2}{3} \times \frac{5}{2} = \frac{5}{3} = 1\frac{2}{3}$ gallons.

8. A: Robert accomplished his task on Tuesday in $\frac{3}{4}$ the time compared to Monday. He must have worked $\frac{4}{3}$ as fast.

9. B: To be directly proportional means that $y = mx$. If x is changed from 5 to 20, the value of x is multiplied by 4. Applying the same rule to the y-value, also multiply the value of y by 4. Therefore, $y = 12$.

10. A: Each bag contributes $4x + 1$ treats. The total treats will be in the form $4nx + n$ where n is the total number of bags. The total is in the form $60x + 15$, from which it is known $n = 15$.

11. D: Denote the width as w and the length as l. Then, $l = 3w + 5$. The perimeter is $2w + 2l = 90$. Substituting the first expression for l into the second equation yields $2(3w + 5) + 2w = 90$, or $8w = 80$, so $l = 10$. Putting this into the first equation, it yields $l = 3(10) + 5 = 35$.

12. B: If 60% of 50 workers are women, then there are 30 women working in the office. If half of them are wearing skirts, then that means 15 women wear skirts. Since none of the men wear skirts, this means there are 15 people wearing skirts.

13. B: The volume of a cube is the length of the side cubed, and 3 inches cubed is 27 in³. Choice A is not the correct answer because that is 2×3 inches. Choice C is not the correct answer because that is 3×3 inches, and Choice D is not the correct answer because there was no operation performed.

14. D: The volume of a cube is the length of the side cubed, and 5 centimeters cubed is 125 cm³. Choice A is not the correct answer because that is 2×5 centimeters. Choice B is not the correct answer because that is 3×5 centimeters. Choice C is not the correct answer because that is 5×10 centimeters.

15. B: This answer is correct because $3^2 + 4^2$ is $9 + 16$, which is 25. Taking the square root of 25 is 5. Choice A is not the correct answer because that is $3 + 4$. Choice C is not the correct answer because that is stopping at $3^2 + 4^2$ is $9 + 16$, which is 25. Choice D is not the correct answer because that is 3×4.

16. A: This answer is correct because $100 - 64$ is 36 and taking the square root of 36 is 6. Choice B is not the correct answer because that is $10 + 8$. Choice C is not the correct answer because that is 8×10. Choice D is also not the correct answer because there is no reason to arrive at that number.

17. A: This answer is correct because $(2 + 2i)(2 - 2i)$, using the FOIL method is: $4 - 4i + 4i - 4i^2 = 8$. Choice B is not the answer because there is no i in the final answer, since the i's cancel out in the FOIL. Choice C, 4, is not the final answer because we add $4 + 4$ in the end to equal 8. Choice D, $4i$, is not the final answer because there is neither a 4 nor an i in the final answer.

18. A: This answer is correct because $(3 + 3i)(3 - 3i)$, using the FOIL method is: $9 - 9i + 9i - 9i2 = 18$. Choice B is not the answer because there is no i in the final answer, since the i's cancel out in the

FOIL. Choice *C* is not the final answer because you have to add the two 9s together in the FOIL method. Choice *D* is not the final answer because there is neither a 9 nor an *i* in the final answer.

19. D: Multiply the top and the bottom by $(2 + 2i)$, the conjugate, to arrive at $\frac{8i}{8}$, which cancels to *i*. Choice *A* is not the answer because the 8's cancel out. Choice *B* is not the answer because the 8's cancel out. Choice *C* is not the answer because 2 is not left, but 8 is.

20. C: First, factor out the 3's: $\frac{1+i}{1-i}$. Then multiply top and bottom by that conjugate: $1 + i \rightarrow \frac{1+2i+i^2}{1-i^2}$. Since *i* is the square root of -1, this goes to: $\frac{1+2i+(-1)}{1-(-1)}$. This equates to $\frac{2i}{2}$. Cancelling out the 2's leaves *i*. Choice *A* is not the correct answer because that only represents the denominator that is part of a fraction that needs to be simplified. Choice *B* is not the correct answer because that only represents the numerator that is part of a fraction that needs to be simplified. Choice *D* is not the final answer because it shows only part of the result from the FOIL method.

21. C: When you simplify $\frac{48°\times\pi}{180}$, you get $\frac{4\pi}{15}$. Choice *A* is not the correct answer because $\frac{\pi}{4}$ is 45°. Choice *B* is not the correct answer because $\frac{\pi}{15}$ is 12°. Choice *D* is not the correct answer because $\frac{3\pi}{4} = 135°$.

22. D: The method to equate the two chord lengths is $3 + x + 2 = x + 3x + 2$, add like terms, $5 + x = 4x + 2$, solve for *x* ($x = 1$), and substitute 1 back into the equation. Choice *A* is not the correct answer because 1 is the solution for *x*, not the length of the chord. Choice *B* is not the correct answer because 2 is one of the terms of the chord length when adding like terms. Choice *C* is not the correct answer because 3 is only the coefficient of one of the terms when solving.

23. A: The method is to equate the two chord lengths: $4 + 2x + 2 = x + 3x + 2$, add the like terms, $6 + 2x = 4x + 2$, solve for $x(x = 2)$, and substitute 2 back into the equation. Choice *B* is not the correct answer because 2 is the solution for *x*, not the length of the chord. Choice *C* is not the correct answer because there is no 1 in the problem. Choice *D* is not the correct answer because 3 is only a coefficient in solving the equation.

24. A: Compare each numeral after the decimal point to figure out which overall number is greatest. In answers *A* (1.43785) and *C* (1.43592), both have the same tenths (4) and hundredths (3). However, the thousandths is greater in answer *A* (7), so *A* has the greatest value overall.

25. D: By grouping the four numbers in the answer into factors of the two numbers of the question (6 and 12), it can be determined that (3 x 2) x (4 x 3) = 6 x 12. Alternatively, each of the answer choices could be prime factored or multiplied out and compared to the original value. 6×12 has a value of 72 and a prime factorization of $2^3 \times 3^2$. The answer choices respectively have values of 64, 84, 108, and 72 and prime factorizations of 2^6, $2^2 \times 3 \times 7$, $2^2 \times 3^3$, and $2^3 \times 3^2$, so answer *D* is the correct choice.

26. C: The sum total percentage of a pie chart must equal 100%. Since the CD sales take up less than half of the chart and more than a quarter (25%), it can be determined to be 40% overall. This can also be measured with a protractor. The angle of a circle is 360°. Since 25% of 360 would be 90° and 50% would be 180°, the angle percentage of CD sales falls in between; therefore, it would be answer *C*.

27. B: Since $850 is the price *after* a 20% discount, $850 represents 80% of the original price. To determine the original price, set up a proportion with the ratio of the sale price (850) to original price (unknown) equal to the ratio of sale percentage:

$$\frac{850}{x} = \frac{80}{100}$$

(where *x* represents the unknown original price)

To solve a proportion, cross multiply the numerators and denominators and set the products equal to each other: (850)(100) = (80)(x). Multiplying each side results in the equation 85,000=80x.

To solve for *x*, divide both sides by 80: $\frac{85,000}{80} = \frac{80x}{80}$, resulting in *x*=1062.5. Remember that *x* represents the original price. Subtracting the sale price from the original price ($1062.50-$850) indicates that Frank saved $212.50.

28. C: To solve for the value of b, both sides of the equation need to be equalized.

Start by cancelling out the lower value of -4 by adding 4 to both sides:

$$5b - 4 = 2b + 17$$

$$5b - 4 + 4 = 2b + 17 + 4$$

$$5b = 2b + 21$$

The variable *b* is the same on each side, so subtract the lower 2b from each side:

$$5b = 2b + 21$$

$$5b - 2b = 2b + 21 - 2b$$

$$3b = 21$$

Then divide both sides by 3 to get the value of *b*:

$$3b = 21$$

$$\frac{3b}{3} = \frac{21}{3}$$

$$b = 7$$

29. D: The total faculty is 15 + 20 = 35. So the ratio is 35:200. Then, divide both of these numbers by 5, since 5 is a common factor to both, with a result of 7:40.

30. C: The first step in solving this problem is expressing the result in fraction form. Separate this problem first by solving the division operation of the last two fractions. When dividing one fraction by another, invert or flip the second fraction and then multiply the numerator and denominator.

$$\frac{7}{10} \times \frac{2}{1} = \frac{14}{10}$$

Next, multiply the first fraction with this value:

$$\frac{3}{5} \times \frac{14}{10} = \frac{42}{50}$$

Decimals are expressions of 1 or 100%, so multiply both the numerator and denominator by 2 to get the fraction as an expression of 100.

$$\frac{42}{50} \times \frac{2}{2} = \frac{84}{100}$$

In decimal form, this would be expressed as 0.84.

31. B: Using the conversion rate, multiply the projected weight loss of 25 lb by 0.45 $\frac{kg}{lb}$ to get the amount in kilograms (11.25 kg).

32. D: First, subtract $1437 from $2334.50 to find Johnny's monthly savings; this equals $897.50. Then, multiply this amount by 3 to find out how much he will have (in three months) before he pays for his vacation: this equals $2692.50. Finally, subtract the cost of the vacation ($1750) from this amount to find how much Johnny will have left: $942.50.

33. B: To solve this correctly, keep in mind the order of operations with the mnemonic PEMDAS (Please Excuse My Dear Aunt Sally). This stands for Parentheses, Exponents, Multiplication, Division, Addition, Subtraction. Taking it step by step, solve the parentheses first:

$$4 \times 7 + (4)^2 \div 2$$

Then, apply the exponent:

$$4 \times 7 + 16 \div 2$$

Multiplication and division are both performed next:

$$28 + 8 = 36$$

34. C: The formula for the perimeter of a rectangle is P=2L+2W, where P is the perimeter, L is the length, and W is the width. The first step is to substitute all of the data into the formula:

$$36 = 2(12) + 2W$$

Simplify by multiplying 2x12:

$$36 = 24 + 2W$$

Simplifying this further by subtracting 24 on each side, which gives:

$$36-24 = 24-24+2W$$

$$12 = 2W$$

Divide by 2:

$$6 = W$$

The width is 6 cm. Remember to test this answer by substituting this value into the original formula: 36 = 2(12) + 2(6).

35. D: To find the average of a set of values, add the values together and then divide by the total number of values. In this case, include the unknown value of what Dwayne needs to score on his next test, in order to solve it.

$$\frac{78 + 92 + 83 + 97 + x}{5} = 90$$

Add the unknown value to the new average total, which is 5. Then multiply each side by 5 to simplify the equation, resulting in:

$$78 + 92 + 83 + 97 + x = 450$$

$$350 + x = 450$$

$$x = 100$$

Dwayne would need to get a perfect score of 100 in order to get an average of at least 90.

Test this answer by substituting back into the original formula.

$$\frac{78 + 92 + 83 + 97 + 100}{5} = 90$$

36. D: For an even number of total values, the *median* is calculated by finding the *mean* or average of the two middle values once all values have been arranged in ascending order from least to greatest. In this case, $(92 + 83) \div 2$ would equal the median 87.5, answer *D*.

37. D: Three girls for every two boys can be expressed as a ratio: 3:2. This can be visualized as splitting the school into 5 groups: 3 girl groups and 2 boy groups. The number of students which are in each group can be found by dividing the total number of students by 5:

650 divided by 5 equals 1 part, or 130 students per group

To find the total number of girls, multiply the number of students per group (130) by how the number of girl groups in the school (3). This equals 390, answer *D*.

38. C: Kimberley worked 4.5 hours at the rate of $10/h and 1 hour at the rate of $12/h. The problem states that her pay is rounded to the nearest hour, so the 4.5 hours would round up to 5 hours at the rate of $10/h. (5h)($10/h)+(1h)($12/h)= $50+$12= $62.

39. D:

$9x + x - 7 = 16 + 2x$	Combine $9x$ and x.
$10x - 7 = 16 + 2x$	
$10x - 7 + 7 = 16 + 2x + 7$	Add 7 to both sides to remove (-7).
$10x = 23 + 2x$	
$10x - 2x = 23 + 2x - 2x$	Subtract 2x from both sides to move it to the other side of the equation.
$8x = 23$	
$\dfrac{8x}{8} = \dfrac{23}{8}$	Divide by 8 to get x by itself.
$x = \dfrac{23}{8}$	

40. C: The first step is to depict each number using decimals. $\dfrac{91}{100} = 0.91$

Multiplying both the numerator and denominator of $\dfrac{4}{5}$ by 20 makes it $\dfrac{80}{100}$ or 0.80; the closest approximation of $\dfrac{2}{3}$ would be $\dfrac{66}{100}$ or 0.66 recurring. Rearrange each expression in ascending order, as found in answer C.

41. B: First, calculate the difference between the larger value and the smaller value.

$378 - 252 = 126$

To calculate this difference as a percentage of the original value, and thus calculate the percentage *increase*, divide 126 by 252, then multiply by 100 to reach the percentage = 50%, answer B.

42. B: Add 3 to both sides to get $4x = 8$. Then divide both sides by 4 to get $x = 2$.

43. A: First simplify the larger fraction by separating it into two. When dividing one fraction by another, remember to *invert* the second fraction and multiply the two as follows:

$$\frac{5}{7} \times \frac{11}{9}$$

The resulting fraction $\dfrac{55}{63}$ cannot be simplified further, so this is the answer to the problem.

44. A: To calculate the range in a set of data, subtract the highest value with the lowest value. In this graph, the range of Mr. Lennon's students is 5, which can be seen physically in the graph as having the smallest difference compared with the other teachers between the highest value and the lowest value.

45. C: 300/80 =30/8 = 15/4 =3.75. But Bernard is only working full days, so he will need to work 4 days, since 3 days is not sufficient.

46. A: Mean. An outlier is a data value that's either far above or below the majority of values in a sample set. The mean is the average of all values in the set. In a small sample, a very high or low number could greatly change the average. The median is the middle value when arranged from lowest to highest. Outliers would have no more of an effect on the median than any other value. Mode is the value that repeats most often in a set. Assuming that the same outlier doesn't repeat, outliers would have no effect on the mode of a sample set.

Science

1. A: One cycle takes 200 months. It starts with the population being low, rising and reaching a peak, and then falling again. It takes 100 months to reach the peak, Choice *B*. Four cycles could be completed in 800 months, Choice *C*, and two cycles could be completed in 400 months, Choice *D*.

2. B: Looking at the Figure 2, the fox is the predator. When the diagram notes that the predator population decreases on the left side, there is only one fox left. As it increases, as noted on the right side, there are two foxes drawn. Foxes are also much larger than rabbits and would be able to catch them much easier than the other way around.

3. D: When the prey population decreases, the predators have less food, i.e. prey, to feed on. This causes the predator population to dwindle. An increase in the prey population, Choice *A*, would actually increase the predator population because they would have more food, which would lengthen survival and increase reproduction. Seasons do not affect the predator population in this situation, Choice *B*. Generally, prey do not have the ability to attack their predators, Choice *C*, due to physical constraints, such as differences in size.

4. A: When the predator population decreases, the rate of survival of the prey population increases and they can then also reproduce more. An increase in the predator population, Choice *B*, would cause the prey population to decrease. Weather and amount of sunlight, Choice *C*, does not affect the growth of the prey population. The prey population is cyclical and does not remain the same size, Choice *D*.

5. C: Prey populations can develop different features to try and hide from and escape the predator population. The features help them blend into their environment, such as Choice *B*, or help them identify predators early and quickly, Choices *A* and *D*. Choice *C* would just allow the predators to hear the prey easily.

6. B: Sunlight comes into the greenhouse as short-wavelength IR. As it is absorbed by surfaces in the greenhouse, it is converted to long-wavelength IR. The long-wavelength IR gets trapped inside the greenhouse and bounces off the surfaces and glass and remains inside the greenhouse. Since short-wavelength IR can enter the greenhouse, it also has the ability to leave the greenhouse, making Choice *A* incorrect. The greenhouse feels warmer, not cooler, than outside, so Choice *C* is incorrect. Water is not involved in the reaction noted in Figure 1, so Choice *D* is also incorrect.

7. D: Looking at the graph in Figure 2, the greenhouse plant grew taller than the outside plant. The bars representing the greenhouse plant are taller at 3 time points that Scientist A measured. Greenhouses trap sunlight, warm air, and gases, such as CO_2 inside the greenhouse, so plants have an increased rate of photosynthesis, allowing them to grow faster. The plants are also protected from pests inside the greenhouse.

8. B: Sunlight enters the greenhouse as short-wavelength IR and get converted to long-wavelength IR. This process also gives off heat and makes the greenhouse feel warmer than the outside climate. Water and oxygen, Choices *A* and *D*, are not involved in this reaction. The plants remain the same and do not get converted into anything else, Choice *C*.

9. A: Short-wavelength IR enters the greenhouse in the form of sunlight. It can pass easily through the glass and can therefore pass easily back out to the outside environment. The long-wavelength IR, Choice *D*, gets trapped inside the greenhouse.

10. C: The plants inside a greenhouse are protected from many pests that can be found in the outside environment. The air is warmer in the greenhouse, so Choice *A* is incorrect. More photosynthesis occurs because of the increased sunlight energy that stays in the greenhouse, making Choices *B* and *D* incorrect.

11. D: The equivalence point occurs when just enough of the unknown solution is added to completely neutralize the known solution. In Figure 1, at the halfway point of the curve, the equivalence point is when 25 volumes of NaOH have been added to the solution. The pH is 7 at this point also, which is a neutralization of the HCl, strong acid.

12. C: The acid dissociation constant is the pK_a of the solution. It is found at the halfway point between the beginning of the curve and the equivalence point, where the solution would have a pH of 7 and be completely neutralized. In Figure 3, it is marked as 4.76.

13. A: Looking at Figure 3, the vertical axis on the left side has information about the pH of the solution. The horizontal axis at the bottom has information about how much basic solution containing OH^- is being added to the acetic acid. When the OH^- is at 0, and none has been added yet, the pH of the acetic acid is marked as 1.

14. B: Looking at the chemical equation in Figure 2, the reactants are on the left side and the products are on the right side. HCl and NaOH, Choices *A* and *C*, are the reactants of the equation. NaCl is the salt that is formed as one of the products of the reaction. The chloride ion, Choice *D*, is not formed in this reaction.

15. A: The equivalence point occurs in all titration reactions when the solution is neutralized. If an acid and base are being titrated, the solution is no longer acidic or basic, Choices *B* and *C*. It reaches a pH of 7 and is considered neutral.

16. A: Oxygen-poor blood is pumped to the lungs before returning to the heart. Oxygen is transferred from the airways of the lungs into the blood. The blood becomes rich with oxygen and then returns to the heart so that it can bring oxygen and nutrients to other organs of the body, such as the brain, stomach, and kidney, Choices *B*, *C*, and *D*.

17. C: The mitral valve has two folds. The tricuspid valve, Choice *B*, has three folds. The valve between the left atrium and ventricle has two valves, as was noted in the descriptive passage. Correlating this information to Figure 1, the name of the valve between these two chambers is the mitral valve. Choices *A* and *D* are vessels that carry blood through them and are not names of valves.

18. D: Arteries carry oxygen-rich blood away from the heart to the rest of the body. The aorta is the largest artery in the body. Veins, Choice *A*, carry oxygen-poor blood to the heart and lungs. Airway, Choice *C*, is found in the respiratory system and carries air in and out of the body.

19. C: A normal heartrate for a child is between 90 and 120 beats per minute. Choice C, 100 beats per minute, falls within this range. Choices A, B, and D are within the normal range for an adult but not for a child. Children's hearts pump blood faster than adults' hearts through the body.

20. B: Looking at Figure 1 and following the red arrow in the aorta backwards, the left ventricle is where the blood is coming from directly before it enters the aorta. Blood flows from the atria to the ventricles, so it enters the left atrium before the left ventricle and then the aorta, Choice D. Oxygen-poor blood is on the right side of the heart and flows from the right atrium to the right ventricle before flowing to the lungs to get re-oxygenated, Choices A and C.

21. C: Lava is a type of molten rock. When molten rock cools down and hardens, it forms igneous rock. Sedimentary and metamorphic rocks, Choices A and B, are not formed from molten rock. Choice D is incorrect because lava does cool down eventually and becomes hard.

22: A: Looking at Figure 1, the granite is found in column A. The description of the rocks in these columns says that these rocks were formed from molten rock. When molten rock cools, it forms igneous rock. Column C describes how metamorphic rocks are formed, Choice B. Column B describes how sedimentary rocks are formed, Choice C. Fossils, Choice D, are not rocks but are formed into sedimentary rock.

23: D: Sedimentary rocks are formed from soft materials, such as sand, shells, and pebbles. This allows for fossils to form because the remains of animals or plants can be pressed into the softer rock material and leave their imprint. Fossils cannot form in igneous, Choice A, or metamorphic, Choice C, rocks. Bones are something that can actually make a fossil imprint, Choice B.

24. B: Rocks that are formed by changes in heat and pressure are called metamorphic rocks, which is how the rocks in Column C are described. Slate is found in Column C of Figure 1. Sandstone and limestone, Choices A and D, are both found in Column B, which describes sedimentary rock. Granite, Choice B, is found in Column A, which describes sedimentary rock.

25. A: Sedimentary rock is formed from sand, shells, and pebbles, all of which are found in abundance at the beach. Shells, Choice B, are something that contribute to the formation of sedimentary rock. Igneous rock, Choice C, is formed from molten rock, which would likely be much too hot to be found on most beaches. The surface environment of a beach likely does not undergo changes in heat and pressure enough to form metamorphic rock, Choice D.

26. D: Water vapor is the gaseous form of water. Looking at Figure 2, Choices A, B, and C are part of the pie chart as greenhouse gases found in the atmosphere. Water vapor is not one of the gases that makes up the chart.

27. B: The two major wedges of the pie chart in Figure 3 are Transportation and Electricity. Using a car, Choice C, produces a lot of carbon dioxide. Walking instead of driving a car would not produce any carbon dioxide. Choices A and D use electricity and leaving either the lights or the television on would need a constant source of electricity, producing lots of carbon dioxide.

28. A: Looking at Figure 2, carbon dioxide, Choice D, takes up the largest wedge of the pie chart at 54.7%. The next largest wedge is methane at 30%. Nitrous oxide, Choice C, takes up only 4.9% and fluorinated gases, Choice B, takes up 0.9%.

29. C: Looking at Figure 1, in the right picture where there are more greenhouse gases, the re-emitted heat arrow is larger as more heat gets trapped in the Earth's atmosphere. Space and the Sun, Choices *A* and *B*, remain outside the Earth's atmosphere. Water vapor, Choice *D*, is not a part of the diagrams for the greenhouse effect.

30. D: Figures 2 and 3 are pie charts. Circular charts that are broken up into wedges, or pie pieces, are called pie charts. Scatter plots, Choice *A*, have specific point markers to mark each data point. In line graphs, Choice *B*, data are represented by connecting lines. In bar graphs, Choice *C*, data are represented by vertical or horizontal bars.

31. A: An anemometer measures air speed. Wind is the movement of air, so an anemometer would be able to measure wind speed. A barometer, Choice *B*, measures air pressure. A thermometer, Choice *C*, measures temperature. A wind vane, Choice *D*, shows which direction the wind is blowing.

32. B: Figure 1 is a graph showing the temperature on different days. Temperature is measured using a thermometer. A rain gauge, Choice *A*, would allow a meteorologist to record amounts of rainfall. A barometer, Choice *C*, measures air pressure. An anemometer, Choice *D*, measures air speed.

33. C: A wind vane shows which direction the wind is blowing. If it is pointing north, the wind is blowing in a northern direction. It would not be blowing in an eastern direction, Choice *A*, or a southern direction, Choice *D*, since that is the opposite direction of north. A wind vane simply tells wind direction and does not determine whether a storm is coming, Choice *B*.

34. A: Looking at the line graph in Figure 2, the lowest point is marked for January, with approximately 2 mm of rainfall. April, Choice *B*, has approximately 23 mm rainfall, September, Choice *C*, has 10 mm of rainfall, and October, Choice *D*, has the highest rainfall at 60 mm.

35. D: Reading the graph in Figure 2, at June, the rainfall is approximately 20 mm. The blue line marks all of the data collected for each month. For June, the blue line is just about at the 20 mm mark from the vertical axis on the left side of the graph.

36. B: Plants use chloroplasts to turn light energy into glucose. Animal cells do not have this ability. Comparing Figures 1 and 2, chloroplasts can be found in the plant cell but not the animal cell.

37. C: The nucleolus is always located inside the nucleus. It contains important hereditary information about the cell that is critical for the reproductive process. Chloroplasts, Choice *A*, are only located in plant cells. It is not found in the mitochondria, Choice *B*, or attached to the cell membrane, Choice *D*.

38. A: Looking at the table in Figure 3, each organelle is described and mitochondria is described as the powerhouse of the cell. The nucleus, Choice *B*, contains the cell's DNA. The ribosomes, Choice *C*, build proteins. The cell wall, Choice *D*, maintains the shape of plant cells and protects its contents.

39. D: Figure 3 describes the functions of the organelles. The cell membrane surrounds the cell and regulates which molecules can move in and out of the cell. Ribosomes build proteins, Choice *A*. Lysosomes, Choice *B*, break down large molecules. The nucleus, Choice *C*, contains the cell's DNA.

40. C: Figure 3 describes the functions of the organelles. Chloroplasts are responsible for photosynthesis in plant cells, which is the process of converting sunlight energy to glucose energy. The cell wall helps maintain the cell's shape, Choice *A*. The nucleus contains the cell's DNA, Choice *B*. Ribosomes build proteins, Choice *D*.

Social Studies

1. C: Map projections, such as the Mercator Projection, are useful for finding positions on the globe, but they attempt to represent a spherical object on a flat surface. As a result, they distort areas nearest the poles, which misrepresent the size of Antarctica, Greenland, and other high latitudinal locations. Map projects can include great detail; some illustrate the physical features in an area, and most include both the northern and southern hemispheres.

2. D: Thematic maps create certain themes in which they attempt to illustrate a certain phenomenon or pattern. The obvious theme of a climate map is the climates in the represented areas. Thematic maps are very extensive and can include thousands of different themes, which makes them quite useful for students of geography. Topographic maps are utilized to show physical features, conformal projections attempt to illustrate the globe in an undistorted fashion, and isoline maps illustrate differences in variables between two points on a map.

3. B: Lines of latitude measure distance North and South. The Equator is zero degrees and the Tropic of Cancer is 23 ½ degrees north of the Equator. The distance between those two lines measures degrees North to South, as with any other two lines of latitude. Longitudinal lines, or meridians, measure distance East and West, even though they run north and south down the Globe. Latitude is not inexact, in that there are set distances between the lines. Furthermore, coordinates can only exist with the use of longitude and latitude.

4. C: Developed Nations have better infrastructural systems, which can include government, transportation, financial, and educational institutions. Consequently, its citizens tend to have higher rates of literacy, due to the sheer availability of educational resources and government sanctioned educational systems. In contrast, developing nations struggle to provide educational resources to their citizens. Nations in the Northern Hemisphere have no greater availability to educational resources than those in the Southern Hemisphere, and centers of trade don't necessarily equate to higher levels of education as many may exist in poorer nations with fewer resources.

5. C: Although it can place a strain on some resources, population density is not a negative demographic indicator. For example, New York City, one of the most densely populated places on Earth, enjoys one of the highest standards of living in the world. Other world cities such as Tokyo, Los Angeles, and Sydney also have tremendously high population densities and high standards of living. High infant mortality rates, low literacy rates, and low life expectancies are all poor demographic indicators that suggest a low quality of life for the citizens living in those areas.

6. C: Longitudinal position, or a place's location either east or west, has no bearing on the place's climate. In contrast, a place's latitudinal position, or its distance away from the direct rays of the sun in the Tropics, greatly affects its climate. Additionally, proximity to mountains, which can block wind patterns, and elevation, which generally lowers temperature by three degrees for every one thousand feet gained, also impacts climate.

7. D: Although nearest the direct rays of the sun, the Tropics are not always warm. In fact, the nations of Ecuador and Peru, which are entirely within the Tropics, are home to the Andes Mountains, which remain snowcapped the entire year. This climatological anomaly is also due to cooler ocean currents and the orographic effect. Choices *A, B,* and *C* are all true of the tropics.

8. B: Developing nations tend to have higher levels of impoverished citizens. As a result, many of their citizens must rely on subsistence farming, or producing enough food to feed their families, in order to survive. In contrast, developed nations tend to produce surpluses of food and very few, if any, of its citizens engage in subsistence farming. Developing nations are less likely to have complex highway systems, stable governments, and economic stability due to financial pressures.

9. A: Although some ethnic groups throughout the world do engage in armed conflicts, the vast majority do not. Most ethnic groups tend to live in relative harmony with others with whom they share differences. Ethnic groups are simply a group of people with a religious, cultural, economic, or linguistic commonality. Additionally, ethnic groups don't always choose to leave places. Many have called certain locations home for centuries. Also, some ethnic groups actually make up the majority in some countries and are not always minority groups.

10. C: Pull factors are reasons people immigrate to a particular area. Obviously, educational opportunities attract thousands of people on a global level and on a local level. For example, generally areas with strong schools have higher property values, due to the relative demand for housing in those districts. The same is true for nations with better educational opportunities. Unemployment, low GDP, and incredibly high population densities may serve to deter people from moving to a certain place and can be considered push factors.

11. A: The use of biotechnology and GMOs has increased the total amount of food on Earth. Additionally, it has helped to sustain the Earth's growing population; however, many activists assert that scientists are creating crops that, in the long run, will be destructive to human health, even though not enough evidence exists to prove such an allegation. Agricultural production has not been affected by poorer soil, plagues of pests, or the use of saline for irrigation purposes.

12. C: Like the boundaries of the United States, political boundaries are constantly changing due to war (South Sudan), religious conflict (India and Pakistan, Israel, East Timor), and differing political ideologies (North and South Korea, Reunification of Germany after the Cold War). The only constant with political boundaries is change. It is not possible to see manmade lines separating countries on Earth, unless they are natural boundaries. Additionally, boundaries are always under dispute, and they have not remained static for centuries.

13. B: Macroeconomics. Macroeconomics studies the economy on a large scale and focuses on issues such as unemployment, interest rates, price levels, and national income. Microeconomics studies more individual or small group behaviors such as scarcity or supply and demand. Scarcity is incorrect because it refers to the availability of goods and services. Supply and demand is also incorrect because it refers to the quantity of goods and services that is produced and/or needed.

14. C: Opportunity cost. Opportunity cost can trade time, power, or anything else of value in exchange for something else. Economic systems determine what is being produced and by whom. Supply and demand refers to the quantity of goods and services that is produced or needed. Finally, inflation refers to how the cost of goods and services increases over time.

15. A: Free. A free market does not involve government interventions or monopolies while trading between buyers and suppliers. However, in a command market, the government determines the price of goods and services. Gross and exchange markets refer to situations where brokers and traders make exchanges in the financial realm.

16. D: Theory of The Firm. Behaviors of firms is not an indicator of economic growth because it refers to the behavior that firms follow to reach their desired outcome. GDP, unemployment, and inflation are all indicators that help determine economic growth.

17. C: Contraction and trough. A recession occurs between the contraction and trough phases of the business cycle. Between expansion and peak phases, employment and productivity are on the rise, causing a "boom." Between the peak and contraction, unemployment rates are starting to fall, but have not yet hit an all-time low. Between trough and expansion phases, the economy is getting back on its feet and starting to increase employment again.

18. C: Federal Reserve. The Federal Reserve is the bank of banks. It is the central bank of the United States and controls the value of money. A commodity is the value of goods such as precious metals. While the Central Reserve and Bank Reserve may sound like good options, the term "bank reserve" refers to the amount of money a bank deposits into a central bank, and the Central Reserve is simply a fictitious name.

19. A: Closed market operations. Monetary policies are sustained by assuring bank reserves, adjusting interest rates, and open market operations. Closed market operations do NOT uphold monetary policies.

20. D: The market. The market, through supply and demand, determines the exchange rate with a "flexible" or "floating" exchange rate. The government is not a correct answer because it is involved in "fixed" exchange rates to help keep exchange rates stable. Taxes is also incorrect because they create government revenue. The Federal Reserve is the bank of banks.

21. B: As inflation increases, purchasing power decreases. As more money is printed, the monetary value of the dollar drops and, in turn, decreases the purchasing power of goods and services. So, as inflation increases, consumers are not spending as much and the value of the dollar is low.

22. B: The value of goods and services matters more than their quantity. For example, in the real estate industry, if a realtor sells ten houses valued at $200,000, his or her commission would be the same as a realtor who sells one house valued at $2,000,000. Even though one realtor sold more homes, the value of 10 houses adds up to the same amount as the single home that the other realtor sold. Therefore, the number of goods and services produced does not determine economic growth—the value of the goods and services does.

23. A: Invasions by Germanic tribes. Large numbers of Franks, Goths, Vandals, and other Germanic peoples began moving south in the fifth century CE. They conquered Rome twice, and the Western Roman Empire finally disintegrated. The Mongol invasion, Choice *B*, pushed westward in the thirteenth century, long after the western Roman Empire was gone. The assassination of Julius Caesar, Choice *C*, led to the end of the Roman Republic and the birth of the Roman Empire. Taoism never spread to Rome, making Choice *D* incorrect.

24. C: Louis the XIV was an absolute monarch who ruled during the sixteenth century. He concentrated power on the throne by forcing nobles to spend most of their time at the royal court. The French Revolution occurred about two hundred years after he died. Absolute monarchs like Louis the XIV bolstered their prestige by claiming they were appointed by God. The Mandate of Heaven was a similar concept, but it was developed by the Zhou Dynasty in China about two thousand years before Louis XIV was born.

25. A: Most scholars already knew the world was round by 1492. On the other hand, the arrival of Europeans in North and South America introduced deadly diseases that killed millions of native peoples. Europeans had developed immunity to diseases such as smallpox, while Native Americans had not. In addition, Europeans introduced a number of new plants and animals to the New World, but they also adopted many new foods as well, including potatoes, tomatoes, chocolate, and tobacco. Finally, Europeans tried to convert Native Americans to Christianity, but Indians did not completely give up their traditional beliefs. Instead, they blended Christianity with indigenous and African beliefs to create new syncretic religions.

26. B: The American Revolution occurred first in 1775, and a number of European soldiers fought for the patriots. The American Revolution, in part, inspired the French Revolution. The Marquis de Lafayette came to America in 1777 and was wounded during the Battle of Brandywine. He returned to France after the American Revolution and became a leader in the French Revolution in 1789.

27. D: The Industrial Revolution is probably one of the most important turning points in world history. The United States and Western Europe, especially Britain, were the first areas to industrialize. Steam engines were used to improve economic and transportation efficiency. They also gave western empires a military advantage over less developed countries in Asia and Africa. Finally, industrialization required large amounts of unskilled labor, which created the working class.

28. A: The atomic bomb was created during World War II (1939 – 1945). Scientists and engineers did develop a number of other weapons in order to break through the heavily entrenched front lines during World War I. Poison gas killed or injured millions of men between 1914 and 1918. Aircraft were used to observe enemy positions and bombard enemy troops. Armored tanks were able to crush barbed wire fences and deflected machine gun bullets.

29. B: Eager to avoid another global conflict, European leaders tried to appease Hitler by letting him occupy Austria and Czechoslovakia. This policy failed because it only emboldened Hitler, and he invaded Poland in 1939. Rather than receiving leniency after World War I, Germany was forced to sign a humiliating peace treaty. Furthermore, the League of Nations failed to prevent conflict because it lacked any real power. This encouraged continued aggression from Italy, Germany, and Japan, which culminated in World War II.

30. A: Nationalism remains a powerful force to this day. Nationalism drove conflict in Ireland, Spain, Yugoslavia, and elsewhere. However, the end of the Cold War removed many of the political barriers that had prevented interaction between the western and Communist blocs. In addition, religious fundamentalism became an increasingly common response to the rapid changes that occurred during the late twentieth and early twenty-first centuries. There was also a rise in cultural and economic globalization, as well as in environmentalism.

31. A: Carolina is divided into two separate states—North and South. Maine was part of Nova Scotia and did not become an American territory until the War of 1812. Likewise, Vermont was not one of the original Thirteen Colonies. Canada remained a separate British colony. Finally, Florida was a Spanish territory. Therefore, by process of elimination, *A* is the correct list.

32. B: Britain was not defeated in the French and Indian War, and, in fact, disputes with the colonies over the new territories it won contributed to the growing tensions. All other options were key motivations behind the Revolutionary War.

33. C: Abraham Lincoln was elected president as part of the new Republican Party, and his plans to limit and potentially abolish slavery led the southern states to secede from the Union.

34. C: The Declaration of Independence occurred during the American Revolution, so it should therefore be considered an effect, not a cause. Similarly, slavery was a cause for the later Civil War, but it was not a primary instigator for the Revolutionary War. Although a single event can have many effects long into the future, it is also important to not overstate the influence of these individual causes; the civil rights movement was only tangentially connected to the War of Independence among many other factors, and therefore it should not be considered a primary effect of it. The French and Indian War (also known as the Seven Years' War) and the Bill of Rights, on the other hand, were respectively a cause and effect from the American Revolution, making Choice *C* the correct answer.

35. D: The president and vice president are part of the executive branch, not the legislative branch. The question focuses specifically on the federal level, so state government should be excluded from consideration. As for the district court and the court of appeals, they are part of the judicial branch. The legislative branch is made up of Congress, which consists of the House of Representatives and the Senate.

GED Practice Test #3

Reading Comprehension

Questions 1–6 are based on the following passage:

What's About to Happen to Mr. Button?

As long ago as 1860 it was the proper thing to be born at home. At present, so I am told, the high gods of medicine have decreed that the first cries of the young shall be uttered upon the anesthetic air of a hospital, preferably a fashionable one. So young Mr. and Mrs. Roger Button were fifty years ahead of style when they decided, one day in the summer of 1860, that their first baby should be born in a hospital. Whether this anachronism had any bearing upon the astonishing history I am about to set down will never be known.

I shall tell you what occurred, and let you judge for yourself.

The Roger Buttons held an enviable position, both social and financial, in ante-bellum Baltimore. They were related to the This Family and the That Family, which, as every Southerner knew, entitled them to membership in that enormous peerage which largely populated the Confederacy. This was their first experience with the charming old custom of having babies— Mr. Button was naturally nervous. He hoped it would be a boy so that he could be sent to Yale College in Connecticut, at which institution Mr. Button himself had been known for four years by the somewhat obvious nickname of "Cuff."

On the September morning <u>consecrated</u> to the enormous event he arose nervously at six o'clock dressed himself, adjusted an impeccable stock, and hurried forth through the streets of Baltimore to the hospital, to determine whether the darkness of the night had borne in new life upon its bosom.

When he was approximately a hundred yards from the Maryland Private Hospital for Ladies and Gentlemen he saw Doctor Keene, the family physician, descending the front steps, rubbing his hands together with a washing movement—as all doctors are required to do by the unwritten ethics of their profession.

Mr. Roger Button, the president of Roger Button & Co., Wholesale Hardware, began to run toward Doctor Keene with much less dignity than was expected from a Southern gentleman of that picturesque period. "Doctor Keene!" he called. "Oh, Doctor Keene!"

The doctor heard him, faced around, and stood waiting, a curious expression settling on his harsh, medicinal face as Mr. Button drew near.

"What happened?" demanded Mr. Button, as he came up in a gasping rush. "What was it? How is she? A boy? Who is it? What—"

"Talk sense!" said Doctor Keene sharply. He appeared somewhat irritated.

"Is the child born?" begged Mr. Button.

Doctor Keene frowned. "Why, yes, I suppose so—after a fashion." Again he threw a curious glance at Mr. Button.

The Curious Case of Benjamin Button, F.S. Fitzgerald, 1922

1. What major event is about to happen in this story?
    a. Mr. Button is about to go to a funeral.
    b. Mr. Button's wife is about to have a baby.
    c. Mr. Button is getting ready to go to the doctor's office.
    d. Mr. Button is about to go shopping for new clothes.

2. What kind of tone does the above passage have?
    a. Nervous and Excited
    b. Sad and Angry
    c. Shameful and Confused
    d. Grateful and Joyous

3. What is the meaning of the word "consecrated" in paragraph 4?
    a. Numbed
    b. Chained
    c. Dedicated
    d. Moved

4. What does the author mean to do by adding the following statement?

"rubbing his hands together with a washing movement—as all doctors are required to do by the unwritten ethics of their profession."

    a. Suggesting that Mr. Button is tired of the doctor.
    b. Trying to explain the detail of the doctor's profession.
    c. Hinting to readers that the doctor is an unethical man.
    d. Giving readers a visual picture of what the doctor is doing.

5. Which of the following best describes the development of this passage?
    a. It starts in the middle of a narrative in order to transition smoothly to a conclusion.
    b. It is a chronological narrative from beginning to end.
    c. The sequence of events is backwards—we go from future events to past events.
    d. To introduce the setting of the story and its characters.

6. Which of the following is an example of an imperative sentence?
    a. "Oh, Doctor Keene!"
    b. "Talk sense!"
    c. "Is the child born?"
    d. "Why, yes, I suppose so—"

Death or Freedom?

Knowing that Mrs. Mallard was afflicted with heart trouble, great care was taken to break to her as gently as possible the news of her husband's death.

It was her sister Josephine who told her, in broken sentences; veiled hints that revealed in half concealing. Her husband's friend Richards was there, too, near her. It was he who had been in the newspaper office when intelligence of the railroad disaster was received, with Brently Mallard's name leading the list of "killed." He had only taken the time to assure himself of its truth by a second telegram, and had hastened to forestall any less careful, less tender friend in bearing the sad message.

She did not hear the story as many women have heard the same, with a paralyzed inability to accept its significance. She wept at once, with sudden, wild abandonment, in her sister's arms. When the storm of grief had spent itself she went away to her room alone. She would have no one follow her.

There stood, facing the open window, a comfortable, roomy armchair. Into this she sank, pressed down by a physical exhaustion that haunted her body and seemed to reach into her soul.

She could see in the open square before her house the tops of trees that were all aquiver with the new spring life. The delicious breath of rain was in the air. In the street below a peddler was crying his wares. The notes of a distant song which some one was singing reached her faintly, and countless sparrows were twittering in the eaves.

There were patches of blue sky showing here and there through the clouds that had met and piled one above the other in the west facing her window.

She sat with her head thrown back upon the cushion of the chair, quite motionless, except when a sob came up into her throat and shook her, as a child who has cried itself to sleep continues to sob in its dreams.

She was young, with a fair, calm face, whose lines bespoke repression and even a certain strength. But now here was a dull stare in her eyes, whose gaze was fixed away off yonder on one of those patches of blue sky. It was not a glance of reflection, but rather indicated a suspension of intelligent thought.

There was something coming to her and she was waiting for it, fearfully. What was it? She did not know; it was too subtle and elusive to name. But she felt it, creeping out of the sky, reaching toward her through the sounds, the scents, and color that filled the air.

Now her bosom rose and fell tumultuously. She was beginning to recognize this thing that was approaching to possess her, and she was striving to beat it back with her will—as powerless as her two white slender hands would have been. When she abandoned herself a little whispered word escaped her slightly parted lips. She said it over and over under her breath: "free, free, free!" The vacant stare and the look of terror that had followed it went from her eyes. They stayed keen and bright. Her pulses beat fast, and the coursing blood warmed and relaxed every inch of her body.

She did not stop to ask if it were or were not a monstrous joy that held her. A clear and exalted perception enabled her to dismiss the suggestion as trivial. She knew that she would weep again when she saw the kind, tender hands folded in death; the face that had never looked save with love upon her, fixed and gray and dead. But she saw beyond that bitter moment a long procession of years to come that would belong to her absolutely. And she opened and spread her arms out to them in welcome.

Excerpt from "The Story of An Hour," Kate Chopin, 1894

7. What point of view is the above passage told in?
   a. First person
   b. Second person
   c. Third person omniscient
   d. Third person limited

8. What kind of irony are we presented with in this story?
   a. The way Mrs. Mallard reacted to her husband's death.
   b. The way in which Mr. Mallard died.
   c. The way in which the news of her husband's death was presented to Mrs. Mallard.
   d. The way in which nature is compared with death in the story.

9. What is the meaning of the word "elusive" in paragraph 9?
   a. Horrible
   b. Indefinable
   c. Quiet
   d. Joyful

10. What is the best summary of the passage above?
    a. Mr. Mallard, a soldier during World War I, is killed by the enemy and leaves his wife widowed.
    b. Mrs. Mallard understands the value of friendship when her friends show up for her after her husband's death.
    c. Mrs. Mallard combats mental illness daily and will perhaps be sent to a mental institution soon.
    d. Mrs. Mallard, a newly widowed woman, finds unexpected relief in her husband's death.

11. What is the tone of this story?
    a. Confused
    b. Joyful
    c. Depressive
    d. All of the above

12. What is the meaning of the word "tumultuously" in paragraph 10?
    a. Orderly
    b. Unashamedly
    c. Violently
    d. Calmly

Question 13 is based on the following passage:

Which Statement is Correct?

In 2015, 28 countries, including Estonia, Portugal, Slovenia, and Latvia, scored significantly higher than the United States on standardized high school math tests. In the 1960s, the United States consistently ranked first in the world. Today, the United States spends more than $800 billion dollars on education, which exceeds the next highest country by more than $600 billion dollars. The United States also leads the world in spending per school-aged child by an enormous margin.

13. If these statements above are factual, which of the following statements must be correct?
    a. Outspending other countries on education has benefits beyond standardized math tests.
    b. The United States' education system is corrupt and broken.
    c. The standardized math tests are not representative of American academic prowess.
    d. Spending more money does not guarantee success on standardized math tests.

Questions 14–17 are based on the following passage:

In history, as in science, the normal order is from obvious facts to hidden causes. The fact of the disastrous fall of Rome is so obvious that every intelligent person is aware of it. Its causes are so obscure that the world is still uncertain what they are. Among the many theories advanced in explanation of this great historical event, one of the most interesting is that of Liebig, which has recently been admirably restated by Professor Simkhovitch. According to the view of these two authors, one of the fundamental factors in the fall of Rome was a marked decline in agriculture. We are told that in the days of the Roman Republic seven jugera, or about four and one-half acres of land, sufficed for the tillage required to support an average family. Agriculture was so intensive that farms of this small size, supplemented presumably by pasture land, supported a contented, self-respecting, and progressive population. The cities, all of which were small, reflected the sturdy independence of the country people, and naturally the government was modeled to fit the citizens who administered it. By the second century before Christ, however, a great change was apparent. Under Scipio in 196 BC, grain began to be distributed from state granaries to poor citizens. Soon came the agrarian troubles with which the names of the Gracchi are associated. Seven jugera were no longer sufficient for the average farmer. Indeed, the farmers in many places were becoming poverty stricken. Instead of sowing their fields with a scientific rotation of carefully tilled crops, they were turning them over to pasturage. Cato declared that good pasturage was the best thing for a farmer, fair pasturage the second best, poor pasturage the third best, and ordinary field crops only the fourth resource. Pessimists declared that in their wheat fields the farmers reaped only four times the seed that they sowed. In later centuries, especially from the second century AD onward, conditions became still worse. Many farms were utterly abandoned; the land was concentrated in the hands of a comparatively few large proprietors. The tenants fell into chronic debt and were little better than slaves. So eager were many of them to escape from the thralldom in which their poverty kept them that they flocked to the cities, until laws were passed which bound them to the soil as serfs. All these and many other evil consequences appear to have flowed from a widespread decline in agriculture, which, though alleviated at times, grew worse and worse until Rome finally fell.

The difference between Roman agriculture in early and in later times has given rise to a warm debate. One side is represented by Durneau de la Malle. As he put it: "A vicious system of agriculture, a biennial rotation, the ignorance of the methods of alternation of crops, the too frequent rotation of wheat on the same land, the insufficient and poor preparation of manure, the slight extent of artificial grasslands, the small number of animals supported on cultivated crops, the imperfection of the methods and instruments of culture, the vicious practice of burning the straw in place of converting it into manure, these and a hundred other deadly practices which it would be too long to enumerate form the conflicting but true picture which Greek and Roman agriculture on the whole present to us." Rodbertus strongly contested this view. He attempted to show that the Romans had a most admirable system of agriculture, being familiar with the rotation of crops and the use of fertilizers, and that more labor was expended per acre than is now spent on the best fields of Germany. That there was agricultural decline he admitted, but he ascribed it to social causes. In the writings of such men as Varro, Cato, Pliny, and Columella, he accepts the parts which indicate that the science of agriculture was highly developed, but says that other portions must be taken "cum grano sallis." He thinks the Latin writers have been misunderstood or that their statements can be explained by other circumstances. For instance, he supposes that when Rome was able to reach out and obtain grain from other lands the Italian farmers turned their attention to vineyards, olive orchards, and cattle raising, and only the worst fields in Italy were devoted to wheat. Hence it was not surprising that the farmers reaped only four times what they had sowed.

Professor Simkhovitch ably shows that these two views are not really contradictory. The picture painted by Rodbertus indicates the condition in the early days, when Rome was in her prime. The other presents the conditions of later times. Simkhovitch ascribes the difference to exhaustion of the soil. Such exhaustion, as he says, is not a necessary consequence of incorrect cultivation, but arises only when unwise methods are pursued. As Van Hise I points out, the most crucial element in the exhaustion of the soil is the depletion of the phosphorus, which can be prevented only by abundant fertilization.

from "Climatic Change and Agricultural Exhaustion as Elements in the Fall of Rome," by Ellsworth Huntington

14. Which answer accurately describes the nature of the evidence used in the text?
    a. Studies of the physical earth that date back to the time of ancient civilizations
    b. Multiple papers published on the idea of climate change and agricultural exhaustion
    c. Textual evidence, observations, and historical records of Roman observers
    d. Accounts of Rome's decline from enemy sources

15. Based on the information in the passage, which answer could best quantify the effect agricultural decline had on the fall of Rome?
    a. The lack of good land to harvest grain contributed to the food shortages that taxed Rome's resources to the brink and brought about economic and civil degradation.
    b. Rome became dependent on other lands for grain, making the empire less reliant on its own resources and prone to collapse.
    c. The Roman empire collapsed as it struggled to maintain economic prosperity.
    d. Lacking sufficient means to feed its armies, Rome could not withstand the attacks of barbarian tribes.

16. Which information serves as the best evidence supporting Rodbertus' following claim about agricultural decline?

"Rodbertus strongly contested this view. He attempted to show that the Romans had a most admirable system of agriculture, being familiar with the rotation of crops and the use of fertilizers, and that more labor was expended per acre than is now spent on the best fields of Germany. That there was agricultural decline he admitted, but he ascribed it to social causes."

a. A series of severe droughts was reported within Rome's last fifteen years of power.
b. Rome sought to colonize other areas of the empire, so many Roman farmers moved to the frontiers.
c. Evidence was found that Romans developed agricultural systems that harvested steady grain supplies even in low yields.
d. Increasing land taxes led to farmers having dwindling resources to produce crops and overworking the land.

17. Huntignton brings in the perspectives of several scholars. Some of his sources support his views, and some disagree with the idea of agricultural decline resulting in the fall of Rome. What does this do for the author's argument?

a. This weakens the argument and confuses the reader; clearly, there are scholars who provide reasons that agricultural decline was not the cause of the fall of the Roman empire.
b. This allows the author to provide a full scope of the idea to the audience; by addressing the conflicting views, he can strengthen his ideas by showing how logic or other evidence shows gaps within the insight of the opposing views.
c. This does nothing for the argument; the author has no argument but to elaborate on a specific historical theory.
d. The author is showing how unfounded the opposing views to the agricultural decline theory are.

Questions 18–23 are based on the following passage:

What is Spinoff Technology?

When researchers and engineers undertake a large-scale scientific project, they may end up making discoveries and developing technologies that have far wider uses than originally intended. This is especially true in NASA, one of the most influential and innovative scientific organizations in America. NASA spinoff technology refers to innovations originally developed for NASA space projects that are now used in a wide range of different commercial fields. Many consumers are unaware that products they are buying are based on NASA research! Spinoff technology proves that it is worthwhile to invest in science research because it could enrich people's lives in unexpected ways.

The first spinoff technology worth mentioning is baby food. In space, where astronauts have limited access to fresh food and fewer options with their daily meals, malnutrition is a serious concern. Consequently, NASA researchers were looking for ways to enhance the nutritional value of astronauts' food. Scientists found that a certain type of algae could be added to food, improving the food's neurological benefits. When experts in the commercial food industry learned of this algae's potential to boost brain health, they were quick to begin their own research. The nutritional substance from algae then developed into a product called life's DHA, which can be found in over 90 percent of infant food sold in America.

Another intriguing example of a spinoff technology can be found in fashion. People who are always dropping their sunglasses may have invested in a pair of sunglasses with scratch resistant lenses—that is, it's impossible to scratch the glass, even if the glasses are dropped on an abrasive surface. This innovation is incredibly advantageous for people who are clumsy, but most shoppers don't know that this technology was originally developed by NASA. Scientists first created scratch resistant glass to help protect costly and crucial equipment from getting scratched in space, especially the helmet visors in space suits. However, sunglass companies later realized that this technology could be profitable for their products, and they licensed the technology from NASA.

18. What is the main purpose of this article?
    a. To advise consumers to do more research before making a purchase
    b. To persuade readers to support NASA research
    c. To tell a narrative about the history of space technology
    d. To define and describe instances of spinoff technology

19. What is the organizational structure of this article?
    a. A general definition followed by more specific examples
    b. A general opinion followed by supporting arguments
    c. An important moment in history followed by chronological details
    d. A popular misconception followed by counterevidence

20. Why did NASA scientists research algae?
    a. They already knew algae was healthy for babies.
    b. They were interested in how to grow food in space.
    c. They were looking for ways to add health benefits to food.
    d. They hoped to use it to protect expensive research equipment.

21. What does the word "neurological" mean in the second paragraph?
    a. Related to the body
    b. Related to the brain
    c. Related to vitamins
    d. Related to technology

22. Why does the author mention space suit helmets?
    a. To give an example of astronaut fashion
    b. To explain where sunglasses got their shape
    c. To explain how astronauts protect their eyes
    d. To give an example of valuable space equipment

23. Which statement would the author probably NOT agree with?
    a. Consumers don't always know the history of the products they are buying.
    b. Sometimes new innovations have unexpected applications.
    c. It is difficult to make money from scientific research.
    d. Space equipment is often very expensive.

Questions 24–29 are based upon the following passage:

How Can We Honor Them?

Four score and seven years ago our fathers brought forth on this continent, a new nation, conceived in liberty, and dedicated to the proposition that all men are created equal.

Now we are engaged in a great civil war, testing whether that nation, or any nation so conceived and so dedicated, can long endure. We are met on a great battlefield of that war. We have come to dedicate a portion of that field, as a final resting place for those who here gave their lives that this nation might live. It is altogether fitting and proper that we should do this.

But, in a larger sense, we cannot dedicate—we cannot consecrate that we cannot hallow—this ground. The brave men, living and dead, who struggled here, have consecrated it, far above our poor power to add or detract. The world will little note, nor long remember what we say here, but it can never forget what they did here. It is for us the living, rather, to be dedicated here to the unfinished work which they who fought here have thus far so nobly advanced. It is rather for us to be here and dedicated to the great task remaining before us—that from these honored dead we take increased devotion to that cause for which they gave the last full measure of devotion—that we here highly resolve that these dead shall not have died in vain—that these this nation, under God, shall have a new birth of freedom—and that government of people, by the people, for the people, shall not perish from the earth.

from Abraham Lincoln's Address Delivered at the Dedication of the Cemetery at Gettysburg, November 19, 1863.

24. The best description for the phrase "Four score and seven years ago" is?
   a. A unit of measurement
   b. A period of time
   c. A literary movement
   d. A statement of political reform

25 What is the setting of this text?
   a. A battleship off of the coast of France
   b. A desert plain on the Sahara Desert
   c. A battlefield in a North American town
   d. The residence of Abraham Lincoln

26. Which war is Abraham Lincoln referring to in the following passage?

Now we are engaged in a great civil war, testing whether that nation, or any nation so conceived and so dedicated, can long endure.

   a. World War I
   b. The War of Spanish Succession
   c. World War II
   d. The American Civil War

27. What message is the author trying to convey through this address?
   a. The audience should consider the death of the people that fought in the war as an example and perpetuate the ideals of freedom that the soldiers died fighting for.
   b. The audience should honor the dead by establishing an annual memorial service.
   c. The audience should form a militia that would overturn the current political structure.
   d. The audience should forget the lives that were lost and discredit the soldiers.

28. What is the effect of Lincoln's statement in the following passage?

But, in a larger sense, we cannot dedicate—we cannot consecrate that we cannot hallow—this ground. The brave men, living and dead, who struggled here, have consecrated it, far above our poor power to add or detract.

   a. His comparison emphasizes the great sacrifice of the soldiers who fought in the war.
   b. His comparison serves as a remainder of the inadequacies of his audience.
   c. His comparison serves as a catalyst for guilt and shame among audience members.
   d. His comparison attempts to illuminate the great differences between soldiers and civilians.

Read the passage below and answer questions 29 & 30:

To Whom It May Concern:

I'm writing in regards to the Writer/Producer position at Shadow Heat. I graduated with my MA degree in English at the University of Texas in May 2016 where I taught technical writing and writing arguments for my fellowship. My years taking and teaching English courses have enabled me to develop strong writing skills, which I believe will contribute greatly to the position in question.

Although a work in progress, my website, attached below, features technical writing, graphic design, blog writing, and creative writing samples. My passion for writing in order to connect with a specific audience is demonstrated by my various publications as well as my degrees that focus heavily on academic and creative writing. I would love to write for your company and hope you'll consider me for this position.

I'm highly motivated, carrying energy and creativity to my work. My nine years' experience in higher education enables me to adapt to changing ideals and trends while also maintaining personal values. I hope that you'll consider me for this position. I look forward to hearing from you!

Thanks!

29. What type of writing does this passage sound like?
   a. A how-to document on teaching
   b. A consumer email to a corporation
   c. A letter of interest for a resume
   d. A memo concerning employees in the workplace

30. Which of the following is correct information?
   a. The writer of the letter is a writer/producer at Shadow Heat.
   b. The writer of the letter has a Master's degree in English.
   c. The writer of the letter has ten years' experience in higher education.
   d. The writer of the letter is applying to be a website designer.

Questions 31–33 are based on the following passage:

Who was George Washington?

George Washington emerged out of the American Revolution as an unlikely champion of liberty. On June 14, 1775, the Second Continental Congress created the Continental Army, and John Adams, serving in the Congress, nominated Washington to be its first commander. Washington fought under the British during the French and Indian War, and his experience and prestige proved instrumental to the American war effort. Washington provided invaluable leadership, training, and strategy during the Revolutionary War. He emerged from the war as the embodiment of liberty and freedom from tyranny.

After vanquishing the heavily favored British forces, Washington could have pronounced himself as the autocratic leader of the former colonies without any opposition, but he famously refused and returned to his Mount Vernon plantation. His restraint proved his commitment to the fledgling state's republicanism. Washington was later unanimously elected as the first American president. But it is Washington's farewell address that cemented his legacy as a visionary worthy of study.

In 1796, President Washington issued his farewell address by public letter. Washington enlisted his good friend, Alexander Hamilton, in drafting his most famous address. The letter expressed Washington's faith in the Constitution and rule of law. He encouraged his fellow Americans to put aside partisan differences and establish a national union. Washington warned Americans against meddling in foreign affairs and entering military alliances. Additionally, he stated his opposition to national political parties, which he considered partisan and counterproductive.

Americans would be wise to remember Washington's farewell, especially during presidential elections when politics hits a fever pitch. They might want to question the political institutions that were not planned by the Founding Fathers, such as the nomination process and political parties themselves.

31. Which of the following statements is logically based on the information contained in the passage above?
   a. George Washington's background as a wealthy landholder directly led to his faith in equality, liberty, and democracy.
   b. George Washington would have opposed America's involvement in the Second World War.
   c. George Washington would not have been able to write as great a farewell address without the assistance of Alexander Hamilton.
   d. George Washington would probably not approve of modern political parties.

32. Which of the following statements is the best description of the author's purpose in writing this passage about George Washington?

    a. To inform American voters about a Founding Father's sage advice on a contemporary issue and explain its applicability to modern times

    b. To introduce George Washington to readers as a historical figure worthy of study

    c. To note that George Washington was more than a famous military hero

    d. To convince readers that George Washington is a hero of republicanism and liberty

33. In which of the following materials would the author be the most likely to include this passage?

    a. A history textbook

    b. An obituary

    c. A fictional story

    d. A newspaper editorial

Questions 34–38 are based on the following passage:

Who First Came to the New World?

Christopher Columbus is often credited for discovering America. This is incorrect. First, it is impossible to "discover" something where people already live; however, Christopher Columbus did explore places in the New World that were previously untouched by Europe, so the term "explorer" would be more accurate. Another correction must be made, as well: Christopher Columbus was not the first European explorer to reach the present day Americas! Rather, it was Leif Erikson who first came to the New World and contacted the natives, nearly five hundred years before Christopher Columbus.

Leif Erikson, the son of Erik the Red (a famous Viking outlaw and explorer in his own right), was born in either 970 or 980, depending on which historian you seek. His own family, though, did not raise Leif, which was a Viking tradition. Instead, one of Erik's prisoners taught Leif reading and writing, languages, sailing, and weaponry. At age 12, Leif was considered a man and returned to his family. He killed a man during a dispute shortly after his return, and the council banished the Erikson clan to Greenland.

In 999, Leif left Greenland and traveled to Norway where he would serve as a guard to King Olaf Tryggvason. It was there that he became a convert to Christianity. Leif later tried to return home with the intention of taking supplies and spreading Christianity to Greenland, however his ship was blown off course and he arrived in a strange new land: present day Newfoundland, Canada.

When he finally returned to his adopted homeland Greenland, Leif consulted with a merchant who had also seen the shores of this previously unknown land we now know as Canada. The son of the legendary Viking explorer then gathered a crew of 35 men and set sail. Leif became the first European to touch foot in the New World as he explored present-day Baffin Island and Labrador, Canada. His crew called the land Vinland since it was plentiful with grapes.

During their time in present-day Newfoundland, Leif's expedition made contact with the natives whom they referred to as Skraelings (which translates to "wretched ones" in Norse). There are several secondhand accounts of their meetings. Some contemporaries described trade between the peoples. Other accounts describe clashes where the Skraelings defeated the Viking explorers with long spears, while still others claim the Vikings dominated the natives. Regardless of the circumstances, it seems that the Vikings made contact of some kind. This happened around 1000, nearly five hundred years before Columbus famously sailed the ocean blue.

Eventually, in 1003, Leif set sail for home and arrived at Greenland with a ship full of timber.

In 1020, seventeen years later, the legendary Viking died. Many believe that Leif Erikson should receive more credit for his contributions in exploring the New World.

34. Which of the following best describes how the author generally presents the information?
    a. Chronological order
    b. Comparison-contrast
    c. Cause-effect
    d. Conclusion-premises

35. Which of the following is an opinion, rather than historical fact, expressed by the author?
    a. Leif Erikson was definitely the son of Erik the Red; however, historians debate the year of his birth.
    b. Leif Erikson's crew called the land Vinland since it was plentiful with grapes.
    c. Leif Erikson deserves more credit for his contributions in exploring the New World.
    d. Leif Erikson explored the Americas nearly five hundred years before Christopher Columbus.

36. Which of the following most accurately describes the author's main conclusion?
    a. Leif Erikson is a legendary Viking explorer.
    b. Leif Erikson deserves more credit for exploring America hundreds of years before Columbus.
    c. Spreading Christianity motivated Leif Erikson's expeditions more than any other factor.
    d. Leif Erikson contacted the natives nearly five hundred years before Columbus.

37. Which of the following best describes the author's intent in the passage?
    a. To entertain
    b. To inform
    c. To alert
    d. To suggest

38. Which of the following can be logically inferred from the passage?
    a. The Vikings disliked exploring the New World.
    b. Leif Erikson's banishment from Iceland led to his exploration of present-day Canada.
    c. Leif Erikson never shared his stories of exploration with the King of Norway.
    d. Historians have difficulty definitively pinpointing events in the Vikings' history.

Questions 39 & 40 are based on the following passage:

Why Should I Stop Smoking?

Smoking tobacco products is terribly destructive. A single cigarette contains over 4,000 chemicals, including 43 known carcinogens and 400 deadly toxins. Some of the most dangerous ingredients include tar, carbon monoxide, formaldehyde, ammonia, arsenic, and DDT. Smoking can cause numerous types of cancer including throat, mouth, nasal cavity, esophagus, stomach, pancreas, kidney, bladder, and cervical.

166

Cigarettes contain a drug called nicotine, one of the most addictive substances known to man. Addiction is defined as a compulsion to seek the substance despite negative consequences. According to the National Institute of Drug Abuse, nearly 35 million smokers expressed a desire to quit smoking in 2015; however, more than 85 percent of those addicts will not achieve their goal. Almost all smokers regret picking up that first cigarette. You would be wise to learn from their mistake if you have not yet started smoking.

According to the U.S. Department of Health and Human Services, 16 million people in the United States presently suffer from a smoking-related condition and nearly nine million suffer from a serious smoking-related illness. According to the Centers for Disease Control and Prevention (CDC), tobacco products cause nearly six million deaths per year. This number is projected to rise to over eight million deaths by 2030. Smokers, on average, die ten years earlier than their nonsmoking peers.

In the United States, local, state, and federal governments typically tax tobacco products, which leads to high prices. Nicotine addicts sometimes pay more for a pack of cigarettes than for a few gallons of gas. Additionally, smokers tend to stink. The smell of smoke is all-consuming and creates a pervasive nastiness. Smokers also risk staining their teeth and fingers with yellow residue from the tar.

Smoking is deadly, expensive, and socially unappealing. Clearly, smoking is not worth the risks.

39. Which of the following best describes the passage?
    a. Narrative
    b. Persuasive
    c. Expository
    d. Technical

40. Which of the following statements most accurately summarizes the passage?
    a. Tobacco is less healthy than many alternatives.
    b. Tobacco is deadly, expensive, and socially unappealing, and smokers would be much better off kicking the addiction.
    c. In the United States, local, state, and federal governments typically tax tobacco products, which leads to high prices.
    d. Tobacco products shorten smokers' lives by ten years and kill more than six million people per year.

Questions 41–45 are based upon the following passage:

How can I find Mr. Hyde?

"Did you ever come across a protégé of his—one Hyde?" He asked.

"Hyde?" repeated Lanyon. "No. Never heard of him. Since my time."

That was the amount of information that the lawyer carried back with him to the great, dark bed on which he tossed to and fro until the small hours of the morning began to grow large. It was a night of little ease to his toiling mind, toiling in mere darkness and besieged by questions.

Six o'clock struck on the bells of the church that was so conveniently near to Mr. Utterson's dwelling, and still he was digging at the problem. Hitherto it had touched him on the intellectual side alone; but; but now his imagination also was engaged, or rather enslaved; and as he lay and tossed in the gross darkness of the night in the curtained room, Mr. Enfield's tale went by before his mind in a scroll of lighted pictures. He would be aware of the great field of lamps in a nocturnal city; then of the figure of a man walking swiftly; then of a child running from the doctor's; and then these met, and that human Juggernaut trod the child down and passed on regardless of her screams. Or else he would see a room in a rich house, where his friend lay asleep, dreaming and smiling at his dreams; and then the door of that room would be opened, the curtains of the bed plucked apart, the sleeper recalled, and, lo! There would stand by his side a figure to whom power was given, and even at that dead hour he must rise and do its bidding. The figure in these two phrases haunted the lawyer all night; and if at anytime he dozed over, it was but to see it glide more stealthily through sleeping houses, or move the more swiftly, and still the more smoothly, even to dizziness, through wider labyrinths of lamplighted city, and at every street corner crush a child and leave her screaming. And still the figure had no face by which he might know it; even in his dreams it had no face, or one that baffled him and melted before his eyes; and thus there it was that there sprung up and grew apace in the lawyer's mind a singularly strong, almost an inordinate, curiosity to behold the features of the real Mr. Hyde. If he could but once set eyes on him, he thought the mystery would lighten and perhaps roll altogether away, as was the habit of mysterious things when well examined. He might see a reason for his friend's strange preference or bondage, and even for the startling clauses of the will. And at least it would be a face worth seeing: the face of a man who was without bowels of mercy: a face which had but to show itself to raise up, in the mind of the unimpressionable Enfield, a spirit of enduring hatred.

From that time forward, Mr. Utterson began to haunt the door in the by street of shops. In the morning before office hours, at noon when business was plenty of time scares, at night under the face of the full city moon, by all lights and at all hours of solitude or concourse, the lawyer was to be found on his chosen post.

"If he be Mr. Hyde," he had thought, "I should be Mr. Seek."

from Robert Louis Stevenson's *The Strange Case of Dr. Jekyll and Mr. Hyde*

41. What is the purpose of the use of repetition in the following passage?
It was a night of little ease to his toiling mind, toiling in mere darkness and besieged by questions.

    a. It serves as a demonstration of the mental state of Mr. Lanyon.
    b. It is reminiscent of the church bells that are mentioned in the story.
    c. It mimics Mr. Utterson's ambivalence.
    d. It emphasizes Mr. Utterson's anguish in failing to identify Hyde's whereabouts.

42. What is the setting of the story in this passage?
   a. In the city
   b. On the countryside
   c. In a jail
   d. In a mental health facility

43. What can one infer about the meaning of the word "Juggernaut" from the author's use of it in the passage?
   a. It is an apparition that appears at daybreak.
   b. It scares children.
   c. It is associated with space travel.
   d. Mr. Utterson finds it soothing.

44. What is the definition of the word *haunt* in the following passage?
   > From that time forward, Mr. Utterson began to haunt the door in the by street of shops. In the morning before office hours, at noon when business was plenty of time scares, at night under the face of the full city moon, by all lights and at all hours of solitude or concourse, the lawyer was to be found on his chosen post.

   a. To levitate
   b. To constantly visit
   c. To terrorize
   d. To daunt

45. The phrase *labyrinths of lamplighted city* contains an example of what?
   a. Hyperbole
   b. Simile
   c. Metaphor
   d. Alliteration

Extended Response

There are two passages below. Read both of the passages carefully all the way through. Then, choose which passage you think is better supported by evidence. In your response, be sure to use your own evidence from the passages. You will have forty-five minutes to plan, write, and edit your response. Your essay should be around 500 words.

Passage I

People who share their lives on social media sites are edging into dangerous territory. Social media sites such as Facebook, Instagram, and Snapchat are black holes for those easily addicted to validation and acceptance. Society should be wary of allowing their kids to have open access to social media sites.

So many people feel a sense of joy at being "liked" or having a certain amount of friends or comments on their pages. This feeling may lead to a false sense of acceptance by peers, and the feeling that one has accomplished something. Friends post vacations, what they ate for lunch, who they are dating, and pictures of themselves and their families. They say that if it's not on social media, it didn't happen. Sharing so much personal information is an invasion of privacy and could prove dangerous. They think sharing personal pictures and details invites predators, cyberbullying, and identity theft.

169

People should take care to stay away from social media and get their validation and acceptance from entities that truly matter, like from themselves or a higher being. Being outside and getting exercise is a good alternative to staring at a screen all day. Those who get out and expand their worlds will definitely experience happier lives.

Passage II

Although there are many negative side effects to social media, such as predatory accounts, cyberbullying, and identity theft, there are many positive sides to social media as well. Carrying around information 24/7 has its perks and can't be all bad—in fact, we are a society thriving on technology and connection. Social media can be seen as a good thing due to its connecting us with family and peers, its possibilities for political support, and its support for at-home businesses and marketers.

Social media is great for staying in touch with family and peers. Last year, when I moved to California, I had bouts of loneliness trying to cope without my family and friends. This is where Skype and Facebook came in handy—I could reach out to family and friends anytime I wanted, with just a click of a button!

Social media is also beneficial for giving and receiving political support. In 2011, young persons in the Egyptian Revolution used social media to form protests and request outside help. They used Twitter and YouTube to reach out to the world and let everyone what was going on with their events and the requests they made to their government. Social media was used as a platform for regular citizens to be heard by their government.

Another reasons social media is beneficial is because many men and women use it to start and maintain at-home businesses. The platforms of Facebook and YouTube are easy ways to set up shop, to create and events, and to create videos to reach out to a particular audience. People can Google certain terms, and those terms will bring them straight to the social media site they are looking for. According to SocialMediaStatsForAtHomeBusiness.org, 75 percent of businesses use social media to supplement their consumer market.

All in all, people should not be afraid of social media when it's able to bring so much opportunity to society. Staying in touch with family and friends, supporting political cries, and creating business opportunities are just some of the ways social media is beneficial to the community.

Mathematical Reasoning

1. $5.88 \times 3.2 =$
   a. 18.816
   b. 16.44
   c. 20.352
   d. 17

2. How will the following number be written in standard form: $(1 \times 10^4) + (3 \times 10^3) + (7 \times 10^1) + (8 \times 10^0)$
   a. 137
   b. 13,078
   c. 1,378
   d. 8,731

3. What is the value of the expression: $7^2 - 3 \times (4 + 2) + 15 \div 5$?

    a. 12.2

    b. 40.2

    c. 34

    d. 58.2

4. Four people split a bill. The first person pays for $\frac{1}{5}$, the second person pays for $\frac{1}{4}$, and the third person pays for $\frac{1}{3}$. What fraction of the bill does the fourth person pay?

    a. $\frac{13}{60}$

    b. $\frac{47}{60}$

    c. $\frac{1}{4}$

    d. $\frac{4}{15}$

5. A student gets an 85% on a test with 20 questions. How many answers did the student solve correctly?

    a. 15

    b. 16

    c. 17

    d. 18

6. What is $\frac{420}{98}$ rounded to the nearest integer?

    a. 4

    b. 3

    c. 5

    d. 6

7. If Danny takes 48 minutes to walk 3 miles, how long should it take him to walk 5 miles maintaining the same speed?

    a. 32 min

    b. 64 min

    c. 80 min

    d. 96 min

8. If $\sqrt{1 + x} = 4$, what is x?

    a. 10

    b. 15

    c. 20

    d. 25

9. $52.3 \times 10^{-3} =$

    a. 0.00523

    b. 0.0523

    c. 0.523

    d. 523

10. Which of the following is a factor of both $x^2 + 4x + 4$ and $x^2 - x - 6$?

    a. $x - 3$

    b. $x + 2$

    c. $x - 2$

    d. $x + 3$

11. Which of the following shows the correct result of simplifying the following expression:

$$(7n + 3n^3 + 3) + (8n + 5n^3 + 2n^4)$$

    a. $9n^4 + 15n - 2$

    b. $2n^4 + 5n^3 + 15n - 2$

    c. $9n^4 + 8n^3 + 15n$

    d. $2n^4 + 8n^3 + 15n + 3$

12. Which of the following inequalities is equivalent to $3 - \frac{1}{2}x \geq 2$?

    a. $x \geq 2$

    b. $x \leq 2$

    c. $x \geq 1$

    d. $x \leq 1$

13. For which of the following are $x = 4$ and $x = -4$ solutions?

    a. $x^2 + 16 = 0$

    b. $x^2 + 4x - 4 = 0$

    c. $x^2 - 2x - 2 = 0$

    d. $x^2 - 16 = 0$

14. What is the solution to the following system of equations?

$$x^2 - 2x + y = 8$$
$$x - y = -2$$

    a. $(-2, 3)$

    b. There is no solution.

    c. $(-2, 0)\ (1, 3)$

    d. $(-2, 0)\ (3, 5)$

15. A line passes through the point (1, 2) and crosses the y-axis at y = 1. Which of the following is an equation for this line?

    a. $y = 2x$

    b. $y = x + 1$

    c. $x + y = 1$

    d. $y = \frac{x}{2} - 2$

16. A company invests $50,000 in a building where they can produce saws. If the cost of producing one saw is $40, then which function expresses the amount of money the company pays? The variable y is the money paid and x is the number of saws produced.

    a. $y = 50,000x + 40$

    b. $y + 40 = x - 50,000$

    c. $y = 40x - 50,000$

    d. $y = 40x + 50,000$

17. If $x > 3$, then $\frac{x^2-6x+9}{x^2-x-6} =$

   a. $\frac{x+2}{x-3}$

   b. $\frac{x-2}{x-3}$

   c. $\frac{x-3}{x+3}$

   d. $\frac{x-3}{x+2}$

18. Is the following function even, odd, neither, or both?

$$y = \frac{1}{2}x^4 + 2x^2 - 6$$

   a. Even
   b. Odd
   c. Neither
   d. Both

19. An investment of $2,000 is made into an account with an annual interest rate of 5%, compounded continuously. What is the total value for the investment after eight years?

   a. $4,707
   b. $3,000
   c. $2,983.65
   d. $10, 919.63

20. What is the 42nd item in the pattern: ▲○○□ ▲○○□ ▲ ...?

   a. ○
   b. ▲
   c. □
   d. None of the above

21. For a group of 20 men, the median weight is 180 pounds and the range is 30 pounds. If each man gains 10 pounds, which of the following would be true?

   a. The median weight will increase, and the range will remain the same.
   b. The median weight and range will both remain the same.
   c. The median weight will stay the same, and the range will increase.
   d. The median weight and range will both increase.

22. Five students take a test. The scores of the first four students are 80, 85, 75, and 60. If the median score is 80, which of the following could NOT be the score of the fifth student?

   a. 60
   b. 80
   c. 85
   d. 100

23. Ten students take a test. Five students get a 50. Four students get a 70. If the average score is 55, what was the last student's score?

    a. 20

    b. 40

    c. 50

    d. 60

24. Given the value of a given stock at monthly intervals, which graph should be used to best represent the trend of the stock?

    a. Box plot

    b. Line plot

    c. Line graph

    d. Circle graph

25. A six-sided die is rolled. What is the probability that the roll is 1 or 2?

    a. $\frac{1}{6}$

    b. $\frac{1}{4}$

    c. $\frac{1}{3}$

    d. $\frac{1}{2}$

26. What is the probability of randomly picking the winner and runner-up from a race of 4 horses and distinguishing which is the winner?

    a. $\frac{1}{4}$

    b. $\frac{1}{2}$

    c. $\frac{1}{16}$

    d. $\frac{1}{12}$

27. A grocery store is selling individual bottles of water, and each bottle contains 750 milliliters of water. If 12 bottles are purchased, what conversion will correctly determine how many liters that customer will take home?

    a. 100 milliliters equals 1 liter

    b. 1,000 milliliters equals 1 liter

    c. 1,000 liters equals 1 milliliter

    d. 10 liters equals 1 milliliter

28. Which of the following statements is true about the two lines below?

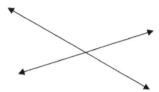

    a. The two lines are parallel but not perpendicular.
    b. The two lines are perpendicular but not parallel.
    c. The two lines are both parallel and perpendicular.
    d. The two lines are neither parallel nor perpendicular.

29. The perimeter of a 6-sided polygon is 56 cm. The length of three sides is 9 cm each. The length of two other sides is 8 cm each. What is the length of the missing side?
    a. 11 cm
    b. 12 cm
    c. 13 cm
    d. 10 cm

30. An equilateral triangle has a perimeter of 18 feet. If a square whose sides have the same length as one side of the triangle is built, what will be the area of the square?
    a. 6 square feet
    b. 36 square feet
    c. 256 square feet
    d. 1000 square feet

31. The area of a given rectangle is 24 centimeters. If the measure of each side is multiplied by 3, what is the area of the new figure?
    a. 48cm
    b. 72cm
    c. 216cm
    d. 13,824cm

32. Apples cost $2 each, while bananas cost $3 each. Maria purchased 10 fruits in total and spent $22. How many apples did she buy?
    a. 5
    b. 6
    c. 7
    d. 8

33. $(4x^2y^4)^{\frac{3}{2}}$ can be simplified to which of the following?
    a. $8x^3y^6$
    b. $4x^{\frac{5}{2}}y$
    c. $4xy$
    d. $32x^{\frac{7}{2}}y^{\frac{11}{2}}$

34. A line passes through the origin and through the point (-3, 4). What is the slope of the line?

a. $-\dfrac{4}{3}$

b. $-\dfrac{3}{4}$

c. $\dfrac{4}{3}$

d. $\dfrac{3}{4}$

35. $3\dfrac{2}{3} - 1\dfrac{4}{5} =$

a. $1\dfrac{13}{15}$

b. $\dfrac{14}{15}$

c. $2\dfrac{2}{3}$

d. $\dfrac{4}{5}$

36. What is the value of $x^2 - 2xy + 2y^2$ when $x = 2, y = 3$?

a. 8

b. 10

c. 12

d. 14

37. The square and circle have the same center. The circle has a radius of r. What is the area of the shaded region?

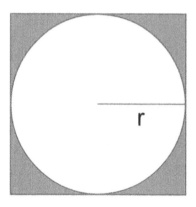

a. $r^2 - \pi r^2$

b. $4r^2 - 2\pi r$

c. $(4 - \pi)r^2$

d. $(\pi - 1)r^2$

38. An equation for the line passing through the origin and the point $(2, 1)$ is

    a. $y = 2x$

    b. $y = \frac{1}{2}x$

    c. $y = x - 2$

    d. $2y = x + 1$

39. What are the coordinates of the two points marked with green dots on this coordinate plane?

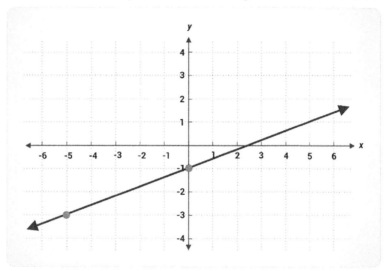

    a. (-3, -5) and (-1, 0)

    b. (5, 3) and (0, 1)

    c. (-5, -3) and (0, -1)

    d. (-3, -5) and (0, -1)

40. What is the value of x for the right triangle shown below?

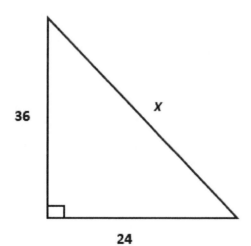

    a. 43.3

    b. 26.8

    c. 42.7

    d. 44.1

41. A cube has sides that are 7 inches long. What is the cube's volume?
    a. $49in^3$
    b. $343in^3$
    c. $294in^3$
    d. $28in^3$

No Calculator Questions

42. 3.4+2.35+4=
    a. 5.35
    b. 9.2
    c. 9.75
    d. 10.25

43. $\frac{3}{25} =$
    a. 0.15
    b. 0.1
    c. 0.9
    d. 0.12

44. 6 is 30% of what number?
    a. 18
    b. 20
    c. 24
    d. 26

45. What is the value of the following expression?
$$\sqrt{8^2 + 6^2}$$

    a. 14
    b. 10
    c. 9
    d. 100

45. $864 \div 36 =$
    a. 24
    b. 25
    c. 34
    d. 18

Science

Passage 1

Questions 1–5 pertain to Passage 1:

Scientists use the scientific method to investigate a theory or solve a problem. It includes four steps: observation, hypothesis, experiment, and conclusion. Observation occurs when the scientist uses one of their senses to identify what they want to study. A hypothesis is a conclusive sentence about what the scientist wants to research. It generally includes an explanation for the observations, can be tested experimentally, and predicts the outcome. The experiment includes the parameters for the testing that will occur. The conclusion will state whether or not the hypothesis was supported.

Scientist A would like to know how sunlight affects the growth of a plant. She says that more sunlight will cause the plant to grow faster. She sets up her experimental groups and tests her hypothesis over 11 days.

Figure 1 below shows the experimental data Scientist A collected over 11 days.

Length and height of plants in the sunlight

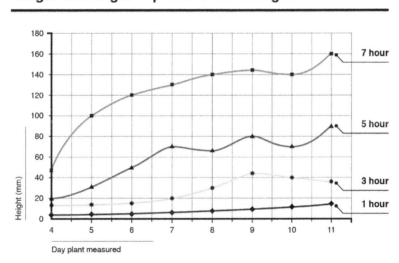

Figure 2 below represents the process of photosynthesis that occurs in plants.

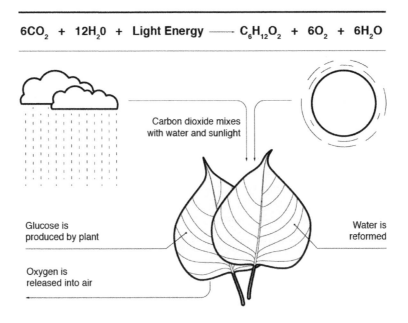

$$6CO_2 \ + \ 12H_2O \ + \ \text{Light Energy} \longrightarrow C_6H_{12}O_2 \ + \ 6O_2 \ + \ 6H_2O$$

1. What is her hypothesis?
    a. More sunlight will cause the plant to grow faster.
    b. She will test her theory over 11 days.
    c. How sunlight affects plant growth.
    d. Plants do not grow well with one hour of sunlight per day.

2. How many experimental groups does she have?
    a. 1
    b. 3
    c. 4
    d. 11

3. What type of chart is represented in the first figure?
    a. Bar graph
    b. Line graph
    c. Pie chart
    d. Pictogram

4. What part of the photosynthesis reaction is provided directly by sunlight?
    a. Light energy
    b. H_2O
    c. CO_2
    d. Glucose

5. What should her conclusion be based on her experimental data?
    a. 5 hours of sunlight is optimal for plant growth.
    b. Plants should only be measured for 11 days.
    c. Less sunlight is better for plant growth.
    d. Providing plants with more sunlight makes them grow bigger.

Passage 2

Questions 6–10 pertain to Passage 2:

The periodic table contains all known 118 chemical elements. The first 98 elements are found naturally while the remaining were synthesized by scientists. The elements are ordered according to the number of protons they contain, also known as their atomic number. For example, hydrogen has an atomic number of one and is found in the top left corner of the periodic table, whereas radon has an atomic number of 86 and is found closer on the right side of the periodic table, several rows down. The rows are called periods and the columns are called groups. The elements are arranged by similar chemical properties.

Each chemical element represents an individual atom. When atoms are linked together, they form molecules. The smallest molecule contains just two atoms, but molecules can also be very large and contain hundreds of atoms. In order to find the mass of a molecule, the atomic mass of each individual atom in the molecule must be added together.

Figure 1 below depicts the trends and commonalities between the elements that can be seen in the periodic table.

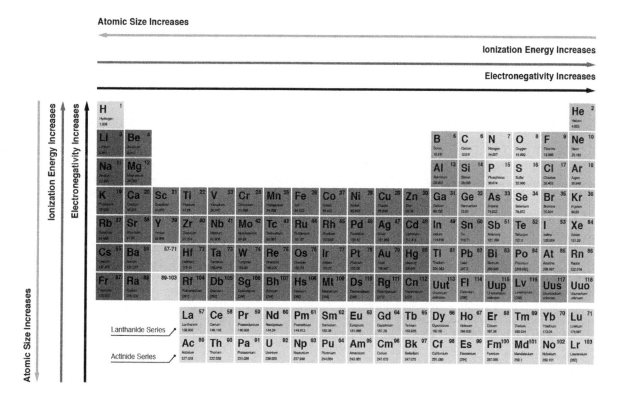

Figure 2 below shows what the information in each element's box represents.

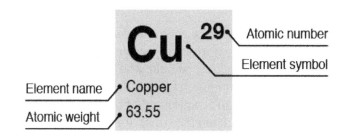

Figure 3 below shows the periodic of table with color coding according to the groups and periods.

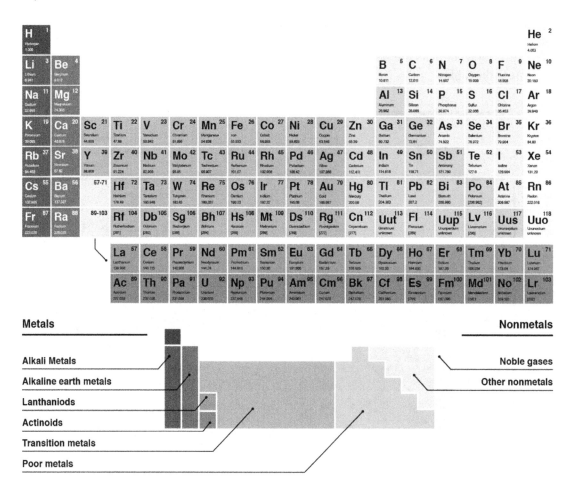

6. What is the atomic mass of NaCl?
   a. 23
   b. 58.5
   c. 35.5
   d. 71

7. Which of the following elements is most electronegative?
   a. Ununoctium (Uuo)
   b. Francium (Fr)
   c. Hydrogen (H)
   d. Helium (He)

8. What is the full name of the element Cr?
   a. Chromium
   b. Copper
   c. Chlorine
   d. Curium

9. Which element has the fewest number of protons?
   a. Radon (Rn)
   b. Boron (B)
   c. Nitrogen (N)
   d. Hydrogen (H)

10. Scientist A needs a noble gas for her experiment. Which of these elements should she consider using?
   a. Nitrogen (N)
   b. Radon (Rn)
   c. Copper (Cu)
   d. Boron (B)

Passage 3

Questions 11–15 pertain to Passage 3:

Physical characteristics are controlled by genes. Each gene has two alleles, or variations. Generally, one allele is more dominant than the other allele and when one of each allele is present on the gene, the physical trait of the dominant allele will be expressed. The allele that is not expressed is called the recessive allele. Recessive alleles are expressed only when both alleles present on the gene are the recessive allele.

Punnett squares are diagrams that can predict the outcome of crossing different traits. In these diagrams, dominant alleles are represented by uppercase letters and recessive alleles are represented by lowercase letters.

Scientist A wants to grow white flowered plants and is doing a series of crossbreeding experiments. She had each plant genetically tested so she knows which alleles comprise each plant. The dominant flowers are red (A) and the recessive allele (a) produces white flowers.

Figure 1 below represents the different flowers that underwent crossbreeding during Round #1A

Round #1A

Crossbreeding #1A			Crossbreeding #2A			Crossbreeding #2A		
	A	a		a	a		a	a
A	AA	Aa	A	Aa	Aa	A	Aa	Aa
A	AA	Aa	A	Aa	Aa	a	aa	aa

Figure 2 below represents the number of flowers that were red and white after the first round of crossbreeding experiments.

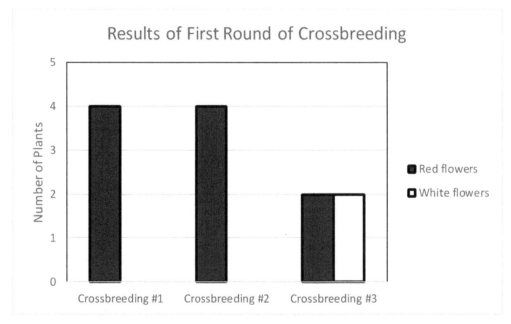

During her second round of crossbreeding, she adds in a plant of unknown genetic makeup with red flowers. She crosses it with a white-flowering plant. The results of her experiment are represented in the next figure.

Figure 3 represents the genetic results from the second round of crossbreeding.

Round #2		
	a	a
?	Aa	Aa
?	aa	aa

Scientist A takes offspring plants from Round #1A and crossbreeds them with each other and calls this Round #1B.

Figure 4 below represents the results of crossbreeding from Round #1B.

Round #1B

Crossbreeding #1B			Crossbreeding #2B			Crossbreeding #2B		
	A	a		A	a		a	a
A	AA	Aa	A	AA	Aa	a	aa	aa
A	AA	Aa	a	Aa	aa	a	aa	aa

11. Crossbreeding which two plants will give her the highest likelihood of obtaining some white plants right away in Round #1A?
   a. AA × Aa
   b. Aa × aa
   c. AA × aa
   d. AA × AA

12. What percentage of plants are white after the first crossbreeding reactions?
   a. 12
   b. 50
   c. 16.7
   d. 25

13. What is the genetic makeup of the unknown plant from the second round of crossbreeding?
   a. aa
   b. Aa
   c. AA
   d. Cannot be determined

14. From which group of crossbreeding in Round #1B can she obtain 100% white flowers by the second generation?
   a. They are all equal.
   b. 1B
   c. 2B
   d. 3B

15. Which of her five senses did she use for the observation step of the scientific method here?
   a. Sight
   b. Smell
   c. Touch
   d. Hearing

Passage 4

Questions 16–20 pertain to Passage 4:

Rainforests cover approximately 6% of the Earth's surface. Tropical rainforests are found in five major areas of the world: Central America, South America, Central Africa, Asia stretching from India to islands in the Pacific Ocean, and Australia. All of these areas are warm and wet areas within ten degrees of the equator. They do not have a substantial dry season during the year.

Rainforests are large areas of jungle that get an abundance of rain. They comprise four layers, each with unique characteristics. The emergent layer is the highest layer and is made up of the tops of the tall trees. There is very good sunlight in this layer. The canopy layer is the next layer, just under the emergent layer. Here, there is some sun but not as much as the emergent layer. The next layer is the understory layer. This layer does not receive very much sunlight. The plants in this layer need to grow very large leaves to reach the sun. The bottom-most layer is the forest floor. Sunlight generally does not reach this layer, so plants do not grow here.

Figure 1 below represents the different layers of the rainforest.

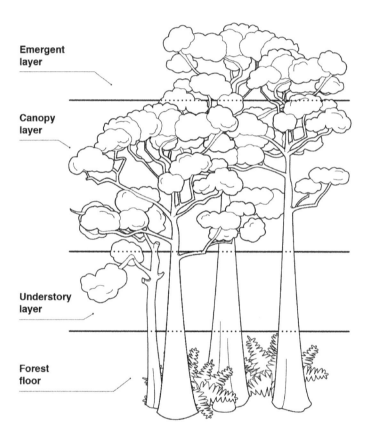

Figure 2 below is a map of the rainforests on Earth and a map of Central America.

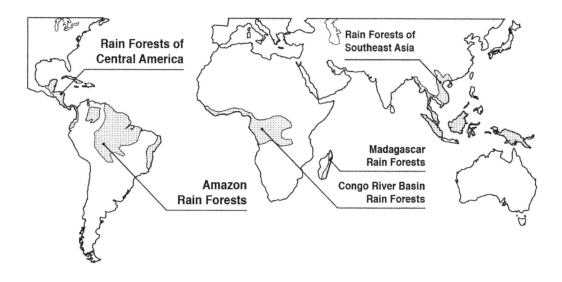

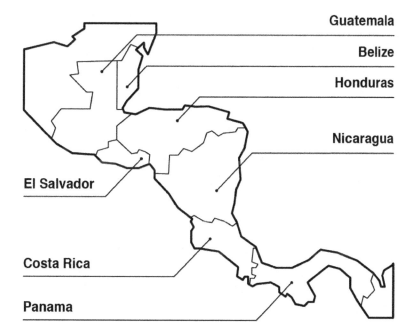

16. What essential part of photosynthesis, which is necessary for plant growth, is lacking on the forest floor and does not allow for plants to grow?
   a. Carbon
   b. Water
   c. Oxygen
   d. Sunlight

17. Which is a country in Central America that contains a rainforest?
    a. India
    b. Panama
    c. Madagascar
    d. Brazil

18. In which layer of the rainforest would birds fly around the most?
    a. Forest floor
    b. Understory layer
    c. Emergent layer
    d. Canopy layer

19. Giant taro plants have the largest leaves in the world that are approximately ten feet in length. In which layer of the rainforest do they reside?
    a. Emergent layer
    b. Canopy layer
    c. Forest floor
    d. Understory layer

20. Which of these plants, based on their listed requirements, would thrive in a rainforest climate?
    a. Giant water lily: warm temperatures, wet environment, has ability to grown large leaves
    b. Cactus: dry environment, long, hot season for growth
    c. Pine tree: dry and sandy soil, lots of sunlight
    d. Black-eyed sun: very hot temperatures, slightly moist soil

Passage 5

Questions 21–25 pertain to Passage 5:

An eclipse occurs when the light from one object in the solar system is completely or partially blocked by another object in the solar system. In 2017, the Earth was a part of two different types of eclipses. One was a solar eclipse, which occurs when the moon passes between the Sun and the Earth and blocks the Sun's light, making it dark during the daytime for several minutes. A total solar eclipse occurs when the moon completely covers the Sun. A partial solar eclipse occurs when the moon only covers part of the Sun. Solar eclipses should not be looked at directly because the Sun's rays can damage a person's eyes even though they appear to be dim while the eclipse is happening. Special viewing devices can be used to look at a solar eclipse indirectly, such as a pinhole camera facing away from the eclipse that allows light from the eclipse to pass through a hole in a piece of cardboard and its image to be reflected on a piece of white paper.

The other type of eclipse that the Earth was a part of was a lunar eclipse. This type of eclipse occurs when the moon passes behind the Earth, into its shadow. The moon is illuminated by the light of the sun, so when it is in the Earth's shadow, the moon becomes dim for a few hours during the night. This type of eclipse is safe to look at without any protection for your eyes.

Figure 1 below represents a solar eclipse.

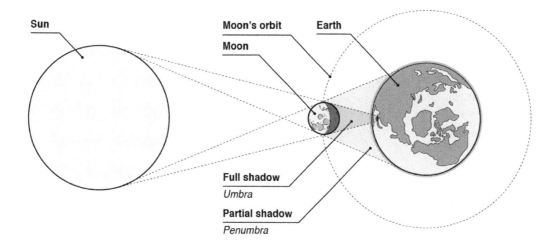

Figure 2 below represents a lunar eclipse.

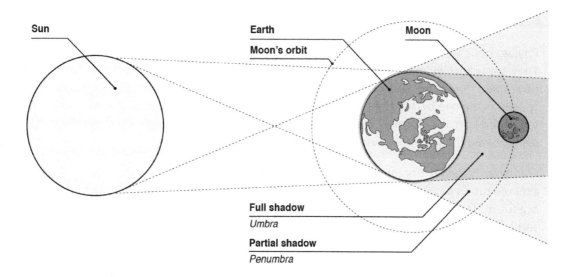

21. Which apparatus would be best to use to look at a solar eclipse?
    a. A telescope facing the eclipse
    b. A pinhole camera facing away from the eclipse
    c. Sunglasses facing the eclipse
    d. Binoculars facing the eclipse

22. What type of eclipse occurs when the moon comes between the Earth and Sun and covers the Sun's light completely?
    a. Total solar eclipse
    b. Partial lunar eclipse
    c. Total lunar eclipse
    d. Partial solar eclipse

23. What object in the solar system becomes dim during a lunar eclipse?
    a. Sun
    b. Earth
    c. Moon
    d. Earth and moon

24. Which type of eclipse could you observe directly using a telescope?
    a. Neither solar nor lunar
    b. Lunar only
    c. Both solar and lunar
    d. Solar only

25. Which type of eclipse is viewed during the daytime?
    a. Both solar and lunar
    b. Solar only
    c. Partial lunar
    d. Total lunar

Passage 6

Questions 26–30 pertain to Passage 6:

Phylogenetic trees are diagrams that map out the proposed evolutionary history of a species. They are branching diagrams that make it easy to see how scientists believe certain species developed from other species. The most recent proposed common ancestor between two species is the one before their lineages branch in the diagram. These diagrams do not attempt to include specific information about physical traits that were thought to be retained or disappeared during the evolutionary process.

Cladograms classify organisms based on their proposed common ancestry but are focused on their common physical traits. Branching points on these diagrams represent when a group of organisms is thought to have developed a new trait. Analogous features are those that have the same function but were not derived from a common ancestor. Homologous features have anatomical similarities, even if the function is no longer the same, due to a proposed common ancestor.

Figure 1 below is a phylogenetic tree of the Carnivora order.

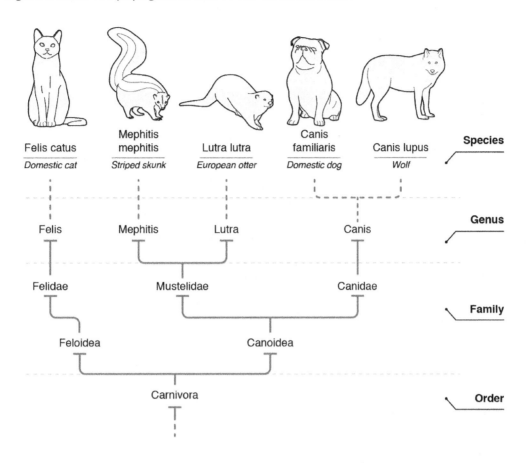

Figure 2 below is a cladogram.

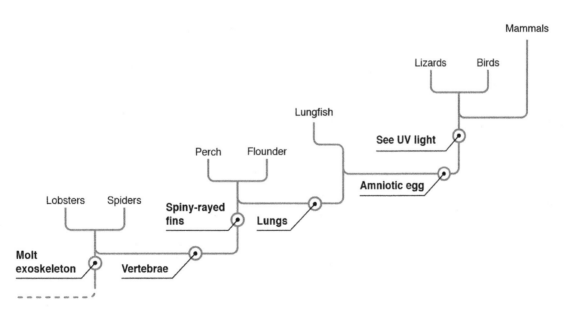

Figure 3 below shows a homologous feature between four different species with a proposed common ancestor.

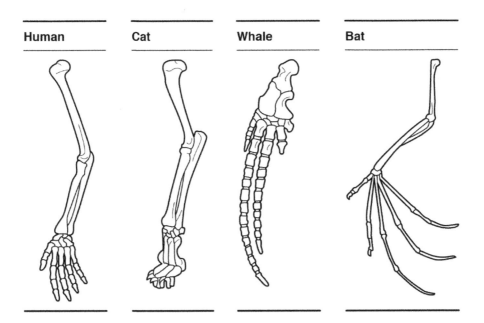

26. Which tool would you use to find out when a common ancestor of two species supposedly developed lungs?
    a. Phylogenetic tree
    b. Cladogram
    c. Punnett square
    d. Photographs

27. According to the earlier details, how are human arms and whale fins related?
    a. They are homologous structures from a common ancestor.
    b. They both have the same number of bones.
    c. They are analogous features.
    d. They are both covered in the same type of skin.

28. According to Figure 1, what common ancestry group do the striped skunk and European otter share?
    a. Mephitis
    b. Felidae
    c. Canidae
    d. Mustelidae

29. What trait do lizards and birds have in common according to Figure 2?
    a. Both see UV light
    b. Both have spiny-rayed fins
    c. Both molt an exoskeleton
    d. They do not have any traits in common.

30. According to Figure 1, at what level of organization are domestic cats and wolves related?
    a. Family
    b. Genus
    c. Order
    d. Species

Passage 7

Questions 31–35 pertain to Passage 7:

Scientists often use an assay called an enzyme-linked immunosorbent assay, or ELISA, to quantify specific substances within a larger sample. An ELISA works based on the specificity of an antibody to an antigen. One type of ELISA is called a sandwich ELISA. In this type of ELISA, a plate is coated with a capture antibody that adheres the antigen in the sample when it is added. Then the primary antibody is added and sticks to any antigen bound to the capture antibody. Next, a secondary antibody is added. Once it attaches to the primary antibody, it releases a colored tag that can be detected by a piece of laboratory equipment. If more color is released, it is indicative of more antigen having been present in the sample.

Figure 1 below describes how a sandwich ELISA works.

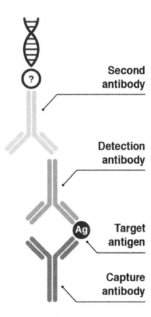

The cytokine protein IL-1β is a marker of inflammation in the body. Scientist A took samples from different locations within the body to find out where there was elevated inflammation in a patient.

193

Figure 2 below is a picture of the ELISA plate from Scientist A's experiment.

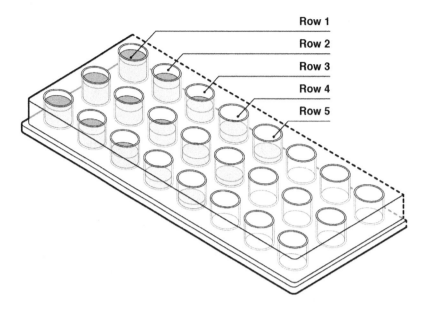

Figure 3 below is a graph of the results of Scientist A's experiment.

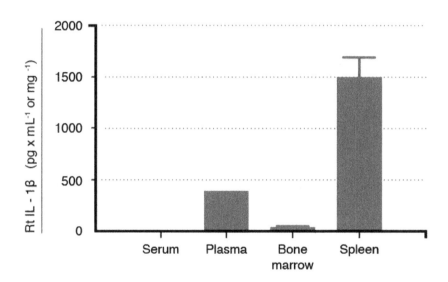

31. Which step of the ELISA allows for the color to be released for detection of the antigen?
    a. Addition of the antigen
    b. Addition of the primary antibody
    c. The presence of the capture antibody
    d. Addition of the secondary antibody

32. According to Figure 2, which row had the largest amount of antigen in the sample?
    a. Row 2
    b. Row 1
    c. Row 5
    d. Row 3

33. According to the ELISA results in Figure 3, which area of the body had the most inflammation?
    a. Serum
    b. Plasma
    c. Spleen
    d. Bone marrow

34. Which two antibodies sandwich the antigen in a sandwich ELISA?
    a. Capture antibody and secondary antibody
    b. Capture antibody and primary antibody
    c. Primary antibody and secondary antibody
    d. Two units of the secondary antibody

35. What is the purpose of an ELISA?
    a. Quantify specific substances within a larger sample
    b. Quantify all substances within a larger sample
    c. To create a colorful pattern with the samples
    d. To develop different antibodies

Passage 8

Questions 36–40 pertain to Passage 8:

> Natural selection is the idea that certain traits make an individual have longer survival and higher reproduction rates than other individuals. It is based on the **phenotype**, or physical appearance, of the individual and not the **genotype**, or genetic makeup. There are three ways in which a phenotype can change due to natural selection. Directional selection occurs when one extreme of a phenotype is favored. Disruptive selection occurs when both extremes of a phenotype are favored. Stabilizing selection occurs when an intermediate phenotype is favored over either extreme phenotype.

> *Scenario 1:* Mice live in an environment that has a mix of light and dark colored rocks. To avoid predators, the mice with intermediate color fur survive longer and produce more offspring.

> *Scenario 2:* The Galapagos Islands experienced a drought and large, tough seeds became abundant. Finches developed large beaks to break up these seeds.

> *Scenario 3:* In Cameroon, seeds are either large or small. Finches in Cameroon have either large beaks or small beaks. They are not found with medium-sized beaks.

36. What type of selection is described in Scenario 1?
    a. Stabilizing selection
    b. Directional selection
    c. Disruptive selection
    d. Color selection

37. What type of selection is described in Scenario 2?
   a. Beak-type
   b. Disruptive
   c. Stabilizing
   d. Directional

38. Why would it be hard for small-beaked finches in the Galapagos Island to survive after the drought?
   a. Too much sand got caught in the small beaks
   b. Beaks would not be able to break up large seeds
   c. Large-beaked finches would attack them
   d. Two extreme phenotypes can never be selected by natural selection

39. What type of selection is described in Scenario 3?
   a. Stabilizing
   b. Directional
   c. Disruptive
   d. Beak-type

40. Which statement is true about natural selection?
   a. Individuals are selected based on their genotype.
   b. An extreme phenotype is always selected.
   c. It only occurs after a drought.

d. Individuals are selected based on phenotypes that are advantageous for survival and reproduction.

Social Studies

1. What's the term for the ability of a ruling body to influence the actions, behavior, and attitude of a person or group of people?
   a. Politics
   b. Power
   c. Authority
   d. Legitimacy

2. Which of the following is NOT a shared characteristic sufficient to form a nation?
   a. Culture and traditions
   b. History
   c. Sovereignty
   d. Beliefs and religion

Question 3 is based on the following passage:

> Upon this, one has to remark that men ought either to be well treated or crushed, because they can avenge themselves of lighter injuries, of more serious ones they cannot; therefore the injury that is to be done to a man ought to be of such a kind that one does not stand in fear of revenge.
>
> From Niccolo Machiavelli's *The Prince*, 1513

3. What advice is Machiavelli giving to the prince?
   a. Lightly injured enemies will overthrow the prince.
   b. Seek to injure everyone you meet.
   c. Hurting people is always the correct course of action.
   d. If you are going to cause an enemy some injury, ensure the injury is fatal.

Question 4 is based on the following passage:

> The creed which accepts as the foundation of morals, Utility, or the Greatest-Happiness Principle, holds that actions are right in proportion as they tend to promote happiness, wrong as they tend to produce the reverse of happiness. By happiness is intended pleasure, and the absence of pain; by unhappiness, pain, and the privation of pleasure.
>
> The utilitarian morality does recognise in human beings the power of sacrificing their own greatest good for the good of others. It only refuses to admit that the sacrifice is itself a good. A sacrifice which does not increase, or tend to increase, the sum total of happiness, it considers as wasted.
>
> From John Stuart Mill's *Utilitarianism*, 1861

4. What is the meaning of the "Utility"?
   a. Actions should be judged based on the net total of pleasure.
   b. Actions requiring sacrifice can never be valuable.
   c. Actions promoting sacrifice that increase happiness are more valuable than actions that only increase happiness.
   d. Actions can be valuable even if the pain outweighs the pleasure.

Question 5 is based on the following passage:

> The history of all hitherto existing society is the history of class struggles.
>
> Freeman and slave, patrician and plebeian, lord and serf, guildmaster and journeyman, in a word, oppressor and oppressed, stood in constant opposition to one another, carried on an uninterrupted, now hidden, now open fight, that each time ended, either in the revolutionary reconstitution of society at large, or in the common ruin of the contending classes.
>
> Let the ruling classes tremble at a Communistic revolution. The proletarians have nothing to lose but their chains. They have a world to win.
>
> Workingmen of all countries unite!
>
> Karl Marx and Friedrich Engels, *The Communist Manifesto,* 1848

5. What's the main idea presented in the excerpt?
   a. Working men are morally superior to the ruling class.
   b. Every society will come to an end at some point.
   c. History is defined by class struggle, and working men must now unite and fight the ruling class to gain freedom.
   d. Working men are in the same position as the slave, plebeian, serf, and journeyman.

Question 6 is based on the following image:

Spectrum of Political Ideologies

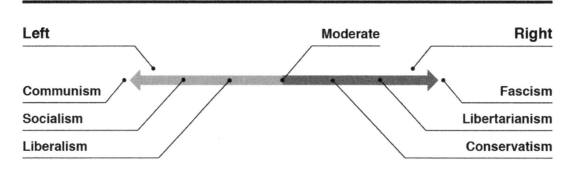

6. Which of the following represents the ideology that advocates for the most radical government intervention to achieve social and economic equality?
    a. Socialism
    b. Liberalism
    c. Libertarianism
    d. Fascism

7. Which of the following represents the ideology that prioritizes stability and traditional institutions within a culture?
    a. Socialism
    b. Liberalism
    c. Conservatism
    d. Libertarianism

8. The central government established under the Articles of Confederation held which of the following powers?
    a. The power to impose taxes
    b. The power to declare war
    c. The power to regulate trade
    d. The power to enforce laws enacted by Congress

Question 9 is based on the following diagram:

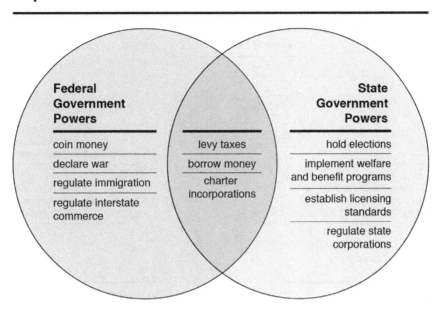

Separation of Powers

Federal Government Powers	levy taxes	State Government Powers
coin money	borrow money	hold elections
declare war	charter incorporations	implement welfare and benefit programs
regulate immigration		establish licensing standards
regulate interstate commerce		regulate state corporations

9. Which of the following terms best describes the missing title?
   a. Reserved powers
   b. Implied powers
   c. Delegated powers
   d. Concurrent powers

Question 10 is based on the following passage:

> Ambition must be made to counteract ambition. The interest of the man must be connected with the constitutional rights of the place. It may be a reflection on human nature, that such devices should be necessary to control the abuses of government. But what is government itself, but the greatest of all reflections on human nature?
>
> If men were angels, no government would be necessary. If angels were to govern men, neither external nor internal controls on government would be necessary. In framing a government which is to be administered by men over men, the great difficulty lies in this: you must first enable the government to control the governed; and in the next place oblige it to control itself.
>
> Alexander Hamilton or James Madison, aka *Publius*, "Federalist No. 50," 1788

10. What is the main idea presented in the excerpt?
   a. Men are inherently immoral and abusive.
   b. The best form of government is the type that angels would construct.
   c. Government reflects human nature.
   d. An effective government requires a separation of powers to regulate itself.

Question 11 is based on the following diagram:

Checks and Balances

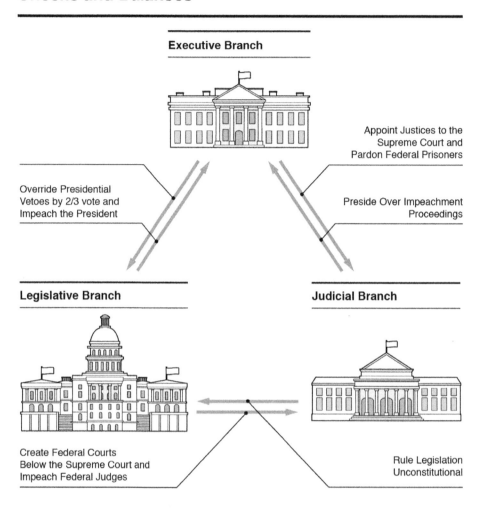

Executive Branch

Appoint Justices to the Supreme Court and Pardon Federal Prisoners

Override Presidential Vetoes by 2/3 vote and Impeach the President

Preside Over Impeachment Proceedings

Legislative Branch

Judicial Branch

Create Federal Courts Below the Supreme Court and Impeach Federal Judges

Rule Legislation Unconstitutional

11. Which of the following answer choices best completes the diagram?
    a. Impeach congressmen and veto legislation
    b. Call special sessions of Congress and refuse to enforce laws
    c. Call special sessions of Congress and veto legislation
    d. Impeach congressmen and refuse to enforce laws

12. What amendment guarantees American citizens the right to keep and bear arms?
    a. First Amendment
    b. Second Amendment
    c. Third Amendment
    d. Fourth Amendment

Question 13 is based on the following table:

Presidential Election of 1824			
Candidate	Electoral Votes	Popular Votes	State Votes in the House of Representatives
Andrew Jackson	99	153,544	7
John Quincy Adams	84	108,740	13
William H. Crawford	41	46,618	4
Henry Clay	37	47,136	0

13. Who won the presidential election of 1824?
    a. Andrew Jackson
    b. John Quincy Adams
    c. William H. Crawford
    d. Henry Clay

14. What electoral system can result in a second round of voting commonly referred to as a runoff?
    a. Majority systems
    b. Plurality systems
    c. Single transferable systems
    d. Party list systems

15. In international relations, which of the following is NOT a basic tenet of realism?
    a. States are the central actors.
    b. States act rationally to advance their self-interest.
    c. States should seek to form international organizations to increase global cooperation and respond to international issues.
    d. All states are interested in maintaining or expanding their power as a means of self-preservation.

16. How did the outcome of the French and Indian War impact the life of American colonists?
    a. The colonies expanded west of the Allegheny Mountains.
    b. Great Britain imposed taxes on the colonies to pay off the British war debt.
    c. A lasting peace developed between the colonists and Native Americans.
    d. The power of self-government increased in the colonies.

Question 17 is based on the following passage:

We hold these Truths to be self-evident: that all Men are created equal; that they are endowed by their creator with certain inalienable rights; that among these are life, liberty, and the pursuit of happiness: that to secure these rights, governments are instituted among men, deriving their just powers from the consent of the governed; that whenever any form of government becomes destructive of these ends, it is the right of the people to alter or abolish it, and to institute new government, laying its foundation on such principles, and organizing its powers in such form, as to them shall seem most likely to affect their safety and happiness.

Prudence indeed will dictate that governments long established should not be changed for light and transient causes; and accordingly all experience hath shown that mankind are more disposed to suffer while evils are sufferable, than to right themselves by abolishing the forms to which they are accustomed. But when a long train of abuses and usurpations begun at a distinguished period and pursuing invariably the same object, evinces a design to reduce them under absolute despotism, it is their right, it is their duty to throw off such government, and to provide new guards for their future security

Declaration of Independence, adopted July 4, 1776

17. What is the main purpose of the excerpt?
    a. Provide a justification for revolution when the government infringes on "certain inalienable rights"
    b. Provide specific evidence of the "train of abuses"
    c. Provide an argument why "all Men are created equal"
    d. Provide an analysis of the importance of "life, liberty, and the pursuit of happiness"

Question 18 is based on the following map:

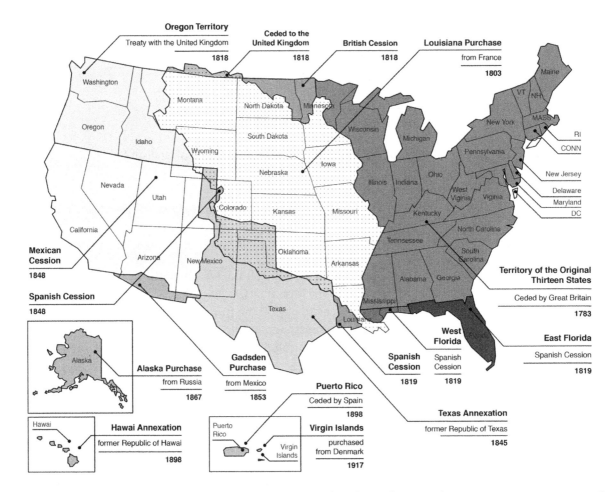

18. What current state did the United States gain through military force with a non-native nation-state?
    a. Nebraska
    b. Missouri
    c. Alaska
    d. Nevada

Question 19 is based on the following passage:

> Now, therefore I, Abraham Lincoln, President of the United States, by virtue of the power in me vested as Commander-in-Chief, of the Army and Navy of the United States in time of actual armed rebellion against the authority and government of the United States, and as a fit and necessary war measure for suppressing said rebellion...
>
> And by virtue of the power, and for the purpose aforesaid, I do order and declare that all persons held as slaves within said designated States, and parts of States, are, and henceforward shall be free; and that the Executive government of the United States, including the military and naval authorities thereof, will recognize and maintain the freedom of said persons.
>
> President Abraham Lincoln, Emancipation Proclamation, January 1, 1863

19. How does President Lincoln justify freeing the slaves in designated areas of the South?
    a. Emancipation is necessary since slavery is evil.
    b. Emancipation is necessary to boost the morale of the North.
    c. Emancipation is necessary to punish for the South seceding from the Union.
    d. Emancipation is necessary to strengthen the war effort of the North.

20. What was a consequence of the industrialization that followed the Civil War?
    a. Decreased immigration
    b. Increased urbanization
    c. Decreased socioeconomic inequality
    d. Increased rights for workers

21. Which of the following best describes how the Treaty of Versailles contributed to the outbreak of World War II?
    a. Forced Germany to assume responsibility for all damage incurred during the war and pay billions of dollars in reparations.
    b. Failed to adequately end the violence of World War I.
    c. Left large tracts of territory unclaimed by any nation-state.
    d. Created the League of Nations.

Question 22 is based on the following passage:

Hand in hand with this we must frankly recognize the overbalance of population in our industrial centers and, by engaging on a national scale in a redistribution, endeavor to provide a better use of the land for those best fitted for the land. The task can be helped by definite efforts to raise the values of agricultural products and with this the power to purchase the output of our cities. It can be helped by preventing realistically the tragedy of the growing loss through foreclosure of our small homes and our farms. It can be helped by insistence that the Federal, State, and local governments act forthwith on the demand that their cost be drastically reduced. It can be helped by the unifying of relief activities which today are often scattered, uneconomical, and unequal. It can be helped by national planning for and supervision of all forms of transportation and of communications and other utilities which have a definitely public character. There are many ways in which it can be helped, but it can never be helped merely by talking about it. We must act and act quickly.

Finally, in our progress toward a resumption of work we require two safeguards against a return of the evils of the old order: there must be a strict supervision of all banking and credits and investments, so that there will be an end to speculation with other people's money; and there must be provision for an adequate but sound currency.

President Franklin D. Roosevelt, Inaugural Address, March 4, 1933

22. Which of the following best describes President Roosevelt's underlying approach to government?
    a. Government must be focused on redistribution of land.
    b. Government must "act and act quickly" to intervene and regulate the economy.
    c. Government must exercise "strict supervision of all banking."
    d. Government must prevent the "growing loss through foreclosure."

Question 23 is based on the following passage:

What, to the American slave, is your 4th of July? I answer: a day that reveals to him, more than all other days in the year, the gross injustice and cruelty to which he is the constant victim. To him, your celebration is a sham; your boasted liberty, an unholy license; your national greatness, swelling vanity; your sounds of rejoicing are empty and heartless; your denunciations of tyrants, brass fronted impudence; your shouts of liberty and equality, hollow mockery; your prayers and hymns, your sermons and thanksgivings, with all your religious parade, and solemnity, are, to him, mere bombast, fraud, deception, impiety, and hypocrisy—a thin veil to cover up crimes which would disgrace a nation of savages. There is not a nation on the earth guilty of practices, more shocking and bloody, than are the people of these United States, at this very hour.

Frederick Douglass, "What to the Slave is the 4th of July?" July 5, 1852

23. What is the specific hypocrisy that Douglass repudiates?
    a. The Declaration of Independence declared that all men are created equal, but Thomas Jefferson owned slaves.
    b. Americans are free, but they do not value their freedom.
    c. The Fourth of July is a celebration about freedom, and slavery remained legal in the United States.
    d. The United States is a Christian nation, but American traditions contradict their faith.

Question 24 is based on the following passage:

> May it please your honor, I shall never pay a dollar of your unjust penalty. All the stock in trade I possess is a $10,000 debt, incurred by publishing my paper—The Revolution—four years ago, the sole object of which was to educate all women to do precisely as I have done, rebel against your man-made, unjust, unconstitutional forms of law, that tax, fine, imprison and hang women, while they deny them the right of representation in the government; and I shall work on with might and main to pay every dollar of that honest debt, but not a penny shall go to this unjust claim. And I shall earnestly and persistently continue to urge all women to the practical recognition of the old revolutionary maxim, that "Resistance to tyranny is obedience to God."

> *An Account of the Proceedings on the Trial of Susan B. Anthony on the Charge of Illegal Voting,* 1874.

24. What is the main idea presented in the excerpt?
    a. Taxation without representation is tyranny.
    b. Domestic abuse and violence against women is the cause of tyranny.
    c. Anthony cannot pay her fine due to debt accumulated from fighting for women's rights.
    d. Denying women the right to vote is tyranny and must be resisted.

25. Which of the following most accurately describes the platform of Ronald Reagan?
    a. Christianity, optimism, and preserving social safety nets
    b. Increased defense spending, deregulation, and tax cuts
    c. Moral majority, international cooperation, and compromise
    d. Conservatism, opposition to abortion, and organized labor

26. How do market economies differ from planned economies?
    a. Unlike market economies, planned economies have a larger number of both buyers and sellers.
    b. Unlike market economies, planned economies distribute resources more efficiently.
    c. Unlike planned economies, market economies allow demand to set prices.
    d. Unlike planned economies, market economies prioritize public services.

Question 27 is based on the following passage:

> Those who are opposed to this proposition tell us that the issue of paper money is a function of the bank and that the government ought to go out of the banking business. I stand with Jefferson rather than with them, and tell them, as he did, that the issue of money is a function of the government and that the banks should go out of the governing business.

> If they dare to come out in the open field and defend the gold standard as a good thing, we shall fight them to the uttermost, having behind us the producing masses of the nation and the world. Having behind us the commercial interests and the laboring interests and all the toiling masses, we shall answer their demands for a gold standard by saying to them, you shall not

press down upon the brow of labor this crown of thorns. You shall not crucify mankind upon a cross of gold.

William Jennings Bryan, "Cross of Gold" speech, 1896

27. What is the main idea presented in the excerpt?
    a. Banks prefer the gold standard.
    b. Most Americans dislike the gold standard.
    c. Violence is justified when the government oppresses the masses.
    d. The government should set the monetary policy based on the will of the people.

Question 28 is based on the following graph:

History of Unemployment in the United States

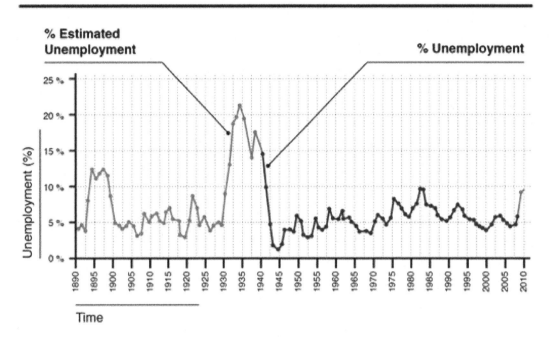

28. Which event caused the second largest increase in unemployment in American history?
    a. Panic of 1893
    b. Depression of 1920
    c. Depression of 1929
    d. Great Recession of 2007

Question 29 is based on the following diagram:

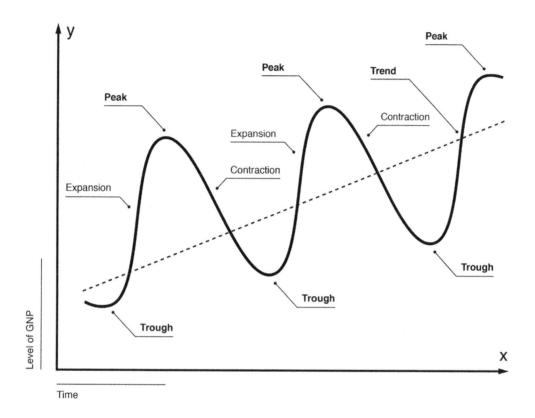

29. Which of the following phases of a business cycle occurs when there is continual growth?
    a. Expansion
    b. Peak
    c. Contraction
    d. Trough

30. Which of the following types of government intervention lowers prices, reassures the supply, and creates opportunity to compete with foreign vendors?
    a. Income redistribution
    b. Price controls
    c. Taxes
    d. Subsidies

31. What type of map would be the most useful for calculating data and differentiating between the characteristics of two places?
    a. Topographic maps
    b. Dot-density maps
    c. Isoline maps
    d. Flow-line maps

Question 32 is based on the following map:

Map of the United States by population density

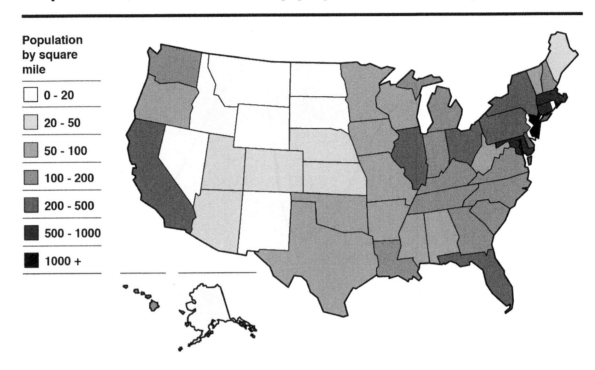

32. According to the map, what area of the United States has the highest population density?
    a. Northwest
    b. Northeast
    c. Southwest
    d. Southeast

33. What accounts for different parts of the Earth experiencing different seasons at the same time?
    a. Differences in the rate of Earth's rotation
    b. Ocean currents
    c. Tilt of the Earth's rotational axis
    d. Elevation

34. Which of the following is NOT a reason why nonrenewable energy sources are used more often than renewables?
    a. Nonrenewable energy is currently cheaper.
    b. Infrastructure was built specifically for nonrenewable sources.
    c. Renewable energy is more difficult and expensive to store for long periods.
    d. Renewable energy cannot be converted into a power source.

Question 35 is based on the following map:

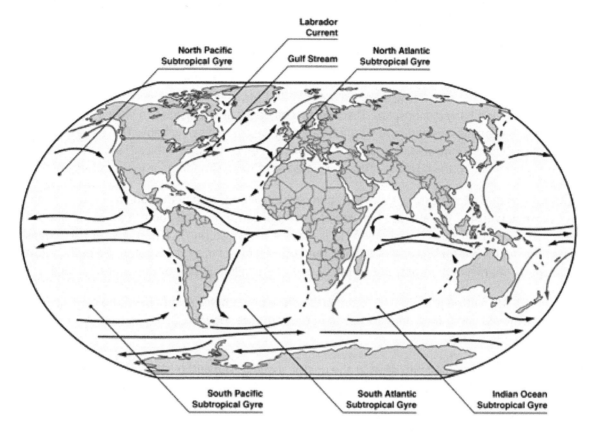

35. Which pair of ocean currents or gyres has the most impact on the weather of the United States?
    a. North Atlantic Subtropical Gyre and South Atlantic Subtropical Gyre
    b. Gulf Stream and North Pacific Subtropical Gyre
    c. North Pacific Subtropical Gyre and South Pacific Subtropical Gyre
    d. Alaskan Current and Indian Ocean Subtropical Gyre

Answer Explanations #3

Reading Comprehension

1. B: Mr. Button's wife is about to have a baby. The passage begins by giving the reader information about traditional birthing situations. Then, we are told that Mr. and Mrs. Button decide to go against tradition to have their baby in a hospital. The next few passages are dedicated to letting the reader know how Mr. Button dresses and goes to the hospital to welcome his new baby. There is a doctor in this excerpt, as Choice *C* indicates, and Mr. Button does put on clothes, as Choice *D* indicates. However, Mr. Button is not going to the doctor's office nor is he about to go shopping for new clothes.

2. A: The tone of the above passage is nervous and excited. We are told in the fourth paragraph that Mr. Button "arose nervously." We also see him running without caution to the doctor to find out about his wife and baby—this indicates his excitement. We also see him stuttering in a nervous yet excited fashion as he asks the doctor if it's a boy or girl. Though the doctor may seem a bit abrupt at the end, indicating a bit of anger or shame, neither of these choices is the overwhelming tone of the entire passage.

3. C: Dedicated. Mr. Button is dedicated to the task before him. Choice *A*, numbed, Choice *B*, chained, and Choice *D*, moved, all could grammatically fit in the sentence. However, they are not synonyms with *consecrated* like Choice *C* is.

4. D: Giving readers a visual picture of what the doctor is doing. The author describes a visual image—the doctor rubbing his hands together—first and foremost. The author may be trying to make a comment about the profession; however, the author does not "explain the detail of the doctor's profession" as Choice *B* suggests.

5. D: To introduce the setting of the story and its characters. We know we are being introduced to the setting because we are given the year in the very first paragraph along with the season: "one day in the summer of 1860." This is a classic structure of an introduction of the setting. We are also getting a long explanation of Mr. Button, what his work is, who is related to him, and what his life is like in the third paragraph.

6. B: "Talk sense!" is an example of an imperative sentence. An imperative sentence gives a command. The doctor is commanding Mr. Button to talk sense. Choice *A* is an example of an exclamatory sentence, which expresses excitement. Choice *C* is an example of an interrogative sentence—these types of sentences ask questions. Choice *D* is an example of a declarative sentence. This means that the character is simply making a statement.

7. C: The point of view is told in third person omniscient. We know this because the story starts out with us knowing something that the character does not know: that her husband has died. Mrs. Mallard eventually comes to know this, but we as readers know this information before it is broken to her. In third person limited, Choice *D*, we would only see and know what Mrs. Mallard herself knew, and we would find out the news of her husband's death when she found out the news, not before.

8. A: The way Mrs. Mallard reacted to her husband's death. The irony in this story is called situational irony, which means the situation that takes place is different than what the audience anticipated. At the beginning of the story, we see Mrs. Mallard react with a burst of grief to her husband's death. However, once she's alone, she begins to contemplate her future and says the word "free" over and over. This is quite a different reaction from Mrs. Mallard than what readers expected from the first of the story.

9. B: The word "elusive" most closely means "indefinable." Horrible, Choice *A*, doesn't quite fit with the tone of the word "subtle" that comes before it. Choice *C*, "quiet," is more closely related to the word "subtle." Choice *D*, "joyful," also doesn't quite fit the context here. "Indefinable" is the best option.

10. D: Mrs. Mallard, a newly widowed woman, finds unexpected relief in her husband's death. A summary is a brief explanation of the main point of a story. The story mostly focuses on Mrs. Mallard and her reaction to her husband's death, especially in the room when she's alone and contemplating the present and future. All of the other answer choices except Choice *C* are briefly mentioned in the story; however, they are not the main focus of the story.

11. D: The interesting thing about this story is that feelings that are confused, joyful, and depressive all play a unique and almost equal part of this story. There is no one right answer here, because the author seems to display all of these emotions through the character of Mrs. Mallard. She displays feelings of depressiveness by her grief at the beginning; then, when she receives feelings of joy, she feels moments of confusion. We as readers cannot help but go through these feelings with the character. Thus, the author creates a tone of depression, joy, and confusion, all in one story.

12. C: The word "tumultuously" most nearly means "violently." Even if you don't know the word "tumultuously," look at the surrounding context to figure it out. The next few sentences we see Mrs. Mallard striving to "beat back" the "thing that was approaching to possess her." We see a fearful and almost violent reaction to the emotion that she's having. Thus, her chest would rise and fall turbulently, or violently.

13. D: Outspending other countries on education could have other benefits, but there is no reference to this in the passage, so Choice *A* is incorrect. Choice *B* is incorrect because the author does not mention corruption. Choice *C* is incorrect because there is nothing in the passage stating that the tests are not genuinely representative. Choice *D* is accurate because spending more money has not brought success. The United States already spends the most money, and the country is not excelling on these tests. Choice *D* is the correct answer.

14. C: The author is not a geologist, and while there could be physical evidence in the ancient soil levels, he does not bring this information into this section of the passage. Choice *A* is incorrect. The author quotes several contemporary sources who have done research on this topic, but they are also basing their research on ancient accounts/sources. These sources can best be described as textual evidence from the Romans themselves. Note how the author cites specific numbers and historical events that contributed to grain shortage and agricultural decline. This information must have been documented at some point in order to reach modern readers. Therefore, Choice *C* is the best description of actual evidence in the text.

15. A: The passage doesn't mention military attack from barbarians, making Choice *D* irrelevant. Choice *C* is vague and doesn't tie back into agricultural decline. The author argues that Rome fell from within, not that its civilization was destroyed. It makes sense that being unable to produce sufficient food in Italy, Rome would have had to rely on other territories for food. This would have taxed Rome greatly and contributed to economic and even political hardships. Choice *B* is a good choice. Poverty, which was mentioned in the text, became more widespread, which also taxed state granaries. This in itself would have made Rome more dependent on external food sources, but essentially a scenario like Choice *B* mentions would be included in Choice *A*'s scenario. Choice *A* more effectively sums up the result of agricultural decline.

16. D: The main point of Rodbertus' stance is that the agricultural decline had less to do with physical circumstances and more to do with social causes. Therefore, the best evidence in favor of this would be details on how the Roman people themselves or the government affected agriculture. Choice *A* is incorrect because this is a natural occurrence. Choice *C* is compelling; this certainly supports Rodbertus' assertion that Romans were keen agriculturalists. Choice *B* is definitely a good option, but just because many farmers left Rome to pursue farming abroad doesn't necessarily mean agriculture suffered an irreparable blow. Choice *D* is the strongest answer. Note how this answer opens with the idea of taxes creating troubles for farmers. Taxes, of course, are instituted by a social structure: the government. The taxes then made farming difficult by placing strains on the farmers which, as a result, led them to overwork the land to a point that crop yields might have been less productive. This illustrates the trickling sequence of social changes and institutions marring agriculture, which is exactly what Rodbertus believes happened. Therefore, Choice *D* is a stronger answer than Choice *C*. Another consideration: Technology and good practice can only go so far when such resources may be limited by external factors such as policy or regulation.

17. B: The author clearly has a specific idea that he's trying to discuss and prove true to the reader. This makes Choice *C* an incorrect answer. Choice *D* is incorrect as well. The opposing information is not easily dismissed; in fact, the author acknowledges that there appears to be validity in some of the other scholars' observations. However, this doesn't weaken the author's argument. By addressing alternative views, the author is providing a greater context of how the evidence can be interpreted. The use of opposing sources actually strengthens his argumentative style because he has the opportunity to illustrate how others might have been overlooked or incorrectly assessed the information regarding agricultural decline. He goes on to assert this through supplementary sources that favor his ideas. Therefore, Choice *B* is correct.

18. D: To define and describe instances of spinoff technology. This is an example of a purpose question—*why* did the author write this? The article contains facts, definitions, and other objective information without telling a story or arguing an opinion. In this case, the purpose of the article is to inform the reader. The only answer choice that is related to giving information is Choice *D*: to define and describe.

19. A: A general definition followed by more specific examples. This organization question asks readers to analyze the structure of the essay. The topic of the essay is about spinoff technology; the first paragraph gives a general definition of the concept, while the following two paragraphs offer more detailed examples to help illustrate this idea.

20. C: They were looking for ways to add health benefits to food. This reading comprehension question can be answered based on the second paragraph—scientists were concerned about astronauts' nutrition and began researching useful nutritional supplements. Choice *A* in particular is not true because it reverses the order of discovery (first NASA identified algae for astronaut use, and then it was further developed for use in baby food).

21. B: Related to the brain. This vocabulary question could be answered based on the reader's prior knowledge; but even for readers who have never encountered the word "neurological" before, the passage does provide context clues. The very next sentence talks about "this algae's potential to boost brain health," which is a paraphrase of "neurological benefits." From this context, readers should be able to infer that "neurological" is related to the brain.

22. D: To give an example of valuable space equipment. This purpose question requires readers to understand the relevance of the given detail. In this case, the author mentions "costly and crucial equipment" before mentioning space suit visors, which are given as an example of something that is very valuable. Choice *A* is not correct because fashion is only related to sunglasses, not to NASA equipment. Choice *B* can be eliminated because it is simply not mentioned in the passage. While Choice *C* seems like it could be a true statement, it is also not relevant to what is being explained by the author.

23. C: It is difficult to make money from scientific research. The article gives several examples of how businesses have been able to capitalize on NASA research, so it is unlikely that the author would agree with this statement. Evidence for the other answer choices can be found in the article: for Choice *A*, the author mentions that "many consumers are unaware that products they are buying are based on NASA research"; Choice *B* is a general definition of spinoff technology; and Choice *D* is mentioned in the final paragraph.

24. B: A period of time. "Four score and seven years ago" is the equivalent of eighty-seven years, because the word "score" means "twenty." Choices *A* and *C* are incorrect because the context for describing a unit of measurement or a literary movement is lacking. *D* is incorrect because although Lincoln's speech is a cornerstone in political rhetoric, the phrase "Four score and seven years ago" is better narrowed to a period of time.

25. C: The setting of this text is a battlefield in Gettysburg, PA. Choices *A, B,* and *D* are incorrect because the text specifies that they "met on a great battlefield of that war."

26. D: Abraham Lincoln is the former president of the United States, so the correct answer is *D,* "The American Civil War." Though the U.S. was involved in World War I and II, Choices *A* and *C* are incorrect because a civil war specifically means citizens fighting within the same country. *B* is incorrect, as "The War of Spanish Succession" involved Spain, Italy, Germany, and Holland, and not the United States.

27. A: The speech calls on the audience to consider the soldiers who died on the battlefield as ideas to perpetuate freedom so that their deaths would not be in vain. Choice *B* is incorrect because, although they are there to "dedicate a portion of that field," there is no mention in the text of an annual memorial service. Choice *C* is incorrect because there is no charged language in the text, only reverence for the dead. Choice *D* is incorrect because "forget[ting] the lives that were lost" is the opposite of what Lincoln is suggesting.

28. A: Choice *A* is correct because Lincoln's intention was to memorialize the soldiers who had fallen as a result of war as well as celebrate those who had put their lives in danger for the sake of their country. Choices *B, C,* and *D* are incorrect because Lincoln's speech was supposed to foster a sense of pride among the members of the audience while connecting them to the soldiers' experiences, not to alienate or discourage them.

29. C: A letter of interest for a resume. The passage mentions teaching, Choice *A,* but it does not fit the format of a how-to document. A how-to document is a set of instructions for the reader to follow. Choice *B* is incorrect; the writer of the letter is not a consumer of products, but trying to apply for a certain position within the company. Choice *D* is also incorrect, as the writer of the letter is not yet an employee, and therefore is incapable of writing the company's memo.

30. B: The writer of the letter has a Master's degree in English. Choice *A* is incorrect because the writer of the letter is applying to be a writer/producer at Shad Heat—they aren't currently a writer/producer there. Choice *C* is also incorrect because the passage states that the writer has nine years' experience in higher education, not ten. Choice *D* is incorrect because the position is listed in the very first sentence: writer/producer, not website designer.

31. D: Although Washington is from a wealthy background, the passage does not say that his wealth led to his republican ideals, so Choice *A* is not supported. Choice *B* also does not follow from the passage. Washington's warning against meddling in foreign affairs does not mean that he would oppose wars of every kind, so Choice *B* is wrong. Choice *C* is also unjustified since the author does not indicate that Alexander Hamilton's assistance was absolutely necessary. Choice *D* is correct because the farewell address clearly opposes political parties and partisanship. The author then notes that presidential elections often hit a fever pitch of partisanship. Thus, it is follows that George Washington would not approve of modern political parties and their involvement in presidential elections.

32. A: The author finishes the passage by applying Washington's farewell address to modern politics, so the purpose probably includes this application. Choice *B* is wrong because George Washington is already a well-established historical figure; furthermore, the passage does not seek to introduce him. Choice *C* is wrong because the author is not fighting a common perception that Washington was merely a military hero. Choice *D* is wrong because the author is not convincing readers. Persuasion does not correspond to the passage. Choice *A* states the primary purpose.

33. D: Choice *A* is wrong because the last paragraph is not appropriate for a history textbook. Choice *B* is false because the piece is not a notice or announcement of Washington's death. Choice *C* is clearly false because it is not fiction, but a historical writing. Choice *D* is correct. The passage is most likely to appear in a newspaper editorial because it cites information relevant and applicable to the present day, a popular format in editorials.

34. D: The passage does not proceed in chronological order since it begins by pointing out Leif Erikson's explorations in America so Choice *A* does not work. Although the author compares and contrasts Erikson with Christopher Columbus, this is not the main way the information is presented; therefore, Choice *B* does not work. Neither does Choice *C* because there is no mention of or reference to cause and effect in the passage. However, the passage does offer a conclusion (Leif Erikson deserves more credit) and premises (first European to set foot in the New World and first to contact the natives) to substantiate Erikson's historical importance. Thus, Choice *D* is correct.

35. C: Choice *A* is wrong because it describes facts: Leif Erikson was the son of Erik the Red and historians debate Leif's date of birth. These are not opinions. Choice *B* is wrong; that Erikson called the land Vinland is a verifiable fact as is Choice *D* because he did contact the natives almost 500 years before Columbus. Choice *C* is the correct answer because it is the author's opinion that Erikson deserves more credit. That, in fact, is his conclusion in the piece, but another person could argue that Columbus or another explorer deserves more credit for opening up the New World to exploration. Rather than being an incontrovertible fact, it is a subjective value claim.

36. B: Choice *A* is wrong because the author aims to go beyond describing Erikson as a mere legendary Viking. Choice *C* is wrong because the author does not focus on Erikson's motivations, let alone name the spreading of Christianity as his primary objective. Choice *D* is wrong because it is a premise that Erikson contacted the natives 500 years before Columbus, which is simply a part of supporting the author's conclusion. Choice *B* is correct because, as stated in the previous answer, it accurately identifies the author's statement that Erikson deserves more credit than he has received for being the first European to explore the New World.

37. B: Choice *A* is wrong because the author is not in any way trying to entertain the reader. Choice *D* is wrong because he goes beyond a mere suggestion; "suggest" is too vague. Although the author is certainly trying to alert the readers (make them aware) of Leif Erikson's underappreciated and unheralded accomplishments, the nature of the writing does not indicate the author would be satisfied with the reader merely knowing of Erikson's exploration (Choice *C*). Rather, the author would want the reader to be informed about it, which is more substantial (Choice *B*).

38. D: Choice *A* is wrong because the author never addresses the Vikings' state of mind or emotions. Choice *B* is wrong because the author does not elaborate on Erikson's exile and whether he would have become an explorer if not for his banishment. Choice *C* is wrong because there is not enough information to support this premise. It is unclear whether Erikson informed the King of Norway of his finding. Although it is true that the King did not send a follow-up expedition, he could have simply chosen not to expend the resources after receiving Erikson's news. It is not possible to logically infer whether Erikson told him. Choice *D* is correct because there are two examples—Leif Erikson's date of birth and what happened during the encounter with the natives—of historians having trouble pinning down important dates in Viking history.

39. B: Narrative, Choice *A*, means a written account of connected events. Think of narrative writing as a story. Choice *C*, expository writing, generally seeks to explain or describe some phenomena, whereas Choice *D*, technical writing, includes directions, instructions, and/or explanations. This passage is definitely persuasive writing, which hopes to change someone's beliefs based on an appeal to reason or emotion. The author is aiming to convince the reader that smoking is terrible. They use health, price, and beauty in their argument against smoking, so Choice *B*, persuasive, is the correct answer.

40. B: The author is clearly opposed to tobacco. He cites disease and deaths associated with smoking. He points to the monetary expense and aesthetic costs. Choice *A* is wrong because alternatives to smoking are not even addressed in the passage. Choice *C* is wrong because it does not summarize the passage but rather is just a premise. Choice *D* is wrong because, while these statistics are a premise in the argument, they do not represent a summary of the piece. Choice *C* is the correct answer because it states the three critiques offered against tobacco and expresses the author's conclusion.

41. D: It emphasizes Mr. Utterson's anguish in failing to identify Hyde's whereabouts. Context clues indicate that Choice *D* is correct because the passage provides great detail of Mr. Utterson's feelings about locating Hyde. Choice *A* does not fit because there is no mention of Mr. Lanyon's mental state. Choice *B* is incorrect; although the text does make mention of bells, Choice *B* is not the *best* answer overall. Choice *C* is incorrect because the passage clearly states that Mr. Utterson was determined, not unsure.

42. A: In the city. The word *city* appears in the passage several times, thus establishing the location for the reader.

43. B: It scares children. The passage states that the Juggernaut causes the children to scream. Choices *A* and *D* don't apply because the text doesn't mention either of these instances specifically. Choice *C* is incorrect because there is nothing in the text that mentions space travel.

44. B: To constantly visit. The mention of *morning*, *noon*, and *night* make it clear that the word *haunt* refers to frequent appearances at various locations. Choice *A* doesn't work because the text makes no mention of levitating. Choices *C* and *D* are not correct because the text makes mention of Mr. Utterson's anguish and disheartenment because of his failure to find Hyde but does not make mention of Mr. Utterson's feelings negatively affecting anyone else.

45. D: This is an example of alliteration. Choice *D* is the correct answer because of the repetition of the *L*-words. Hyperbole is an exaggeration, so Choice *A* doesn't work. No comparison is being made, so no simile or metaphor is being used, thus eliminating Choices *B* and *C*.

Mathematical Reasoning

1. A: This problem can be multiplied as 588×32, except at the end, the decimal point needs to be moved three places to the left. Performing the multiplication will give 18,816, and moving the decimal place over three places results in 18.816.

2. B: 13,078. The power of 10 by which a digit is multiplied corresponds with the number of zeros following the digit when expressing its value in standard form. Therefore, $(1 \times 10^4) + (3 \times 10^3) + (7 \times 10^1) + (8 \times 10^0) = 10,000 + 3,000 + 70 + 8 = 13,078$.

3. C: 34. When performing calculations consisting of more than one operation, the order of operations should be followed: *Parenthesis, Exponents, Multiplication/Division, Addition/Subtraction*. Parenthesis: $7^2 - 3 \times (4 + 2) + 15 \div 5 = 7^2 - 3 \times (6) + 15 \div 5$. Exponents: $7^2 - 3 \times 6 + 15 \div 5 = 49 - 3 \times 6 + 15 \div 5$. Multiplication/Division (from left to right): $49 - 3 \times 6 + 15 \div 5 = 49 - 18 + 3$. Addition/Subtraction (from left to right): $49 - 18 + 3 = 34$.

4. A: To find the fraction of the bill that the first three people pay, the fractions need to be added, which means finding common denominator. The common denominator will be 60. $\frac{1}{5} + \frac{1}{4} + \frac{1}{3} = \frac{12}{60} + \frac{15}{60} + \frac{20}{60} = \frac{47}{60}$. The remainder of the bill is $1 - \frac{47}{60} = \frac{60}{60} - \frac{47}{60} = \frac{13}{60}$.

5. C: 85% of a number means multiplying that number by 0.85. So, $0.85 \times 20 = \frac{85}{100} \times \frac{20}{1}$, which can be simplified to $\frac{17}{20} \times \frac{20}{1} = 17$.

6. A: Dividing by 98 can be approximated by dividing by 100, which would mean shifting the decimal point of the numerator to the left by 2. The result is 4.2 and rounds to 4.

7. C: 80 min. To solve the problem, a proportion is written consisting of ratios comparing distance and time. One way to set up the proportion is: $\frac{3}{48} = \frac{5}{x} \left(\frac{distance}{time} = \frac{distance}{time} \right)$ where x represents the unknown value of time. To solve a proportion, the ratios are cross-multiplied: $(3)(x) = (5)(48) \rightarrow 3x = 240$. The equation is solved by isolating the variable, or dividing by 3 on both sides, to produce $x = 80$.

8. B: Start by squaring both sides to get $1 + x = 16$. Then subtract 1 from both sides to get $x = 15$.

9. B: Multiplying by 10^{-3} means moving the decimal point three places to the left, putting in zeroes as necessary.

10. B: To factor $x^2 + 4x + 4$, the numbers needed are those that add to 4 and multiply to 4. Therefore, both numbers must be 2, and the expression factors to $x^2 + 4x + 4 = (x + 2)^2$. Similarly, the expression factors to $x^2 - x - 6 = (x - 3)(x + 2)$, so that they have $x + 2$ in common.

11. D: The expression is simplified by collecting like terms. Terms with the same variable and exponent are like terms, and their coefficients can be added.

12. B: To simplify this inequality, subtract 3 from both sides to get $-\frac{1}{2}x \geq -1$. Then, multiply both sides by -2 (remembering this flips the direction of the inequality) to get $x \leq 2$.

13. D: There are two ways to approach this problem. Each value can be substituted into each equation. A can be eliminated, since $4^2 + 16 = 32$. Choice B can be eliminated, since $4^2 + 4 \cdot 4 - 4 = 28$. C can be eliminated, since $4^2 - 2 \cdot 4 - 2 = 6$. But, plugging in either value into $x^2 - 16$, which gives $(\pm 4)^2 - 16 = 16 - 16 = 0$.

14. D: This system of equations involves one quadratic function and one linear function, as seen from the degree of each equation. One way to solve this is through substitution. Solving for y in the second equation yields $y = x + 2$. Plugging this equation in for the y of the quadratic equation yields $x^2 - 2x + x + 2 = 8$. Simplifying the equation, it becomes $x^2 - x + 2 = 8$. Setting this equal to zero and factoring, it becomes $x^2 - x - 6 = 0 = (x - 3)(x + 2)$. Solving these two factors for x gives the zeros $x = 3, -2$. To find the y-value for the point, each number can be plugged in to either original equation. Solving each one for y yields the points $(3, 5)$ and $(-2, 0)$.

15. B: From the slope-intercept form, $y = mx + b$, it is known that b is the y-intercept, which is 1. Compute the slope as $\frac{2-1}{1-0} = 1$, so the equation should be $y = x + 1$.

16. D: For manufacturing costs, there is a linear relationship between the cost to the company and the number produced, with a y-intercept given by the base cost of acquiring the means of production, and a slope given by the cost to produce one unit. In this case, that base cost is $50,000, while the cost per unit is $40. So, $y = 40x + 50,000$.

17. D: Factor the numerator into $x^2 - 6x + 9 = (x - 3)^2$, since $-3 - 3 = -6, (-3)(-3) = 9$. Factor the denominator into $x^2 - x - 6 = (x - 3)(x + 2)$, since $-3 + 2 = -1, (-3)(2) = -6$. This means the rational function can be rewritten as:

$$\frac{x^2 - 6x + 9}{x^2 - x - 6} = \frac{(x - 3)^2}{(x - 3)(x + 2)}$$

Using the restriction of x > 3, do not worry about any of these terms being 0, and cancel an $x - 3$ from the numerator and the denominator, leaving $\frac{x-3}{x+2}$.

18. A: The equation is *even* because $f(-x) = f(x)$. Plugging in a negative value will result in the same answer as when plugging in the positive of that same value. The function:

$$f(-2) = \frac{1}{2}(-2)^4 + 2(-2)^2 - 6 = 8 + 8 - 6 = 10$$

yields the same value as:

$$f(2) = \frac{1}{2}(2)^4 + 2(2)^2 - 6 = 8 + 8 - 6 = 10$$

19. C: The formula for continually compounded interest is $A = Pe^{rt}$. Plugging in the given values to find the total amount in the account yields the equation $A = 2000e^{0.05*8} = 2983.65$.

20. A: o. The core of the pattern consists of 4 items: ▲oo□. Therefore, the core repeats in multiples of 4, with the pattern starting over on the next step. The closest multiple of 4 to 42 is 40. Step 40 is the end of the core (□), so step 41 will start the core over (▲) and step 42 is o.

21. A: If each man gains 10 pounds, every original data point will increase by 10 pounds. Therefore, the man with the original median will still have the median value, but that value will increase by 10. The smallest value and largest value will also increase by 10 and, therefore, the difference between the two won't change. The range does not change in value and, thus, remains the same.

22. A: Lining up the given scores provides the following list: 60, 75, 80, 85, and one unknown. Because the median needs to be 80, it means 80 must be the middle data point out of these five. Therefore, the unknown data point must be the fourth or fifth data point, meaning it must be greater than or equal to 80. The only answer that fails to meet this condition is 60.

23. A: Let the unknown score be x. The average will be $\frac{5 \cdot 50 + 4 \cdot 70 + x}{10} = \frac{530 + x}{10} = 55$. Multiply both sides by 10 to get $530 + x = 550$, or $x = 20$.

24. C: Line graph. The scenario involves data consisting of two variables, month, and stock value. Box plots display data consisting of values for one variable. Therefore, a box plot is not an appropriate choice. Both line plots and circle graphs are used to display frequencies within categorical data. Neither can be used for the given scenario. Line graphs display two numerical variables on a coordinate grid and show trends among the variables.

25. C: A die has an equal chance for each outcome. Since it has six sides, each outcome has a probability of $\frac{1}{6}$. The chance of a 1 or a 2 is therefore $\frac{1}{6} + \frac{1}{6} = \frac{1}{3}$.

26. D: $\frac{1}{12}$. The probability of picking the winner of the race is $\frac{1}{4}$ $\left(\frac{number\ of\ favorable\ outcomes}{number\ of\ total\ outcomes}\right)$. Assuming the winner was picked on the first selection, three horses remain from which to choose the runner-up (these are dependent events). Therefore, the probability of picking the runner-up is $\frac{1}{3}$. To determine the probability of multiple events, the probability of each event is multiplied: $\frac{1}{4} \times \frac{1}{3} = \frac{1}{12}$.

27. B: $12 \times 750 = 9,000$. Therefore, there are 9,000 milliliters of water, which must be converted to liters. 1,000 milliliters equals 1 liter; therefore, 9 liters of water are purchased.

28. D: The two lines are neither parallel nor perpendicular. Parallel lines will never intersect or meet. Therefore, the lines are not parallel. Perpendicular lines intersect to form a right angle (90°). Although the lines intersect, they do not form a right angle, which is usually indicated with a box at the intersection point. Therefore, the lines are not perpendicular.

29. C: Perimeter is found by calculating the sum of all sides of the polygon. $9 + 9 + 9 + 8 + 8 + s = 56$, where s is the missing side length. Therefore, 43 plus the missing side length is equal to 56. The missing side length is 13 cm.

30. B: An equilateral triangle has three sides of equal length, so if the total perimeter is 18 feet, each side must be 6 feet long. A square with sides of 6 feet will have an area of $6^2 = 36$ square feet.

31. C: 216cm. Because area is a two-dimensional measurement, the dimensions are multiplied by a scale that is squared to determine the scale of the corresponding areas. The dimensions of the rectangle are multiplied by a scale of 3. Therefore, the area is multiplied by a scale of 3^2 (which is equal to 9): $24cm \times 9 = 216cm$.

32. D: Let a be the number of apples and b the number of bananas. Then, the total cost is $2a + 3b = 22$, while it also known that $a + b = 10$. Using the knowledge of systems of equations, cancel the b variables by multiplying the second equation by -3. This makes the equation $-3a - 3b = -30$. Adding this to the first equation, the o values cancel to get $-a = -8$, which simplifies to a = 8.

33. A: Simplify this to $(4x^2y^4)^{\frac{3}{2}} = 4^{\frac{3}{2}}(x^2)^{\frac{3}{2}}(y^4)^{\frac{3}{2}}$. Now, $4^{\frac{3}{2}} = (\sqrt{4})^3 = 2^3 = 8$. For the other, recall that the exponents must be multiplied, so this yields $8x^{2\cdot\frac{3}{2}}y^{4\cdot\frac{3}{2}} = 8x^3y^6$.

34. A: The slope is given by $m = \frac{y_2-y_1}{x_2-x_1} = \frac{0-4}{0-(-3)} = -\frac{4}{3}$.

35. A: These numbers to improper fractions: $\frac{11}{3} - \frac{9}{5}$. Take 15 as a common denominator: $\frac{11}{3} - \frac{9}{5} =: \frac{55}{15} - \frac{27}{15} = \frac{28}{15} = 1\frac{13}{15}$ (when rewritten to get rid of the partial fraction).

36. B: Each instance of x is replaced with a 2, and each instance of y is replaced with a 3 to get $2^2 - 2 \cdot 2 \cdot 3 + 2 \cdot 3^2 = 4 - 12 + 18 = 10$.

37. C: The area of the shaded region is the area of the square, minus the area of the circle. The area of the circle will be πr^2. The side of the square will be $2r$, so the area of the square will be $4r^2$. Therefore, the difference is $4r^2 - \pi r^2 = (4 - \pi)r^2$.

38. B: The slope will be given by $\frac{1-0}{2-0} = \frac{1}{2}$. The y-intercept will be 0, since it passes through the origin. Using slope-intercept form, the equation for this line is $y = \frac{1}{2}x$.

39: C. The two points are at -5 and 0 for the x-axis and at -3 and at -1 for y-axis respectively. Therefore, the two points have the coordinates of (-5, -3) and (0, -1).

40. A: The Pythagorean theorem states that for right triangles $c^2 = a^2 + b^2$, with c being the side opposite the 90° angle. Substituting 24 as a and 36 as b, the equation becomes $c^2 = 24^2 + 36^2 = 576 + 1296 = 1872$. The last step is to square both sides to remove the exponent, $c = \sqrt{1872} = 43.3$.

41. B: The formula for the volume of a cube is $V = s^3$. Substitute the side length of $7in$ to get $V = 7^3 = 343in^3$.

No Calculator Questions

42. C: The decimal points are lined up, with zeroes put in as needed. Then, the numbers are added just like integers:

$$
\begin{array}{r}
3.40 \\
2.35 \\
+\underline{4.00} \\
9.75
\end{array}
$$

43. D: The fraction is converted so that the denominator is 100 by multiplying the numerator and denominator by 4, to get $\frac{3}{25} = \frac{12}{100}$. Dividing a number by 100 just moves the decimal point two places to the left, with a result of 0.12.

44. B: 30% is 3/10. The number itself must be 10/3 of 6, or $\frac{10}{3} \times 6 = 10 \times 2 = 20$.

45. B: 8 squared is 64, and 6 squared is 36. These should be added together to get $64 + 36 = 100$. Then, the last step is to find the square root of 100 which is 10.

46. A: The long division would be completed as follows:

$$
\begin{array}{r}
24 \\
36\overline{)864} \\
-72\downarrow \\
\hline
144
\end{array}
$$

Science

1. A: The hypothesis is the sentence that describes what the scientist wants to research with a conclusive expected finding. Choice *A* describes how she believes sunlight will affect plant growth. Choice *B* includes details about the experiment. Choice *C* is not a conclusive theory. Choice *D* describes the data that she found after conducting the experiment.

2. C: Looking at Figure 1, four experimental groups are shown on the graph for which data were collected: plants that received 1 hour of sunlight, 3 hours of sunlight, 5 hours of sunlight, and 7 hours of sunlight. Choices *A* and *B* could be describing two of the experimental groups and how much sunlight they received. Choice *D* describes how many days' data was collected.

3. B: After the data was collected, it was compiled into a line graph. The data points were collected, and then a line was drawn between the points. Data is represented by horizontal or vertical bars in bar graphs, Choice *A*. Pie charts are circular charts, with the data being represented by different wedges of the circle, Choice *C*. Pictograms use pictures to describe their subject, Choice *D*.

4. A: Looking at Figure 2, the sun provides light energy that drives forward the process of photosynthesis, which is how plants make their own source of energy and nutrients. Choices *B* and *C* are found in the environment around the plants. They combine with light energy to make the photosynthesis reaction work. Choice *D* is a product of photosynthesis.

5. D: Looking at the Figure 1, the experimental group that received 7 hours of sunlight every day grew taller than any of the other groups that received less sunlight per day. Therefore, it is reasonable to conclude that more sunlight makes plants grow bigger. Choice *A* is not a reasonable conclusion because it did not have the tallest plants. The scientist decided to measure the plants only for 11 days, but that does not describe a conclusion for the experiment, Choice *B*. Choice *C* is the opposite of the correct conclusion and does not have evidence to support it.

6. B: The atomic mass of a molecule can be found by adding the atomic mass of each component together. Looking at Figure 2, the atomic mass of each element is found below its symbol. The atomic mass of Na is 23, Choice A, and the atomic mass of Cl is 35.5, Choice C. The sum of those two components is 58.5, Choice B. Choice D is equal to two Cl atoms joined together.

7. D: Figure 1 shows the trends of the periodic table. Looking at the black arrows representing electronegativity, it is shown that electronegativity increases going towards the top row of the table and also increases going towards the right columns of the table. Therefore, the most electronegative element would be found in the top right corner of the table, which is where the element Helium is found. Choices A and B are found at the bottom of the table. Choice D is found on the left side of the table.

8. A: Looking at Figure 2, the element name is found under the symbol in each box on the periodic table. Looking at Figure 1 or 3, the full name of element Cr is Chromium. Copper, Choice B, is represented by Cu. Chlorine, Choice C, is represented by Cl. Curium, Choice D, is represented by Cm.

9. D: The atomic number of an element represents the number of protons. Looking at Figure 2, the atomic number is located at the top of the box, above the element's symbol. Hydrogen (H) has an atomic number of 1 and has the least number of protons of any other element in the periodic table. Radon (Rn), Choice A, has 86 protons. Boron (B), Choice B, has 5 protons. Nitrogen (N), Choice C, has 7 protons.

10. B: Looking at Figure 3, the elements are color coded in periods and groups according to their similar properties. Noble gases are located in the right most column of the table. Radon (Rn) is the only one of the element choices marked as a noble gas and would be the right choice for Scientist A. Nitrogen (N) and Boron (B), Choices A and D, are nonmetals. Copper (Cu), Choice C, is a transition metal.

11. B: Looking at Figures 1 and 2, crossbreeding experiment #3 in round #1 produces plants that are completely recessive and would have white flowers. Choices A and C, crossbreeding experiments #1 and 2, respectively, only produce flowers with a dominant allele present, making red flowers. Choice D does not have any recessive alleles, so white flowers are not a possibility.

12. C: Looking at Figure 2, which represents the number of plants that were produced from each crossbreeding experiment, it can be seen that only 2 plants produced white flowers out of 12 plants total, 4 from each experiment. To find the percentage, divide 2 by 12 and multiply by 100. The result is 16.7%. Choice A is the total number of plants that were produced. Choice B represents the percentage of white flowers in experiment #3 alone.

13. B: In a Punnett Square, each box represents one allele from each of the parent's genes. To find the genetic makeup of the second parent, take out the allele that was contributed from the first parent. Here, the first parent contributed a recessive allele, a, to each offspring. In the top row, that leaves a dominant allele, A, and in the bottom row, that leaves a recessive allele, a. Therefore, the genetic makeup of the second parent is Aa.

14. D: Crossbreeding the plants with only recessive alleles will result in 100% white flowering plants. All four offspring have white flowering plants. Choice B gives 100% red flowering plants. Choice C gives 25%, 1 out of 4 plants, with white flowers.

15. A: The observation step of the scientific method involves using your senses to identify the results of the experiment. In this case, the experiment depended on identifying the color of the flowers. This was done using sight. If the experiment had involved different scents produced by the flowers, Choice B would have worked. If it has involved different textures of the flowers, Choice *C* would have worked. Flowers generally do not make any noise, so Choice *D* would not have been useful.

16. D: The process of photosynthesis requires carbon dioxide and water to combine with sunlight to produce glucose, which is used as an energy source by plants. The forest floor does not get a lot of sunlight since it is shaded by the growth of so many trees and plants in the rainforest. Carbon, Choice *A*, is available through the air. Plants expel carbon dioxide. Water, Choice *B*, is abundant in the humid climate of the rainforest. Oxygen, Choice *C*, is always available in the Earth's atmosphere.

17. B: Central America is one of the five major areas of the world that has a rainforest. Looking at Figure 2, it can be seen that the southern countries of Central America contain rainforests. Comparing this map to the map of Central America, it is clear that Panama is a country that has rainforests. Choices *A*, *C*, and *D* are not found in Central America.

18. C: Birds fly above the trees of the rainforest the most. There, they have unobstructed skies, unlike the dense growth of the trees and plants in the other layers of the rainforest.

19. D: The understory layer is the third layer from the top of the rainforest. It does not receive much sunlight, so the plants need to grow large leaves to absorb as much sunlight as possible. Giant taro leaves would grow well in this layer since they have large leaves. The emergent layer, Choice *A*, gets plenty of sunlight since it is the topmost layer. The canopy layer, Choice *B*, receives enough sunlight for plants to grow without needing to increase their leaf size. The forest floor, Choice *C*, does not receive sunlight, and plants generally do not grow here.

20. A: Rainforests have warm and wet climates. They do not have long dry seasons and tend to have temperate temperatures. The giant water lily is ideal for the rainforest because it can grow large leaves and needs a wet environment to grow in. They grow in the shallow basins of rainforest rivers. Choices *B* and *C* need dry environments. Choice *D* needs a very hot environment, which is not characteristic of rainforests.

21. B: Solar eclipses should not be looked at directly. The rays of the Sun do not seem as bright as normal but can still cause damage to the eyes. A pinhole camera facing away from the eclipse allows the viewer to see a reflection of the eclipse instead of the actual eclipse. Choices *A*, *C*, and *D* all require looking directly at the solar eclipse.

22. A: When the moon comes between the Earth and Sun, a solar eclipse occurs. If the sun is far enough away and is completely blocked by the moon, it is a total solar eclipse. If it is only partially blocked by the moon, it is a partial solar eclipse, Choice *D*. A lunar eclipse occurs when the moon is on the opposite side of the Earth as the Sun and the Sun creates a shadow of the Earth on the moon, so that the moon becomes completely dark, Choice *C*, or partially dark, Choice *B*.

23. C: During a lunar eclipse, the Sun and moon are on opposite sides of the Earth. They line up so that the Sun's light that normally illuminates the moon is blocked by the Earth. This causes the moon to become dim. Sunlight can still be seen, Choice *A*, and the Earth does not become dark, Choices *B* and *D*.

24. B: The moon does not produce harmful light rays that can damage the eyes, so lunar eclipses can be viewed directly. A telescope would allow the lunar eclipse to be magnified and seen more clearly. During a solar eclipse, the Sun's rays appear to be dim and easy to see directly but they are still harmful to the eyes.

25. B: Solar eclipses are viewed during the daytime because they involve viewing the Sun while it is out during normal daytime hours. Lunar eclipses, Choices *C* and *D*, are viewed at nighttime when the moon is in the sky during its normal hours. The moon is normally illuminated by the Sun that is on the other side of the Earth. When the Sun is on the other side of the earth, it is nighttime for people looking at the moon.

26. B: A cladogram is a diagram that organizes proposed ancestral relations based on the development of physical features. A branching point would be seen on the cladogram where the development of lungs was noted. A phylogenetic tree, Choice *A*, does not note phenotypic features on it. Punnett squares, Choice *C*, are used to determine the possible genetic makeup of offspring and are not related to evolution. Photographs, Choice *D*, may reveal species that look alike but would not reveal if they truly had a common ancestor.

27. A: According to Figure 3, human arms and whale fins are homologous structures that were derived from a common ancestor. They have anatomical similarities, although their function is not the same. They have different numbers of bones, so Choice *B* is incorrect. Since they are proposed to be developed from a common ancestor, they are not analogous features, Choice *C*. Whales have blubber covering their bodies and not layered skin like humans, so Choice *D* is incorrect.

28. D: According to the phylogenetic tree in Figure 1, the common ancestor of the striped skunk and European otter is the one that is noted before they branch into separate lineages, which is Mustelidae. Mephitis, Choice *A*, is the genus for only the striped skunk. Felidae, Choice *B*, and Canidae, Choice *C*, are completely different branches of the Carnivora order than the one that leads to the striped skunk and European otter.

29. A: According to Figure 2, the common trait that is listed on the branch of the cladogram that leads to lizards and birds is seeing UV light. They also have the common traits listed on the main branch of the cladogram before their lineages are branched off, which are vertebrae, lungs, and amniotic eggs. Perch and flounder branch from the main common ancestor and develop spiny-rayed fins, Choice *B*. Lobsters and spiders branch from the main common ancestor and develop the ability to molt an exoskeleton, Choice *C*.

30. C: Domestic cats and wolves are proposed to be related at the point where they share a common line before any branching occurs to separate their lineages. Figure 1 shows this as Carnivora, which is noted as the Order on the left side of the figure.

31. D: The color reagent is attached to the secondary antibody. It is released only when the secondary antibody attaches to the activated primary antibody. The antigen, primary antibody, and capture antibody, Choices *A*, *B*, and *C*, do not have any color reagent attached to them, so only the secondary antibody can cause the color reaction.

32. B: The color reagent is attached to the secondary antibody. If more antigen is present, more primary and secondary antibody will be attached to it and more color reagent will be released. Row 1 has the darkest green color of all the samples tested in the plate in Figure 2.

33. C: Looking at the graph in Figure 3, the highest amount of IL-1β is found in the spleen. IL-1β is a marker of inflammation and indicates that the spleen had the most inflammation of the areas tested. Serum, Choice *A*, had no IL-1β in the sample. Plasma, Choice *B*, had the second highest amount of IL-1β in the sample, and bone marrow, Choice *D*, had the second lowest amount of IL-1β.

34. B: Looking at the diagram in Figure 1, the antigen is located between the capture antibody and the primary antibody. The capture antibody keeps the antigen attached to the surface of the plate. The primary antibody recognizes the specific antigen. The secondary antibody generally recognizes the primary antibody is not specific to the antigen.

35. A: ELISAs are used to analyze specific substances within a larger sample. The antibodies used in an ELISA are designed specifically for a particular antigen. Sandwich ELISAs are generally used to quantify one antigen and not all substances in a larger sample, making Choice *B* incorrect. When used to quantify an antigen, the antibodies need to already be developed and able to detect the antigen, making Choice *D* incorrect.

36. A: Stabilizing selection occurs when an intermediate phenotype is favored over two extreme phenotypes. In Scenario 1, the mice develop an intermediate colored fur so that they can blend in with the rocks in their environment. Developing one or both extremes, Choices *B* and *C*, would make them more visible to predators. Color selection, Choice *D*, is not a type of natural selection.

37. D: Directional selection occurs when one extreme of a phenotype is favored. In Scenario 2, large beaks are favored over medium- or small-sized beaks. The large beaks help the finches break up the tough seeds that became abundant after the drought. Finches with medium and small beaks had trouble breaking up the large seeds and did not survive as well as those with large beaks.

38. B: Small-beaked finches had trouble breaking up the large seeds after the drought, and therefore could not gain enough nutrition for survival. Natural selection is based on the idea that the individuals who adapt to their environment in the best way are the ones that have enhanced survival and reproduction. Finches with large beaks were most able to adapt to the large seeds and continue with their regular feeding schedule. There was no evidence of Choices *A* or *C* in the passage. Two extremes can be selected by natural selection in disruptive selection but that was not the case here, Choice *D*.

39. C: Disruptive selection occurs when both extremes of a phenotype are selected. In Cameroon, the finches had both large and small beaks, but did not survive well with medium beaks. If medium beaks were selected, it would have been stabilizing selection, Choice *A*. If only one of the extremes had been favored, it would have been directional selection, Choice *B*.

40. D: Natural selection is the idea that individuals are selected to survive and reproduce based on their ability to adapt to the environment. Their phenotypes are advantageous for survival and reproduction over those of other individuals. It is solely based on the phenotype of the individual, not the genotype, Choice *A*. Extreme phenotypes, Choice *B*, may be selected but are not always the most advantageous. It occurs all time, not just in extreme weather conditions, such as a drought, Choice *C*.

Social Studies

1. B: Choice *B* is correct, as power is the ability of a ruling body to influence the actions, behavior, and attitude of a person or group of people. Choice *A* is incorrect, as politics is the process of governance typically exercised through the enactment and enforcement of laws over a community, most commonly a state. Although closely related to power, Choice *C* is incorrect, because authority refers to a political entity's justification to exercise power. Legitimacy is synonymous with authority, so Choice *D* is also incorrect.

2. C: Choice *C* is correct. There are no definitive requirements to be a nation. Rather, the nation only needs a group bound by some shared characteristic. Examples include language, culture, religion, homeland, ethnicity, and history. Choice *C* isn't a requirement to be a nation, though it is required to be a state.

3. D: Choice *D* is correct. Machiavelli was an Italian diplomat, politician, and historian, and *The Prince* is his best-known political treatise. The excerpt instructs the Prince that if he injures a man, then he must ensure the injury is "of such a kind that one does not stand in fear of revenge." Choices *B* and *C* contradict the first sentence of the excerpt, which says that men "ought either to be well treated or crushed." Choice *A* is close, but the selection goes too far, assuming revenge will result in overthrowing the Prince.

4. A: Choice *A* is correct. John Stuart Mill was an English philosopher and political economist who advocated for utilitarianism and women's rights. In the excerpt, "utility" is defined as actions that are "right in proportion as they tend to promote happiness, wrong as they tend to produce the reverse of happiness." The excerpt then explains that happiness is measured by pleasure, and the reverse is pain. Therefore, Mill calls for actions to be evaluated based on the net total of pleasure. Choice *D* contradicts the definition provided in the excerpt. The excerpt doesn't support Choice *C*, as there's no evidence that pleasure-generating sacrifices merit special status. Choice *B* is incorrect because sacrifice can still be valuable if it leads to more pleasure than pain.

5. C: Choice *C* is correct. Karl Marx, a philosopher, social scientist, historian, and revolutionary, is considered the father of communism. All the answer choices contain true statements or reasonable assumptions from the passage; however, Choice *C* best articulates the main idea—society is the history of class struggle, and working men must unite and fight a revolutionary battle like their historical ancestors.

6. A: Choice *A* is correct. On the political spectrum, ideologies on the left side of the axis emphasize socioeconomic equality and advocate for government intervention, while ideologies on the right axis seek to preserve society's existing institutions and oppose government intervention. Therefore, the answer will be the farthest left on the axis, making Choice *A* correct.

7. C: Choice *C* is correct, as it most closely corresponds to the provided definition. Conservatism prioritizes traditional institutions. In general, conservatives oppose modern developments and value stability. Socialism and liberalism both feature the desire to change the government to increase equality. Libertarianism is more concerned with establishing a limited government to maximize personal autonomy.

8. B: Choice *B* is correct. The Articles of Confederation were the first form of government adopted in the American colonies. Under the Articles of Confederation, the central government (the Continental Congress) was granted very limited powers, rendering it largely ineffective. Although the choices describe what would appear to be basic functions of government, the central government could only declare war.

9. D: Choice *D* is correct. The missing title is in the overlap between federal and state government powers. Concurrent powers are shared between federal and state governments. Reserved powers are the unspecified powers of the states not expressly granted to the federal government or denied to the state by the Constitution, and left to the states by the Tenth Amendment. Implied powers are the unstated powers that can be reasonably inferred from the Constitution. Delegated powers are the specific powers granted to the federal government by the Constitution.

10. D: Choice *D* is correct. The Federalists supported the expansion of the federal government, and the anti-Federalists feared that a stronger central government would weaken the states. *The Federalist Papers* argued for the ratification of the Constitution to establish a more powerful central government. The main idea of this excerpt is to argue that the Constitution establishes a central government powerful enough to rule, while also providing checks and balances to ensure the government doesn't abuse its power. Separation of powers is the concept behind checks and balances, so Choice *D* is the correct answer. Choices *A* and *C* are true statements, but they don't identify the main idea. Choice *B* references a theoretical assertion from the excerpt, but it's not the main idea.

11. C: Choice *C* is the correct answer. Checks and balances refer to the powers granted to ensure other branches don't overstep their authority. The other arrows in the diagram identify checks and balances, so the correct answer is the executive branch's checks and balances on the legislative branch. The executive branch can call special sessions of Congress and veto legislation, so Choice *C* is correct. Unlike the judicial and executive branches, members of the legislative branch cannot be impeached by another branch, though the legislative branch can expel its own members. The executive branch cannot refuse to enforce laws.

12. B: Choice *B* is correct. The Second Amendment states, "A well regulated Militia, being necessary to the security of a free State, the right of the people to keep and bear Arms, shall not be infringed." The First Amendment provides freedom of religion, speech, and the press, the right to assemble, and the right to petition the government. The Third Amendment establishes the right to refuse to house soldiers in times of war. The Fourth Amendment establishes a series of protections for citizens accused and charged with crimes.

13. B: Choice *B* is correct. The Electoral College determines the winner of presidential races, but if a candidate doesn't win a majority of electoral votes, the Twelfth Amendment requires the House of Representatives to decide the presidency, with each state delegation voting as a single bloc. The candidate with the most votes in the House wins the election. The table shows that Andrew Jackson won a plurality of electoral and popular votes, but he didn't receive a majority. John Quincy Adams received the most votes in the House of Representatives, so he won the presidency.

14. A: Choice *A* is correct. Electoral systems dictate how the members of the ruling body are selected, how votes translate into positions, and how seats are filled in the political offices at each level of government. In a majority system, a candidate must receive a majority of votes in order to be awarded a seat, but if none of the candidates reach a majority, a second round of voting occurs, commonly referred to as a runoff.

15. C: Choice *C* is correct. The two major theories of international relations are Realism and Liberalism. Realism analyzes international relations through the interactions of states under the assumption that states act rationally to maintain or expand power a means of self-preservation, which inevitably leads to conflict in an anarchical system. The question asks for the choice that doesn't adhere to Realism, and the other choices state three of the four basic tenets of Realism. In contrast, Choice *C* states a principle of Liberalism. Realists don't value international organizations or prioritize global cooperation.

16. B: Choice *B* is correct. Following the French and Indian War, the British government amassed an enormous war debt, and Great Britain imposed taxes on the colonists to generate more revenue. King George III argued that British resources defended the colonists from French and Native American forces, so the colonists should share in the expenses. The other choices are factually incorrect. The Royal Proclamation of 1763 prevented the colonies from expanding west of the Allegheny Mountains. No lasting peace ever occurred between the colonists and Native Americans. Self-government decreased in the colonies after the French and Indian War.

17. A: Choice *A* is correct. Heavily influenced by the Enlightenment, the Declaration of Independence repudiated the colonies' allegiance to Great Britain. The main purpose of the excerpt is to justify the colonists' revolutionary ambitions due to Great Britain's tyranny and the role of consent in government to protect the natural rights of citizens. Although the excerpt alludes to abuses, the purpose isn't to list specific evidence. This occurs later in the Declaration of Independence. Choices *C* and *D* are supporting evidence for the main purpose.

18. D: Choice *D* is correct. The question asks for a territory that the United States didn't gain from war. Any territory gained via purchase is incorrect. Missouri and Nebraska became American territories through the Louisiana Purchase, and the United States purchased Alaska from Russia. In contrast, Mexico ceded Nevada as part of the peace agreement ending the Mexican-American War.

19. D: Choice *D* is correct. President Lincoln issued the Emancipation Proclamation to free the slaves in the Confederacy, allowing the institution to continue in states and territories that didn't secede. The excerpt justifies the decision as a "fit and necessary war measure for suppressing said rebellion." Therefore, per the excerpt, emancipation was necessary to strengthen the war effort for the North. Choice *C* is the second-best answer, but the excerpt supports the contention that emancipation was part of an active war effort, rather than merely a punishment. Nothing in the excerpt describes the evil of slavery or the effect of emancipation on morale in the North.

20. B: Choice *B* is correct. Industrialization directly caused an increase in urbanization. Factories were located near cities to draw upon a large pool of potential employees. Between 1860 and 1890, the urbanization rate increased from about 20 percent to 35 percent. The other three choices are factually incorrect. Immigration increased during industrialization, as immigrants flooded into America to search for work. Socioeconomic problems plagued the period due to the unequal distribution of wealth and the social ills caused by rapid urbanization. Labor unrest was common as unions advocated for workers' rights and organized national strikes.

21. A: Choice *A* is correct. The Treaty of Versailles contained a clause that required Germany to assume responsibility for damages incurred during the conflict. Thus, the Treaty ordered Germany to pay $31.4 billion, the equivalent of $442 billion in 2017. World War I ravaged the German economy, and the country couldn't afford the war debt. The resulting poverty contributed to the rise of the Nazi Party, leading to World War II.

22. B: Choice *B* is correct. President Franklin D. Roosevelt introduced the New Deal, a series of executive orders and laws passed by Congress in response to the Great Depression. The excerpt describes how President Roosevelt intended to fight poverty by using the government's power to intervene and regulate the economy. Although the other answer choices correctly identify specific activities referenced in the excerpt, they are examples of the underlying philosophy in action. The underlying philosophy is an active role for government in the nation's economic affairs.

23. C: Choice *C* is correct. Frederick Douglass escaped from slavery and worked as an abolitionist for the rest of his life. The excerpt references the hypocrisy of the Fourth of July, as the holiday celebrates freedom in a country with millions of slaves. The other answer choices identify hypocritical aspects surrounding the slavery debate, but Choice *C* directly states the specific hypocrisy attacked in the excerpt.

24. D: Choice *D* is correct. Along with Lucy Stone and Elizabeth Cady Stanton, Susan B. Anthony was one of the most outspoken advocates for women's suffrage. Women couldn't vote in the United States until Congress passed the Nineteenth Amendment in 1920. Choice *D* accurately expresses the main idea of the excerpt. Denying women the right to vote is tyranny, so Anthony will not pay a fine for voting illegally. Choice *A* is the second-best answer, but it's too general to be the main idea of an excerpt specifically about women's suffrage.

25. B: Choice *B* is correct. Ronald Reagan won the presidential election of 1980 and promised to restore America's military power through defense spending, cutting government regulations, and reducing taxes. Evangelical Christians and the Moral Majority fiercely supported President Reagan's agenda, particularly his opposition to abortion and his conservative approach to social issues. The other answer choices include at least one mischaracterization. Choice *A* is incorrect because President Reagan generally opposed social programs. Choice *C* is incorrect because President Reagan valued American leadership more than international cooperation. In addition, his platform was far more radically conservative than compromising. Choice *D* is incorrect because President Reagan fought labor unions on several fronts, most notably when he broke a strike organized by an air traffic controllers' union.

26. C: Choice *C* is correct. In a market economy, privately owned businesses, groups, or individuals price goods or services and set prices based on demand. In contrast, the government or central authority determines prices and quantity of production in a command economy. Of the two economic systems, the market economy more efficiently uses resources. Choice *C* is the only accurate statement.

27. D: Choice *D* is correct. William Jennings Bryan's "Cross of Gold" is one of the most famous speeches in American history, launching his candidacy in the 1896 presidential election. The speech advocates for abolishing the gold standard and adopting a bimetallic system to provide more government control over monetary policy. The excerpt condemns the influence of banks in monetary policy, and without some reform, the masses should act to remove the gold standard. Although the other answer choices accurately state assertions from the excerpt, they aren't the main idea.

28. A: Choice *A* is correct. The Depression of 1929, commonly referred to as the Great Depression, is the largest increase to unemployment, but the question stem asks for the second-largest increase. According to the graph, the Panic of 1893 increased unemployment by approximately ten percent; the Depression of 1920 increased unemployment by approximately six percent; the Depression of 1929 increased unemployment by approximately fifteen percent; and the Great Recession of 2007 increased unemployment by approximately four percent. Thus, the Panic of 1893 marks the second-largest increase to unemployment.

29. A: Choice *A* is correct. A business cycle is when the gross domestic product (GDP) moves downward and upward over a long-term growth trend, and the four phases are expansion, peak, contraction, and trough. An expansion is the only phase where employment rates and economic growth continually grow. Contraction is the opposite of expansion. The peak and trough are the extreme points on the graph.

30. D: Choice *D* is correct. The government can intervene in the economy by imposing taxes, subsidies, and price controls to increase revenue, lower prices of goods and services, ensure product availability for the government, and maintain fair prices for goods and services. Subsidies lower prices, reassure the supply, and create opportunity to compete with foreign vendors, so Choice *D* is correct.

31. C: Choice *C* is correct. Isoline maps are used to calculate data and differentiate between the characteristics of two places. In an isoline map, symbols represent values, and lines can be drawn between two points to determine differences. The other answer choices are maps with different purposes. Topographic maps display contour lines, which represent the relative elevation of a particular place. Dot-density maps and flow-line maps are types of thematic maps. Dot-density maps illustrate the volume and density of a characteristic of an area. Flow-line maps use lines to illustrate the movement of goods, people, or even animals between two places.

32. B: Choice *B* is correct. The map is a density map illustrating population density by state in the United States. Accordingly, the darker areas have higher population density. The darkest area of the map is the Northeast, so Choice *B* is correct.

33. C: Choice *C* is correct. The tilt of the Earth's rotation causes the seasons due to the difference in direct exposure to the Sun. For example, the northern hemisphere is tilted directly toward the Sun from June 22 to September 23, which creates the summer in that part of the world. Conversely, the southern hemisphere is tilted away from the Sun and experiences winter during those months. Choice *A* is factually incorrect—the rate of Earth's rotation is constant. Choice *B* and *D* are factors in determining climate, but differences in climate don't cause the seasons.

34. D: Choice *D* is correct. Nonrenewable energy resources are oil, natural gas, and coal, collectively referred to as fossil fuels. Nonrenewable energy is more widely used due to its abundance and relatively cheap price. In addition, countries have tailored their existing infrastructure to nonrenewable energy. Currently, the technology to store renewable energies for long periods is either nonexistent or expensive. Choice *D* is correct because it's inaccurate. Renewable energy can be converted into a power source, but the issue is scale of use. For example, the United States converts renewable resources to derive ten percent of the country's energy.

35. B: Choice *B* is correct. Ocean currents dramatically impact the climate by storing heat from the Sun and transporting the warmth around the globe. The evaporation of ocean water increases the temperature and humidity in the nearby landmasses. A gyre is a system of circulating currents. Countries are most impacted by the currents and gyres closest to their shores. The question stem asks what currents have the most impact on the United States. According to the map, the North Atlantic Gyre, North Pacific Gyre, California Current, Alaskan Current and Gulf Stream impact the United States. Choice *B* is the only answer with a pair of those currents or gyres.

Dear GED Test Taker,

We would like to start by thanking you for purchasing this practice test book for your GED exam. We hope that we exceeded your expectations.

We strive to make our practice questions as similar as possible to what you will encounter on test day. With that being said, if you found something that you feel was not up to your standards, please send us an email and let us know.

We would also like to let you know about other books in our catalog that may interest you.

HiSET

This can be found on Amazon: amazon.com/dp/1628455039

GED

Amazon.com/dp/1628454962

SAT

amazon.com/dp/1628455217

ACT

amazon.com/dp/1628454709

ACCUPLACER

amazon.com/dp/162845492X

We have study guides in a wide variety of fields. If the one you are looking for isn't listed above, then try searching for it on Amazon or send us an email.

Thanks Again and Happy Testing!
Product Development Team
info@studyguideteam.com

Interested in buying more than 10 copies of our product? Contact us about bulk discounts:

bulkorders@studyguideteam.com

FREE Test Taking Tips DVD Offer

To help us better serve you, we have developed a Test Taking Tips DVD that we would like to give you for FREE. **This DVD covers world-class test taking tips that you can use to be even more successful when you are taking your test.**

All that we ask is that you email us your feedback about your study guide. Please let us know what you thought about it – whether that is good, bad or indifferent.

To get your **FREE Test Taking Tips DVD**, email freedvd@studyguideteam.com with "FREE DVD" in the subject line and the following information in the body of the email:

     a. The title of your study guide.

     b. Your product rating on a scale of 1-5, with 5 being the highest rating.

     c. Your feedback about the study guide. What did you think of it?

     d. Your full name and shipping address to send your free DVD.

If you have any questions or concerns, please don't hesitate to contact us at freedvd@studyguideteam.com.

Thanks again!

95701100R10133

Made in the USA
Middletown, DE
30 October 2018